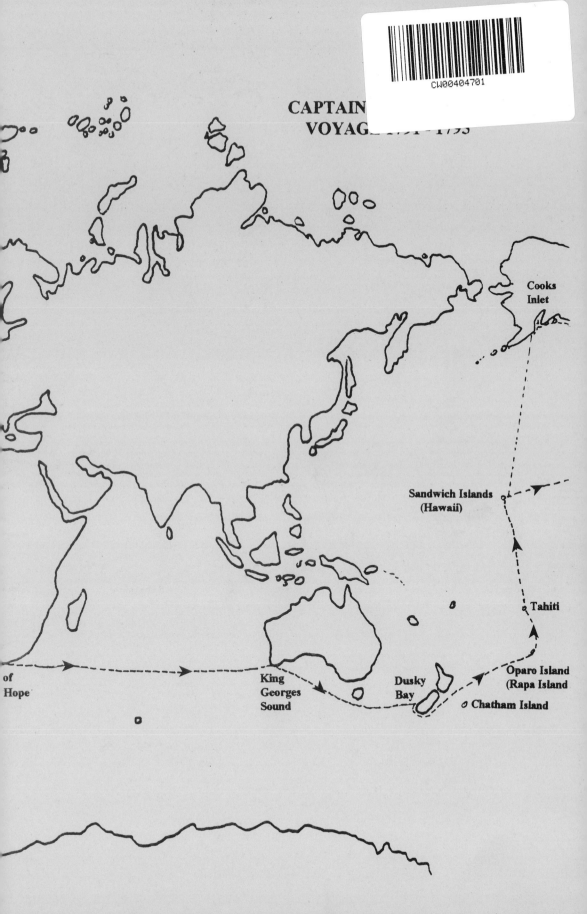

CAPTAIN
VOYAGE 1791-1793

Cooks
Inlet

Sandwich Islands
(Hawaii)

Tahiti

Oparo Island
(Rapa Island

Chatham Island

Dusky
Bay

King
Georges
Sound

of
Hope

CAPTAIN VANCOUVER
NORTH WEST NAVIGATOR

CAPTAIN VANCOUVER
NORTH WEST NAVIGATOR

by

E. C. COLEMAN

CAEDMON OF WHITBY

ISBN 0 905355 53 9

Set in Monotype Bembo

Published in 2000 by
CAEDMON OF WHITBY
128 Upgang Lane
Whitby
North Yorkshire

Printed and bound by
SMITH SETTLE
Ilkley Road, Otley, West Yorkshire LS21 3JP

CONTENTS

ACKNOWLEDGEMENTS

Not being one of nature's 'self-starters' I needed the support and encouragement of a number of people, all of whom were to prove vital to the completion of this work. My thanks are due to people such as John and Inga Howse, who provided food and shelter to a sailor as he frequently passed through Calgary, Alberta; and to Sarah Goodall and her family who looked after me so splendidly at Vancouver, British Columbia. To Dan and Jonolyn Weinstein, whose American sense of 'go for it' made me feel embarrassed even at the thought of failure - and also for their repeated kindnesses to me and my family. To Margaret Moodie and her family for much information on her native City of Vancouver B.C. To George Meagan and his Alaskan friends who looked after me as the ice lay thick on Cook's Inlet, and to Margaret Bertulli of Yellowknife, Northwest Territories, for her never-failing support. To William Mills and Shirley Sawtell of the Scott Polar Research Institute, Cambridge, for their encouragement of someone distinctly non-academic. To Ann and Graeme Paterson who, without complaint, sacrificed much shoe-leather on the north-west of North America in search of maps and charts, and to Kay Drummond who allowed me to use the facilities of her late, much lamented, and deeply missed, husband, Angus. To Mrs Cordelia Stamp - my publisher - both for her initiative in starting the project and for her slave-driving tendencies without which I could have easily fallen by the wayside. And finally to my wife, Joy, who, as I day-dreamed of one day finishing the story of George Vancouver, went out to work and brought home my beer-tokens.

E. C. COLEMAN
Lincoln
2000

Chapter One

KINGS LYNN

Near to the eastern extremity of England's coast, close by the wide, shallow, inlet known as The Wash, Bridget Vancouver gave birth to a son she named George. So began a life visited by a glorious share of fame and good fortune, liberally laced by disinterested fate and downright bad luck. Fate began looking the other way very early in Vancouver's life. Not only is there no certainty about his place of birth, but even the date of the event itself is in some doubt. What is known of his early life and the position of his parents leads to the idea that he was born in the Norfolk coastal town of King's Lynn, but a suggestion that his mother was across the county border with Lincolnshire at the assumed date of his birth throws doubt on any presumptions about his birthplace. Vancouver, himself, however, regarded Kings Lynn as 'the place of my nativity'. As far as the late 19th century 'Dictionary of National Biography' was concerned, Vancouver was born in 1758. But an examination of the Baptismal records of Saint Margaret's church, Kings Lynn – after showing that Vancouver was baptised on 16th March, 1761 – reveals in an additional note by the Reverend Charles Bagge that he was born on 22nd June, 1757, eight years to the day after his parent's wedding. Strangely, in an age when children were baptised early in fear of the infant mortality rate, Vancouver was not baptised until he was almost four years old. The additional note, furthermore, was added by a minister who spelt Vancouver's father's middle name as 'Gasper' instead of 'Jasper'.

With two brothers and three sisters ahead of him, Vancouver was the last of the children born to John and Bridget. His father held the post of Deputy Collector of Customs at Kings Lynn, a position he combined with the appointment as Collector of the Town Dues. The actual post of Customer and Collector of Customs was a sinecure worth £1,200 a year and was held by Charles Turner, a leading figure in the town's society. The work of collecting the customs was carried out by the Deputy Collector, a position of no small responsibility as, at the time of Vancouver's birth, Kings Lynn followed only London, Bristol, Liverpool and Hull in the amount of custom dues collected.

True to form, there is no certainty among the roots of Vancouver's family background. He might have been descended from refugees who fled persecution in The Netherlands during the 16th century, or his ancestors might be found among the engineers who came from The Netherlands to Norfolk and Lincolnshire to help drain the low-lying fens west of The Wash. What is reasonably certain, however, is that the name 'Vancouver' is an adaptation of 'van Coevorden' – a distinguished family who took their name from the town of Coevorden in eastern Holland. A member of this family – Reint Wolter van Coeverden – married an Englishwoman who had been appointed as lady in waiting to German royalty. Their son, Lucas Hendrik, settled in England and married a woman named Sarah

17(*1761 Baptisms S. Margaret in Kings Lyn. Norfolk.* Day.

January 1761

Susanna D. Henry and Mary Harrison · · 25

February

Frances D. William and Mary Claxton · · · 1.

Elisabeth D. William and Anne Cox · · · 2.

Anne D. John and Mary Sneath · · 5.

Thomas S. Thomas and Mary Spicer. · · 8.

Mary D. Henry and Mary Fill. · · 8.

March

Elisabeth D. John and Mary Burch. · · 8.

William S. William and Eleanor Hall. · 13.

Anne D. Vincent and Anne Knowles · · 15.

George S. Mr John Gasper Vancouver and Bridget his Wife · · 16
     Born 22 June 1757.

Anne D. Messor and Elisabeth Atmore · 30.

April

John S. Thomas and Mary Hardin · · 2.

Chas Bagge. Minister

Record of George Vancouver's baptism

whose surname is unknown. It is generally accepted that this Sarah is the same person as Sarah Vancouver – George Vancouver's grandmother. Sarah's son, John, married Bridget Berners, a descendent of Sir Richard Grenville whose gallant and doughty fight in the *Revenge* against fifty-three Spanish ships earned him undying fame in the annals of the Royal Navy. The marriage produced six children – Bridget, Sarah, Mary, Charles, John, and George.

Little is known about Vancouver's childhood in the busy port of Kings Lynn. It is reasonably assumed that he attended the local Grammar School held above the charnel house attached to St. Margaret's church. He would have been unable to avoid the attractions offered by the bustling harbour with its wall lined with sailing ships delivering cargoes from all points of the compass. The town's streets would have been crowded with seamen full of tales of foreign lands as they kept a weather eye on the town's 'Rendezvous'. From that detested site the Royal Navy's Impress Service would send out press gangs to persuade seamen to enter the King's service. Vancouver, being the son of a gentleman and without experience at sea, would not have been among the press gang's targets – although young volunteers were always welcome at the Rendezvous. Instead, secure in an ambition to go to sea, Vancouver would find a route that would side-step the press gangs and offer a glittering path towards the promise of fame and glory.

Chapter Two

UNDER COOK'S COMMAND

'A Quiet inoffensive young man.'

W hen, in July 1771, Lieutenant James Cook, commander of the *Endeavour*, returned from his voyage of discovery to the South Seas he found himself lionised by the upper reaches of society. The Admiralty, the Royal Society and the king himself listened with appropriate attention to Cook's account of his voyage. In accordance with the Society's instructions a transit of Venus across the face of the sun had been observed at Otaheite (Tahiti) – although with modest success thanks to the planet's hazy outline – before Cook, following his Admiralty instructions, headed off southwards in search the great continent believed to exist in high southern latitudes. Having reached 39 degrees South with no sign of such a continent, Cook tacked westwards towards New Zealand. Unvisited for over a hundred years since it was discovered by the Dutch navigator Abel Tasman, New Zealand was believed by some to be a promontory or peninsular of the supposed southern continent. Among those who held to this belief was one of the *Endeavour*'s supernumaries – the wealthy amateur botanist and Fellow of the Royal Society, Joseph Banks. But Cook's circumnavigation of the two islands comprising New Zealand not only put an end to such speculation, but produced a chart of the country that was astonishing in its accuracy.

Leaving New Zealand to the east, Cook had then crossed over to the coast of New Holland (Australia) – again unvisited since Tasman's time. Landing at Botany Bay and a number of other sites in his cruise northwards, Cook carefully charted the unknown coast before the almost total disaster of a grounding on the Great Barrier Reef was averted through superb seamanship. With the Torres Strait achieved, Cook was able to head for Batavia, the chief port of the Dutch East Indies. So far, thanks to Cook's insistence on hygiene and the supply of fresh or pickled vegetables, the ship's company of the *Endeavour* had remained fit and healthy, but the malaria and dysentery rife at Batavia accounted for twenty-eight deaths before the coast of England rose above the horizon.

The deaths apart (which were not considered as unusual for the time), Cook's achievements – especially the placing of New Zealand and much of New Holland under British sovereignty – placed him at the forefront of naval navigators, a position far too important to be allowed to rest idle on half-pay. Within four weeks of his arrival, Cook had been appointed Master and Commander and sent to command the sloop *Scorpion*, a former fireship intended for surveying duties but, in practice, used to keep an otherwise unemployed officer's name on her books, thus retaining him in active service.

Soon after his return, Cook was talking of a voyage in continued search of the supposed continent waiting to be found at high southern latitudes. Banks was convinced that such a continent existed and his position in society allowed him to apply pressure to the Admiralty for the search to be continued. In late September, 1771, the Navy Board received orders from the Admiralty for the purchase of two vessels suitable for a voyage of exploration. It had been decided that two ships would be used as the *Endeavour*'s experience on the Great Barrier Reef had clearly demonstrated the risks involved in using a single vessel. Furthermore, the vessels ordered were to be of the same type as the *Endeavour* – Whitby-built colliers intended for the east coast coal trade, shallow in draught but capacious and strong. Not surprisingly, Cook was ordered to oversee the purchase. After little search, and upon his advice, the Navy Board purchased the 460 ton *Marquis of Granby*, and the 340 ton *Marquis of Rockingham*.

Under Admiralty instructions the vessels were re-named *Drake* and *Raleigh* and classed as sloops. It was not long, however, before someone pointed out that, as the ships would be operating in the Pacific – much of which was claimed by the Spanish – the names *Drake* and *Raleigh* might be considered somewhat undiplomatic. Accordingly, the Admiralty authorised the names to be changed to *Resolution* and *Adventure* – names which Cook considered to be "much properer".

With the minimum of surprise, retaining his appointment as Master and Commander, James Cook was appointed to the command of the *Resolution* and her ship's complement of 112. For his first lieutenant he selected Robert Palliser Cooper (Captain Palliser – an early patron of Cook's – was the Comptroller of the Navy, head of the Navy Board). Charles Clerke, formerly of the *Endeavour*, and with even earlier experience in the Pacific and two circumnavigations to his credit, was appointed as the second lieutenant. Richard Pickersgill – formerly a master's mate in the *Endeavour* (and known for 'liking ye grog') – entered as third lieutenant.

Command of the *Adventure* went to Lieutenant Tobias Furneaux – also appointed Master and Commander for the voyage. Another experienced circumnavigator, Furneaux had been senior to Cook as a lieutenant by nine years and, under normal circumstances, his seniority as a lieutenant should have made him senior to Cook regardless of the date of his appointment. The Admiralty, however, were quite clear about who was to command the expedition. The *Adventure*'s first lieutenant was Joseph Shank, Arthur Kempe was second.

Furneaux's acceptance of second position probably stemmed from the promise the voyage held out. There was no war in progress in which glory, promotion and prize money could be earned, and a voyage under Cook was the best that could be hoped for amongst men of ambition. The same hopes and ambition would have affected the large number of young men hoping for a place on the ships as midshipmen, master's mates, or as other 'young gentlemen', all eager to find a foothold on the ladder leading to an eventual commission as a naval officer.

The key to naval ambition was 'interest'. Interest was earned through a vast and complicated network of nepotism, acquaintance, favouritism, and social advancement. With the rare exception of Admiralty-appointed 'Midshipmen Ordinary' (who had completed a course at the Royal Naval Academy), other midshipmen, along with master's mates, were appointed with the personal approval of the ship's captain (regardless of whatever rank – lieutenant, master and commander, or 'post' captain – he held at the time). It was to the captain, therefore, that all appeals for employment were made. The reasons behind the eventual selection were legion. If he wished to curry favour, he might choose sons of the aristocracy or of other powerful men. He might feel obliged to repay some interest or favour shown him in the past and take sons of senior naval officers or, indeed, any other naval officer. He could select a young man for a previously demonstrated and particular skill such as drawing or surveying, or he might simply do a favour for a friend. Cook would have had many appeals from people with interest eager to have their, or other people's sons, join him on the forthcoming voyage. Two of his eventual choices have left a record of their personal interest and how it was used to gain a berth in the *Resolution*.

John Elliott's uncle was a close acquaintance of the same Captain Sir Hugh Palliser who had earlier been a patron of Cook and was now the Comptroller of the Navy. With one kinsman already on board as the first lieutenant, Palliser had no difficulty in getting Elliott introduced to Cook, and Cook had no difficulty in repaying Palliser's earlier interest in his own career by appointing Elliott as one of his midshipmen.

Twenty-one years old James Burney had been in the Royal Navy since the age of ten and had already passed his lieutenant's examination. His father was a noted musician, Dr Charles Burney, and his sister was Francis ('Fanny') Burney, a writer and diarist. Dr Burney not only knew the First Lord of the Admiralty – the Earl of Sandwich – well, but had also met Cook when they had dined at the Earl's home. Not surprisingly, James Burney was given a place in the *Resolution*'s midshipman's mess.

Midshipmen were not the only 'young gentlemen' to seek a place in the *Resolution*. To qualify as a midshipman it was necessary to have served for three years in a Royal Navy ship and to have reached the skills required of an able seamen (ie. to be able to 'hand, reef, and steer'). To achieve this first rung on the ladder the Royal Navy indulged in a gentle piece of fiction. Each officer was entitled to a number of servants according to his rank and seniority. A captain of a ship with a ship's company of over one hundred men would be entitled to four servants, a junior lieutenant to one. Instead of taking actual servants, the officers would (or could, if they so desired) do one of two things with the position available. Firstly, he could simply take the name of a suitable young gentleman – often aged ten years old or even younger – and put it on the ship's books. This would mean that, after three years, the 'servant' would have appeared to have completed his three years 'sea-time' and would be eligible for the immediate rating of midshipman (the 'able seaman' qualification would have to be learned as a midshipman). The advantage of this system was that it allowed the young man to remain at school and broaden his education before eventually stepping on the deck of a man-of-war. Two of the names on the ship's book of the *Resolution* were James and Nathaniel – both sons of the ship's captain, James Cook. The second method of turning 'servants' into midshipmen was for the young men actually to enter the ship and 'learn the ropes' at first-hand. He would be rated as an able seaman but would live with the midshipmen and master's mates. After three years he could apply to be rated midshipman or master's mate. Midshipmen were trained for eventual command of ships, the master's mates learned the skills required to become ship's masters – warrant officers skilled in the sailing and navigation of the ship. It was not at all unusual for midshipmen to transfer to master's mates, or master's mates to midshipmen in order to broaden their skills. Both ratings could also be reverted to the rating of able seamen for short periods if it was felt that they needed extra training, or that – as the number of midshipmen was fixed by the Admiralty – that someone else should gain the experience of minor office. After two years as a midshipman, and having reached the age of twenty-two (although no-one looked too closely at birth certificates), the young man could apply to be examined for his lieutenant's certificate.

Dr Burney was not only a friend of the First Lord of the Admiralty and Commander James Cook, he was also acquainted with John Vancouver. As organist at Saint Margaret's church, Kings Lynn, Burney had been a neighbour of the Customs Collector and, although there remains no evidence, it seems that a word from Burney in the right ear might have secured a place in the *Resolution* for the fourteen year old George Vancouver as a servant to one of the officers – even, perhaps, to Cook himself. Altogether there were eleven young gentlemen in the midshipman's mess.

With a single chest containing all his clothes and other possessions for the forthcoming voyage, Vancouver joined the *Resolution*'s ship's company at Deptford on 22nd January, 1772. To a young man, even one with experience of ships alongside the harbour wall at Kings Lynn, the sight that greeted him would have been one of seeming chaos and disorder. The ships had to be ready to sail by April and had only been in dockyard hands for less than two months. Extra cabins had to be built, a manger constructed for the livestock, and the apparatus for the experimental rendering of salt water into fresh had to be fitted. A vast range of stores had to be stowed – everything from wheat and lemons to carrot marmalade and Dr James's Fever Powders. Scientific instruments, including a Gregory's improved compass, Jesse Ramsden's sextants, and chronometers supplied by Larcum Kendall and John Arnold, were carefully secured on board. All such hectic activity was part of the normal preparations for any voyage but, for the *Resolution*, there was an even greater problem.

It was obvious to all concerned that Joseph Banks should head the expedition's scientific effort. With his previous experience with Cook, the work he had done for the Royal Society, and through his friendship with the First Lord of the Admiralty, Banks was appointed and promptly began to amass a large number of servants and assistants to accompany him on the voyage. In addition, he collected a prodigious amount of scientific instruments and personal luggage. Owing to her design, however, the *Resolution* could not accommodate Bank's extra requirements so he demanded that he take over Cook's quarters and that an extra deck be built complete with a superimposed cabin for the captain. Cook was appalled at the idea but, as Banks had the support of the Navy Board, he had no other option but to go along with the scheme. When the work had been completed, Cook believed that the ship would prove to be 'crank' and Clerke told Banks that he was prepared to go to sea in a 'grog tub' but thought the *Resolution* was the most dangerous ship he had ever seen. Both were proved to be right when the ship carried out trials from Deptford. Even a modest amount of canvas threatened to capsize her and the Thames pilot refused to remain in her beyond the Nore. On the ship's return all the new work was removed and the ship returned to stability. Banks – outraged at this challenge to his authority – withdrew himself and his staff and set off on an expedition to Iceland.

In the place of Banks, the Royal Society sent a Prussian of Scottish descent, Johann Reinhold Forster, who reported on board bringing his son, George, as his assistant. George proved to be an amiable addition to the ship but his father took little time in convincing all in his vicinity that his most redeeming quality was his lack of humour. The able and experienced William Wales was appointed astronomer in the *Resolution* whilst William Bayly was given the same position in the *Adventure*.

The two ships mustered at Plymouth in late June for the final setting of the chronometers and for Cook to receive his instructions. These – written in part by himself – ordered him to collect wine at Madeira and fresh supplies at the Cape of Good Hope before heading south in search of Cape Circumcision (last seen in 1739) which was believed to be a possible promontory of the great, unknown, southern continent. If nothing came of the search, Cook was to complete a circumnavigation in high southern latitudes before returning home via the Cape of Good Hope.

The two ships departed from Plymouth Sound in the early dawn of 13th July. Their voyage was expected to keep them away from home for the next two, or even three, years.

Vancouver would have known little of Cook's instructions. All he needed to do was to keep himself and his personal belongings clean, obey his orders promptly, and study hard. He was considered by his messmate, Elliott, to be '*a Quiet inoffensive young man*' and almost certainly came under the guidance of the experienced Burney. The captain was keen that no time should be wasted in getting the members of the midshipman's mess to play an active role in the ship's activities. Elliott noted that: '*In the Early part of the Voyage, Captn Cook made all us young gentlemen, do the duty aloft the same as the Sailors, learning to hand, and reef the sails, and Steer the ship, Exercise Small Arms &c thereby making us good Sailors, as well as good Officers.*'

Cook believed that the way to avoid disease was by keeping a clean ship. The bilges were kept as dry as possible by regular pumping, the decks were frequently scrubbed and dried using charcoal fires, the seamen and marines were ordered to wash their clothing whenever possible and to air their bedding. Furneaux in the *Adventure* was much more relaxed in such matters and, before the ship reached the Cape, two of his midshipmen had died of a fever.

The equator was crossed on 8th September and Vancouver would not have escaped the age-old ceremony of 'Crossing the Line.' King Neptune, along with his queen and entourage, would have clambered over the ship's bows and demanded that all those crossing the equator for the first time would have to pay a penalty. Generally such a forfeit took the shape of being 'shaved' with a gruesome-looking razor, swallowing a 'pill' made of a foul-tasting substance, and being tipped unceremoniously into a canvas bath of sea-water. The rough-and-tumble of such an event was good-natured with just the occasional score being settled. Furneaux did not allow the ceremony to take place in the *Adventure*, being alarmed at the thought of the indiscipline it might encourage.

Table Bay was reached on 30th October. There were delays in obtaining the supplies needed, but the time was used to allow the ship's companies to exercise ashore and for the scientist to test their equipment. Lieutenant Shank, the first lieutenant in the *Adventure* had developed gout and had to be put ashore. Lieutenant Kempe was promoted to first lieutenant, his place being taken by Vancouver's friend and messmate, James Burney, newly promoted to lieutenant. A new addition to *Resolution's* ship's company arrived in the shape of a Swedish botanist, Anders Sparrman. The elder Forster had met Sparrman ashore and had persuaded Cook to allow him to bring the Swede on board as an assistant.

At last they left the Cape on 22nd November with the ship's bows headed directly south. Before long the temperature had dropped to a level where Cook authorised the issue of clothing made from 'fearnaught' – a dense, heavy, woollen mixture intended to keep the cold at bay. The livestock on board began to suffer and Cook ordered the birds and animals to be killed and either issued or preserved. On 10th December, as the thermometers fell below freezing, the first icebergs were seen. Four days later Cook found himself hard up against pack ice and was forced to follow its edge to the south-east. Hazardous in every other way, Cook found that the ice provided him with unlimited fresh water.

Christmas Day found the weather calm so Cook allowed his ship's company a day of celebration. Increasing the supply of rum (to supplement the alcohol the seamen had been hoarding) Cook entertained his officers as his men enjoyed a day of 'mirth and good humour'. Forster, however, was not impressed by the 'savage noise and drunkenness' and Sparrman was perplexed by the bloody noses brought about 'by fighting in the English fashion, which is called boxing.'

On 3rd January, 1773, Cook found himself both south and west of the position of Cape Circumcision. He had not found the land, but whatever it was (an island, later named Bouvet Island after its discoverer), he knew from his position that it could not be connected to any land to the south. He, therefore, abandoned the search and headed south-east, threading his way through massed icebergs. Two weeks later, at 11.15am on the 17th, the Antarctic Circle was crossed: 'undoubtedly the first and only ship that ever crossed that line.' The following day ice drove the ships northwards once again.

Cook had told Furneaux that, should the ships be separated, they were to head for Queen Charlotte Sound, New Zealand and, when the ships parted in thick fog on 8th February, Furneaux did just that. Cook, however, kept as close to the Antarctic Circle as he could just in case a southward path lay open. But no opening in the ice appeared and, in mid-March, he tacked to the north-east and headed for New Zealand.

CAPTAIN COOK

From the introduction to his Second Voyage:

It is the production of a man who has not had the advantage of much school education, but who has been constantly at sea from his youth; and though with the assistance of a few good friends, he has passed through all the stations belonging to a seaman from an apprentice in the coal trade to a post captain in the Royal Navy, he has had no opportunity of cultivating letters.

After this account of myself the public must not expect from me the elegance of a fine writer or the plausibility of a professed book maker, but will, I hope, consider me as a plain man, zealously exerting himself in the service of his country and determined to give the best account he is able of his proceedings ...

Captain Cook's Statue in Whitby U.K.

CAPTAIN VANCOUVER

From the introduction to
Vancouver's Voyage of Discovey ...

It will readily appear to the candid perusers of this voyage that, as the primary design of the undertaking was to obtain useful knowledge, so it became an indispensible duty on my part to use my utmost exertions in doing justice to the original intention ... And when the writer alleges that from the age of thirteen, his whole life has been devoted to constant employment in His Majesty's naval service, he feels, and with all possible humility, that he has some claims to the indulgence of a generous public; who, under such circumstances will not expect to find elegance of diction, purity of style, or unexceptionable grammatical accuracy; but will be satisfied with 'a plain unvarnished' relation, given with a rigid attention to the truth of such transactions and circumstances as appeared to be worthy of being recorded by a naval officer, whose greatest pride is to deserve the appellation of being zealous in the service of his king and country.

Captain Vancouver's Statue in
Vancouver B.C.

Chapter Three

FURTHEST SOUTH

Ne plus ultra!

After four months without the sight of land, and after covering almost eleven thousand miles since leaving the Cape, Cook hauled into Dusky Bay on the western coast of New Zealand's south island. Lieutenant Pickersgill found a harbour so secure that Cook could moor the *Resolution* almost alongside the steeply-rising shore. The botanists landed to record and collect, a survey of the coastline was carried out, a camp was established ashore for the ship's artisans to carry out repairs, and a local version of 'spruce beer' was brewed. Eventually contact was made with the natives of the area and a trade in souvenirs for metal nails was soon under way.

Cook had no intention of remaining at Dusky Bay – or any other part of New Zealand – for the winter. Six weeks after his arrival he sailed up the western coast and found the *Adventure* in Queen Charlotte's Sound. Furneaux, required to stay in the area until Cook's arrival, had already began to prepare his ship for a wintering at his anchorage in Ship Cove and Cook was soon lending him men to prepare her for sea.

For five weeks the ships reached eastwards in search of new lands before Cook ordered them to tack northwards towards the green-clad grandeur of Tahiti. His intention to land at Vaitepiha Bay to obtain fresh supplies almost proved disastrous as an onshore breeze pushed both ships towards the reef. At one time it looked as if the *Resolution* would not only be driven on to the threatening coral but would also be rammed by the *Adventure*. At last, however, the anchors held and both ships were warped into safety aided by a slight change in wind direction. The Swede, Sparrman, was deeply impressed by the calm manner in which the ship's companies had behaved during the crisis, but was equally appalled by the language used by Cook as he took command of the situation.

At his old anchorage in Matavai Bay, Cook renewed old friendships and, taking on board a young Tahitian named Porio, sailed north-west towards Huahine and its neighbouring islands. Porio succumbed to the charms of one of the women of Huahine and was replaced by a native of Bora Bora named Odiddy. Furneaux gave passage to Omai, a young native from Raiatea who was keen to go to England. Two islands were discovered and named as the Hervey Island (now part of the Cook Islands) but no landing was made before the ships reached Amsterdam, Rotterdam, and Middleburg islands – first reached by Tasman in 1643. So overwhelming was the welcome the islanders gave to the first white men they had ever seen that Cook renamed the islands as the Friendly Islands (Tonga). Stacked to the gunwales with fresh fruit, live pigs, and chickens, the ships sailed south for another attempt to find the missing southern continent.

Before Cook reached Queen Charlotte Sound bad weather had caused the ships to separate. As before, the *Adventure* was expected to be encountered in the great bay but, despite Cook delaying his departure until 25th November, no sign of the ship was seen. Five days after Cook had left, the *Adventure* dropped anchor in Ship Cove. A message from Cook was found, but it contained no definite rendezvous for Furneaux to head for. With his ship leaky and 'crank', and with sickness – including scurvy – breaking out amongst his ship's company, Furneaux was beginning to lose heart. The final, horrifying, blow came when Lieutenant Burney was sent ashore to find a missing party of men who had been sent to collect fruit. Burney stumbled across a cannibal's feast at which the fare had been Master's Mate John Rowe and eight seamen. With no stomach for instant retribution Furneaux sailed for home and reached England in July, 1774. His native islander, Omai, was taken under the wing of the upper reaches of society, learned to skate, and greeted King George with the words 'How do, King Tosh'.

Meanwhile Cook had left New Zealand on a south-east course and, by mid-December, was back among icebergs. A minor retreat was required before another push took the *Resolution* south of the Antarctic Circle where Christmas day was spent shivering beneath ice-hung rigging. Forced north once again by a sea full of icebergs, Cook spent two weeks recovering from the experience before crossing the Antarctic Circle for the third time. On this occasion he was able to reach an astonishing 71 degrees, 10' South – just 1250 miles from the South Pole – before the pack ice forced him to order the ship about. Just as the order was being given, according to his own account, the sixteen years old George Vancouver – still rated as an able seaman – ran along the *Resolution*'s bowsprit until he reached its end. There, waving his hat to gain everyone's attention, Vancouver shouted out *'Ne plus ultra!'*. He was indeed the most southerly person in the world. But indifferent fate ensured that his claim was short-lived as Sparrman, whose cabin was at the stern of the ship, was looking out of his cabin scuttle as the *Resolution* came about and claimed that the stern drifted further south than the bowsprit had penetrated. Whether true or not, Sparrman's claim ensured that the lustre had gone from the young Vancouver's great moment.

The Antarctic Circle was crossed twice again before Cook, in consultation with his officers, and much to the delight of the lower deck, decided to head north. His first port of call was to be Easter Island, a rarely-visited place with little to offer in the way of food and water. The natives showed no hostility towards the strangers who remarked upon the tattoos and extended ears of the native men. Nothing, however, compared to the astonishing sight of huge stone statues, some raised on platforms, others toppled, and some rearing out of the soil itself. Bearing features unlike that of the natives, it seemed that neither they nor Cook's men could account for their existence.

A brief visit was made to the Marquesas Islands before Tahiti was gained in April. The stay was not to be long before the ship sailed to survey a wide archipelago which Cook named 'New Hebrides' and a large island he called 'New Caledonia'. The uninhabited, yet beautiful, 'Norfolk Island' was visited before Cook arrived

at Queen Charlotte's Sound where he found the natives unaccountably wary –
Furneaux had left no message warning of the local taste for cannibalism. The
Resolution stayed for three weeks until sailing on 11th November for the tip of
South America. Cape Horn was rounded on 29th December and, to complete his
circumnavigation in high southern latitudes, Cook headed eastwards until hopes
were suddenly raised by the sight of land ahead. With the chance that the land
might be part of the unknown continent, Cook closed with its soaring snow-clad
peaks and multitude of glaciers pouring out of its much-broken shoreline. Taking
possession of the land in the name of his sovereign, Cook skirted the coast until –
at 'Cape Disappointment' – he realised he had fallen in with yet another island.
Naming its stark beauty 'Isle of Georgia' (South Georgia) Cook left to discover
another group of desolate islands he named the 'South Sandwich Islands' before
continuing eastwards to cross the track he had made in search of Cape Circumcision
more than two years before. With his circumnavigation complete, Cook tacked
towards the Cape of Good Hope. He was tired and dispirited by his lack of success
in finding the missing continent. He was 'tired of these high latitudes where there
is nothing to be found but ice and thick fogs.' Another explorer might probe
further south than he had been able to do but 'I shall not envy him the honour of
the discovery, but will be bold enough to say that the world will not be benefited
by it.' The ships company were also pleased to be returning home. One of the
Resolution's seaman, Thomas Perry, wrote new verses to the tune 'Heart of Oak'.
The first ran –

> It is now my brave boys we are clear of the ice
> And keep a good heart if you'll take my advice
> We are out of the cold my brave boys do not fear
> *For the Cape of Good Hope with good hearts we do steer.*

Following a delayed departure from the Cape due to a damaged rudder, the
Resolution dropped anchor at Spithead on 30th July, 1775. She had been away for
three years and eighteen days. Cook's achievements were swiftly recognised. Ten
days after his return he was presented to the King and promoted to captain. A short
holding appointment followed before he was appointed as one of the captains of
Greenwich Hospital – a palatial home given by a grateful nation for its aged and
infirm seamen. It was an opportunity for the forty-six year old Cook to rest on his
laurels. Not only was his new post an appointment for life but, having achieved
the rank of captain, all he had to do was sit back and wait for his eventual promotion
to flag rank with its enhanced status and income. Cook, however, was not entirely
sure that was what he really wanted to do – 'I must confess it a fine retreat and a
pretty income, but whether I can bring myself to like ease and retirement time will
show.'

George Vancouver's return was deeply clouded when he learned that his father
had died almost two-and-a-half years earlier. His brother John had succeeded to
the post of Deputy Collector of Customs and it was almost certainly to his house
in Kings Lynn that Vancouver repaired on his return. Although he had served with
the rating of able seaman on one of the great voyages of the age, neither he, nor

the Royal Navy, were under any obligation towards each other. Clearly, Vancouver's time in the *Resolution* had been well spent, and he had served long enough to qualify for an appointment as a midshipman. But there was still the need for 'interest' to weigh in his favour. His best hope probably lay in one of the *Resolution*'s officers receiving an appointment which allowed him to recommend Vancouver to his captain. In the meantime, all he could do – like hundreds of other 'young gentlemen' – was to hope.

Chapter Four

PACIFIC TRAGEDY

'taking care not to loose any time in exploring rivers or inlets.'

For well over two hundred years before the return of Cook's second voyage many men's minds had been occupied with the problem of the 'Northwest Passage'. This was an assumed passage believed to exist across the top of north America, linking the Atlantic and the Pacific oceans. If such a passage existed it would drastically reduced the time of voyages to China and India, both sources of great wealth. Cabot, Frobisher, Hudson, Davis and Baffin were just a few of the men who had given much of their effort – and sometimes their lives – in the search for the passage. More recently, in 1742, Vitus Bering had proved the existence of a strait between north-west America and north-east Asia and there was every likelihood that Bering's Strait would prove to be a western gateway to the passage. Another vitally important clue was found by Samuel Hearne – a Hudson's Bay Company employee and former Royal Navy midshipman – who had travelled down the Coppermine River as it cut through the vast Barren Lands that compose much of the northern edge of north America. Reaching the mouth of the river, Hearne found himself looking out across an ice-rimmed, but open, sea. He was the first European to gaze upon the Arctic Ocean and part of the Northwest Passage. For a maritime trading nation like Great Britain such indications could not afford to be missed, and the Admiralty set about raising expeditions to look into the problem from both ends of the supposed passage. To look at the eastern side they appointed Lieutenant Pickersgill to the command of *HMS Lyon* with instructions to protect the whaling fleet from marauding Americans and to find an entrance to the passage.

Their Lordships then decided that Cook's old ship *Resolution* should be used for the western part of the enterprise. As the *Adventure* was not fit to join her on such a service (she was to end up as a fireship before being sold in 1783), Cook was asked to advise on a replacement. Not surprisingly he selected yet another Whitby-built vessel, the *Diligence* soon to be re-named *Discovery*.

All that then remained was the appointment of the man to command the voyage. With a marked lack of subtlety the First Lord of the Admiralty invited Cook to dinner along with Sir Hugh Palliser and Phillip Stephens – the Secretary to the Admiralty. The express purpose of the dinner was to consult Cook on the choice of leader for the expedition. To the surprise of few, Cook's request to be appointed was received within days and accepted within hours.

Next came the question of appointing the other officers. Command of the *Discovery* and her ship's company of 69 went to Charles Clerke, formerly second lieutenant in the *Resolution* and now promoted to Master and Commander for his third voyage under Cook. Cook's first lieutenant was to be John Gore, an

American-born officer who had already circumnavigated the globe before he had joined Cook in the *Endeavour*. He had then accompanied Banks on his voyage to Iceland and may have played a part in bringing Cook and Banks back together after their falling out over Banks's attempts to re-design the *Resolution*. The second lieutenant was James King, a likeable, well-educated, young officer with connections in high political circles. John Williamson was appointed as third lieutenant. Much given to a violent temper, Williamson was to prove the most unpopular officer of the voyage. The *Resolution's* master was William Bligh. Only twenty-one, Bligh had been in the Royal Navy since he was fourteen years old. In those six short years he had demonstrated an extraordinary capability as a surveyor, navigator, and seaman – so extraordinary in fact that his three master's mates (all who had served previously under Cook), Henry Roberts, William Harvey, and William Lanyon, were all older than him.

Clerke's first lieutenant was to be none other than James Burney. Having returned in the *Adventure*, Burney had served on the America Station where unrest among the colonists was beginning to make itself felt. The second lieutenant was John Rickman. The master of the *Discovery* was Thomas Edgar. Not in the same class as Bligh, Edgar, nevertheless, proved to be a competent navigator and surveyor.

With such names already well-known to him – and he to them – Vancouver clearly had several opportunities to write asking for an appointment. Even a letter to Cook himself would not have been amiss. However, it was almost certainly a combination of Burney and Clerke that saw him appointed to the *Discovery*. Such a choice could only mean that Vancouver matched the demanding requirements of the ship's two most senior officers, neither of whom would have been likely to have wasted an appointment on someone for whom they had little esteem. Once again, Vancouver was appointed as an able seaman but, within three weeks he was rated as a midshipman and would soon have been dressed in the dark blue uniform of his new position complete with tri-corn hat, gilt buttons, and with white 'turn-backs' lighting up his standing collar – his three years as an able seaman ensuring his qualification for the new rating.

As the time for departure drew near, Cook found himself with an unusual, and irritating, problem. His second-in-command, the captain of the *Discovery*, Charles Clerke, had been locked up in prison. Clerke had stood surety for debts accumulated by his naval officer brother, Captain Sir John Clerke. Sir John, no doubt believing in the old naval officer's tradition that 'all debts are cancelled with the first raising of a sail' had left to take up an appointment on the India Station leaving his brother to face the debtors. With Clerke inside the debtor's prison, it was left to Burney to take the *Discovery* to Plymouth, soon to be joined by an agitated Cook. Eventually, Cook could wait no longer and, with the native Omai on board to be returned to his island home, sailed on 12th July, 1776. He left, somewhat optimistic, orders for Clerke to follow him. Fortune, however, proved to be on Clerke's side. With revolutionary noises from the other side of the Atlantic becoming more and more clamorous, with the French and possibly even the

Spanish taking a keen interest in events, the British Government realised that it could not have a large number of its military and naval officers in debtor's prisons. Accordingly, 'An Act for the Relief of Insolvent Debtors; and for the Relief of Bankrupts in Certain Cases' was passed by Parliament. Just in time, Clerke was able to negotiate himself out of prison and into the *Discovery*. He sailed three weeks after Cook, writing to Banks about his excitement and eagerness to catch up with the *Resolution* – 'Huzza my Boys heave away'.

And 'heave away' they did until the *Discovery* joined Cook off Cape Town on 18th November. All were keen to press on to 'our intended attack on the North Pole' but, before leaving, Cook gave Clerke a copy of his official instructions and arranged that, should the vessels be separated, they should head for the usual rendezvous at Queen Charlotte Sound. They sailed from Cape Town unaware that the eastern part of the search for the Northwest Passage had collapsed in ignominy. Pickersgill had sailed too late to achieve a high latitude through the Davis Strait and had found his path barred by ice. The well-meaning, easy-going lieutenant found he was not up to the task ahead and sought solace in the bottle. Bringing the *Lyon* home less than six months after he had sailed, Pickersgill was court-martialled and dismissed from the Service. He eventually found employment as the captain of a privateer. One night, returning on board after drinking heavily ashore, he fell overboard and was drowned.

Cook and Clerke's voyage brought them to the Prince Edward and Crozet Islands before spending Christmas in the lee of the bleak shores of Kerguelen Island. Van Dieman's Land (Tasmania) was visited and contact made with the natives, but the time spent there did not allow Cook to determine whether or not the land was part of New Holland or was actually an island. They reached Queen Charlotte Sound on 12th February, 1777. It was found that the natives fully expected reprisals for their cannibalism of some of the *Adventure*'s men and were bemused to find that Cook had no intention of extracting revenge. After two weeks at Queen Charlotte Sound, Cook set a course for Tahiti. He was, by now, too late to reach the north-west coast of America that year, a situation underlined by contrary winds which prevented him from taking a direct passage to Tahiti. Instead, he visited several previously unknown islands before calling in at the Friendly Islands where he and his ships companies spent an idyllic twelve weeks. Tahiti was reached on 12th August to a warm welcome. Cook's rheumatic pains were massaged away by a team of twelve women before he amazed the local people by – in company with Clerke – riding horses around Matavai Bay. There was bad news as well. Clerke had begun to show signs of tuberculosis – possibly contracted during his stay in prison.

Omai was returned to his home on Huahine before Cook set off north again crossing the equator on 22nd December. An uninhabited, barren, island was found two days later and named 'Christmas Island'. A week was spent on its flat, sandy, surface; the seamen catching fish and turtles as the officers observed and recorded an eclipse of the sun.

As dawn broke on the 18th January, 1778, they saw land rising to the north-east. This was soon joined by more peaks to the north. Cook had fallen in with Kauai and Niihau, the northernmost of his 'Sandwich Islands' (Hawaiian Islands). Unknown to Europeans, the islanders proved to be of the same Polynesian race as the people of Tahiti, yet neither knew of the others existence. Eager to trade (and with the same propensity to remove any item not bolted down as other Pacific islanders), the natives proved to be friendly and outgoing. A dramatic change, however, was brought about when Lieutenant Williamson was sent ashore with three boats to find water. With their task completed the men were about to return when the natives began to grab at their oars and at any loose items. Williamson, losing control of the situation, open fire with his pistol shooting a native man through the head. Instead of reporting the incident to Cook, Williamson remained quiet about it and, when Cook went ashore, he was understandably surprised to find that the natives prostrated themselves in his presence, remaining prone until he ordered them to rise. Much to his chagrin, Cook was not to learn of Williamson's action until he had left the island.

At last, on 2nd February, the ship's bows were pointing to the north-east and to the west coast of America. Cook's instructions from the Admiralty read –

> *'Upon your arrival on the Coast of New Albion you are to put into the first convenient Port to recruit your wood and water and procure refreshments, and then to proceed northward along the coast as far as the latitiude of 65 degrees, or farther, if you are not obstructed by lands or ice,* **taking care not to lose any time in exploring rivers or inlets, until you get into the before-mentioned latitude of 65 degrees,** *where we would wish you to arrive in the middle of June next. When you get to that length you are very carefully to search for and to explore such rivers or inlets as may appear to be of considerable extent and pointing towards Hudsons or Baffins Bays.'*

He was to reach the coast in the latitude of 45 degrees North whilst being very careful of avoiding any diplomatic incidents –

> 'You are also, in your way thither, strictly enjoined not to touch any part of the Spanish Dominions on the Western Continent of America, unless driven thither by some unavoidable accident, in which case you are to stay no longer there than shall be absolutely necessary, and to be very careful not to give umbrage or offence to any of the inhabitants or subjects of His Catholic Majesty. And if in your farther progress to the Northward, as hereafter directed, you find any subjects of any European Prince or State upon any part of the coast you may think it proper to visit, you are not to disturb them or give them any just cause for offence, but on the contrary to treat them with civility and friendship.'

Although the Spanish had every reason not to come to the aid of revolting colonists, they – like the French – would seize any opportunity to revenge the drubbing inflicted on them during the Seven Years War. Cook reached the American coast on 7th March, The French declared war in July, and the Spanish opened hostilities in April, 1779.

Cook had more immediate problems than diplomacy or threats of war. Strong westerly gales threatened to drive him on to the coast as he struggled to make his way to the north. Amongst his first sightings of land appeared to be a northernmost limit of the coast, he named it 'Cape Foul Weather' before being driven out to sea once again. This action – or a night passage – caused Cook to miss the wide opening of the Strait of Juan de Fuca where, according to legend, a Greek pilot named Juan de Fuca was sent in 1592 by the Viceroy of Mexico. de Fuca returned with the claim that he had sailed through a strait all the way to the Atlantic and back. Such a passage suited the Spanish well as they believed that the English would now use that route rather than pass through Spanish territories in the south Pacific. The passage, however, had never been re-discovered and de Fuca's name was given to an open waterway with Cape Foul Weather on its southern edge. A week after being driven out to sea, Cook saw land again. It was an imposing sight with snow-covered mountains sheltering densely-wooded valleys. A large opening caught Cook's attention and, as he was desperately keen to carry out repairs to the *Resolution's* masts, spars, and rigging, he ordered the ships into the wide inlet with its central island ('Bligh Island'). Under gentle weigh, searching for an anchorage, the two vessels were suddenly surrounded by canoes containing men who either sang to the beat of their paddles or gesticulated whilst shouting 'Nootka, Itchme Nootka, Itchme'. The shouting was an attempt to get Cook to enter deeper into the inlet but Cook, and others, took the words as the name of the people – thus they became 'Nootkas'.

Once contact had been established, the natives proved to be friendly enough, keen to trade and quick to remove anything that could be carried. Unaccustomed to washing, and smelling strongly of fish oil, they painted their faces black, white and red and hung copper trinkets from their ears and noses. One man provided a surprise when Lieutenant Gore noticed that he had two silver spoons hung round his neck – both turned out to be Spanish.

The ships spent almost a month in preparation for the thrust to the north. The site was ideal for the supply of spare and replacement masts and, confident in their repairs, sails were bent and the ships secured for sea. At noon on the 26th April, to a farewell chorus from the natives, Cook departed from the inlet after giving it the name 'King George's Sound' (Nootka Sound).

The two ships were greeted by a five day storm that again drove them from the coast. On his achieving the land again, Cook could recognise nothing from Bering's account of his voyage and so began naming the prominent features; Mount and Cape Edgecumbe, Mount and Cape Fairweather, Kaye Island (Kayak Island), Cape Suckling, Controller Bay. At Snug Corner Cove in Sandwich Sound (Prince William Sound), the *Resolution* was heeled over and had the seams between her planks recaulked with oakum.

To the north of Sandwich Sound, the wide entrance to – what appeared to be – a river was found. Cook, disregarding his instructions, accepted Gore's plea to enter the mountain-lined waterway. After several miles the water divided and Cook sent Bligh to examine the smaller of the two arms whilst he looked into the other. Bligh's venture ran out very quickly and Cook could make little headway along his route. Eventually he retreated, giving his east trending arm the name 'Turnagain River' (Turnagain Arm). So disappointed was he by this wasted time and effort that Cook failed to name the wide waterway up which he had initially travelled. It was later named by Lord Sandwich as 'Cook's River' (Cook Inlet).

The Alaskan peninsular was pierced at Unalaska, one of the broken line of Aleutian islands that extended the peninsular almost to the west, and a visit was paid to the island's Samgoonoodha harbour (English Bay). Fog held the ships off the coast for much of the voyage northwards until, after briefly touching the Asian coast, the *Resolution* and the *Discovery* entered the Bering Sea. It was mid-August and the temperature was falling dramatically but, to everyone's delight, the sea ahead was clear of ice. Soon the officers were calculating the distance to Baffin's Bay and Clerke, his debts still outstanding, was, no doubt, anticipating his share of the £20,000 reward authorised by Parliament for the first voyage through the Northwest Passage. But it was not to be that easy. After three days, a bright edge appeared on the northern horizon – it was 'ice blink', the sure sign that ice lay ahead.

The solid ice-field, rearing ten feet above the surface, was met at 70 degrees 41'. A careful cruise along its edge brought them to 70 degrees 44'. This was to be Cook's most northerly achievement and almost exactly matched his furthest south. A probe to the east brought the shore into view and the ships into great danger. Just as the bottom began to shoal, giving the ships considerably less sea-room, a northerly wind not only threatened to drive them ashore, but also drove the mass of ice at them. It was probably a change in the wind to a more easterly source that saved them, allowing both ships to escape to the south-west. Before leaving the area, Cook honoured a low, ice-fringed, headland with the name 'Icy Cape'. Clearly, although the Arctic summer had only just ended, at that season the western entrance to the Northwest Passage (if,indeed, that is where Cook had found himself) had proved to have a deeply unforgiving nature. After leaving the Bering Sea, and spending a few days on Unalaska carrying out repairs, Cook took his ships south of the Tropic of Cancer – to the Sandwich Islands for a winter of recuperation.

Among the gods of the people of Owhyee (Hawaii), Lono was the god of light and peace. Folk tradition had it that Lono would arrive on the island in a large canoe bringing with him his special qualities of harmony. With no knowledge of this, Cook was almost overwhelmed by the welcome which awaited him as he brought his ships into Kealakekua Bay. Lieutenant King estimated that ten thousand natives, paddling fifteen hundred canoes, took to the waters of the bay to greet the newcomers. Thousands more lined the beach as hundreds of young women and boys swam around the ships. The local chief, accompanied by a priest, went on board the *Resolution* and offered Cook gifts before cloaking him in red cloth. This was followed by speeches in which the word 'Lono' was frequently heard. That afternoon, Cook went ashore where, much to his embarrassment, he found the natives prostrating themselves in his presence. This time the gesture had none of the fearful element that had appeared after Williamson had shot one of the natives on the previous visit – even Cook could not avoid the fact that he was being treated as a divinity, something he regarded as 'a confounded inconvenience'. There followed much tiresome ceremony and sacrificing of pigs until a week after their arrival the island's king – Terreeoboo – broke off warfare with a neighbouring island and came to meet Cook. On his arrival, the king took off the splendid cloak and helmet of red and yellow feathers and put them on Cook. From then on, every member of both ships companies were treated as honoured guests. The constant feasting, hospitality, and the excessive favours shown by the local women were readily enjoyed. To what extent Midshipman Vancouver joined in is not known, but he mingled enough with the natives to gain an understanding of their language.

After two weeks of sheer indulgence, Cook felt the time had come to move on. A point of view probably not unwelcomed by the natives who were beginning to feel the strain on their resources of too much celebration. Early on the morning of 4th February, 1779, the two ships sailed with the escort of a huge flotilla of canoes, their occupants waving their farewells to Lono.

Four days out, the *Resolution*'s foremast was damaged in a gale and Cook, not unreasonably, decided to return to Kealakekua Bay for repairs. This time, however, the welcome was much more muted although Clerke was able to swap a feather cloak for nine long iron daggers. Where before there had been adoration, now there was only insolence – the legend of Lono had said nothing about his return for a second time.

On the afternoon of 13th February, after a morning of trouble in which a watering party had been stoned by the natives, Cook went ashore with King to inspect the work being done on the faulty mast. Vancouver was in the *Discovery* when his attention was attracted by a commotion on board. A native had stolen some of the armourer's tools and was making for the shore in a canoe. Clerke order the marines to open fire with their muskets, but the canoe was quickly out of range. The ship's master, Thomas Edgar, climbed into the ship's cutter with two men and Vancouver joined him as he set of in pursuit. Just as they reached the shore where the canoe had been abandoned, Cook and King could be seen running along the beach having heard the sound of gun-fire. King shouted out to the cutter and Vancouver pointed in the direction of the canoe and gesticulated that the thief had run inland. As the cutter grounded, it was joined by the *Discovery*'s pinnace – and a large crowd of hostile natives. None of the officers or seamen were armed as a shower of stones fell around them and the natives advanced with hoisted clubs. With the pinnace receiving the worst attention, Edgar got out of the cutter and stood knee-deep in the water as Vancouver went to the pinnace to lend a hand. Finding that the pinnace was, in fact, being abandoned by its crew, Vancouver jumped out just in time to receive a hard blow from a broken oar that had originally been aimed at Edgar. Sent sprawling full length into the shallows and losing his hat, Vancouver recovered enough to help Edgar who had decided to grab the thief's canoe in recompense for the stolen tools. Unfortunately, the canoe belonged to a chief who ran forward to prevent its being taken away, an act rewarded by a blow on the head by an oar wielded by one of the pinnace's seamen. This act drove the crowd to even greater fury. They rushed en mass at Edgar and Vancouver and were only stopped by the chief – a friend of Vancouver's – who ordered them back. The momentary pause in the assault allowed the two officers to climb into the pinnace and, using its single effective oar, push themselves into deeper water to join the cutter. They set off in search of Cook pursued by the chief in his canoe trying to return Vancouver's hat.

That night, despite marine sentries being alert for attack, the *Discovery*'s large cutter was stolen. Cook, tired and on edge, was furious. First he ordered boats out to blockade the harbour and try to capture native canoes. He then decided to take King Terreeoboo prisoner and hold him to ransom until the cutter was returned. Taking marine lieutenant Molesworth Phillips and nine marine privates with him, Cook landed in the launch ordering its officer, Lieutenant Williamson, to lay a few yards offshore and await his return. An accompanying cutter, under the command of Master's Mate Henry Roberts, followed suit.

They did not have to wait for long. The unmistakable sound of an approaching mob was followed by the sight of Cook and the marines walking purposefully back to the beach. The king had been taken, but before long, had fallen to the ground with terror in the belief that he was about to be killed. Cook, appalled by the indignity of the whole event, had abandoned his plan and ordered Phillips to return to the boats. Just as they neared the beach a chief landed from a canoe nearby and told the crowd that one of the blockading boats had opened fire on a canoe killing one of the natives. At this, the crowd grew even more hostile and several long iron daggers – which could only have come from the ships – were produced. One of the natives, wearing protective matting armour, lunged at Cook who replied by firing one of the charges in his double-barrelled musket. The charge was only of shot which had little or no effect upon the protected native. The yelling crowd rushed forward, Phillips fended off a knife attack, as Cook fired his other barrel – this time loaded with ball – killing a man. Phillips opened fire, ordering the other marines to do likewise, as Cook shouted out 'Take to the boats!'. Seeing Cook wave his arm ordering the boats to approach the rocks where the fighting was taking place, Roberts and his crew pulled in desperation as one or more of the red-coated marines was seen to fall. In the launch, closer to Cook than the cutter, Williamson sat immobile as his agitated crew shouted at him for orders to rescue their captain. The lieutenant's response was to order them further from the beach. As the cutter closed with the action five of the marines and the, by now, wounded Phillips tumbled into the boat. One of the men fell back into the water and Phillips, despite his injuries and the danger, jumped out and rescued him. Cook, now left alone on the rocks, turned to look at Williamson – now no more than a few yards away. As he did so, he was clubbed on the back of his head and fell to one knee. A native sprang forward with a dagger and thrust it into the helpless man's neck causing him to pitch forward into the water. He was followed by a flailing mass of natives, hacking, stabbing, and clubbing. A volley of musket fire from the cutter forced the natives back leaving Cook's body floating in blood-stained water. Roberts looked across to Williamson only to see that the senior officer had ordered his boat's crew to start back for the ships. Seething with silent rage, Roberts followed.

With Cook's death, command of the expedition fell on to Charles Clerke, already so weak from tuberculosis that even remaining on deck was an effort. Nevertheless, he had himself taken across to the *Resolution* and appointed Lieutenant Gore to the command of the *Discovery*. Although desperate to obtain the body of Cook and the marines, Clerke knew that his most important task was to recover the foremast and the scientific equipment which still remained ashore. An armed party under Lieutenant King landed and retrieved the mast and other items against the threat of attack from a crowd of natives. Some stones were thrown but a few rounds from the *Resolution*'s four-pounder cannon drove the attackers away. That evening Clerke sent King, Burney, and Vancouver ashore under a flag of truce to try and retrieve the bodies. Fortunately, they were met by the chief who had saved Edgar's and Vancouver's life the day before and who seemed pleased that Vancouver was present as he 'best understood them'. The party learned that parts of Cook's body had been distributed among various chiefs of the island but, as an act of conciliation, the parts would be collected and made available the next day. King, unsure of how to proceed, sent Vancouver over to Clerke for instructions. On his return, Vancouver told King he was to return on board after informing the natives that if the body was not ready for collection the next day 'their town & People should be destroy'd.' The boat had just pushed off from the beach when a number of natives turned their backs on the landing party and exposed their buttocks as others laughed and jeered. King, possessed by a sudden rage, picked up his musket and aimed at the nearest offending native. Burney, remaining calm, instantly pleaded with King not to open fire. His urgent request was heard and King lowered the gun, possibly preventing a further outbreak of violence.

It was not until the sun had set on the following day that a priest arrived at the *Resolution* with a piece of flesh which, he claimed, had been cut from Cook's thigh. Only bones, said the priest, otherwise remained. Clerke, weak from his illness and busy with the re-stepping of the foremast, demanded that all the bones be brought to him. At noon on the 20th, a procession was seen making its way towards the beach. Clerke went to meet them in the pinnace and was presented with a bundle covered by a cloak made of black and white feathers. Returning on board, Clerke had the bundle opened and found a scalp, a skull, all the limb bones and two hands preserved in salt. The ribs and backbone, it was explained , had been lost with the flesh in a fire. The following day, the feet and jawbone were handed over. Of the dead marines, nothing remained.

On the 21st of February, 1779, as lowered flags hung limp at the halliards and the boom of minute guns echoed around the bay, the last remains of the Royal Navy's great navigator was committed to the still waters of the bay.

Now it was time for Clerke and his ships to leave. He intended to follow Cook's plan for a return to the western entrance to the Northwest Passage and to follow that supposed route to the Atlantic. Sweeping first west then north in an unsuccessful search for more discoveries, the ships arrived at the Kamchatka port of Petrapavlovsk. Despite the re-issue of warm clothing, many of the ship's companies suffered in the bitter cold as they had swapped much of their other clothing for female comforts at Hawaii. Petrapavlovsk proved to be a cheerless place but the local Russian commander was unstinting in his hospitality. As he was soon to leave for St Petersburg, he also offered to take letters and copies of Cook's and Clerke's journals for onward transmission to England.

Bering's Strait was penetrated on 6th July. To his great disappointment, Clerke found the waters around him 'Choak'd with Ice'. For two weeks he tried to find a way through but only succeeded in damaging his ships as they bumped into the main pack or collided with loose floes. With no hope in that direction, he ordered his ships back to Petrapavlovsk. On the 22nd July, with the coast of Kamchatka in view, the thirty-eight years old Charles Clerke died. He was buried at the port.

Command now fell upon Lieutenant Gore. King was given command of the *Discovery*. Her first lieutenant was now to be the deeply despised Williamson who had spent much of the voyage since Hawaii being ignored – the marine officer, Phillips, in particular, using every opportunity to slight him or even tempt him into a duel.

There was little for Gore to do. In consultation with his officers he decided to return home via the Cape. At Macao they learned that, not only had the American colonists persisted in their revolution, it was still continuing. Even more urgent was the news that France had joined in on the colonist's side.

This news placed an urgency on their speedy return, with a war against France in progress there was always the opportunity for glory, promotion, and prize-money.

More news was obtained at the Cape. Spain had joined France in a coalition against the British but, in splendid recognition of the value of exploration over war, both countries – and the Americans – had guaranteed not to attack the *Resolution* and the *Discovery*. Also at the Cape a rumour grew that Phillips and Williamson had fought a duel – there had been no injuries, but Williamson's behaviour did little to restore his reputation.

The ships dropped anchor at the Nore on 4th October, 1780, having been away for four years, two months, and twenty-two days. Their arrival caused no great fuss. It was already known that Cook had died, and the country was fighting a war.

Both Gore and King were promoted to captain. The former died ten years later and King, after editing Cook's account of his third voyage of exploration, died four years after his return. The *Resolution*'s young master, William Bligh, went on to achieve undeserved ignominy for the events surrounding his voyage in the *Bounty*. In October, 1797, at the Battle of Camperdown, Bligh distinguished himself as captain of the *Director* in cannonading his way down the enemy line to come to the aid of his sorely-pressed admiral. The captain of *HMS Agincourt* in the same battle was John Williamson who had managed to be promoted to captain despite his conduct during the affray in which Cook lost his life. True to form, at the end of the battle, Williamson was court-martialled for *'cowardice, negligence or disaffection'*. He was dismissed the Service.

Chapter Five

WEST INDIES

'A Spaniard chased is a Spaniard taken.'

There may have been some eagerness about Midshipman George Vancouver to visit his brother John at Kings Lynn and tell tall tales of his visit to the Pacific in the company of Captain Cook. There were, however, other pressing needs that had to be addressed. England was at war, and no young man of spirit wanted to miss the chance of glory or prize money. Better still would be to take part as a commissioned sea officer. Vancouver's time as a midshipman was well in excess of the requirements for the Lieutenant's examination and many of his contemporaries already held the rank (Horatio Nelson – a fellow Norfolk man – was a year younger than Vancouver, and was already a captain). Applying to take the examination immediately on his return, Vancouver was called to the Admiralty to be examined on 19th October. The examination was no mere formality. It had been introduced the previous century by Samuel Pepys as a means of preventing well-connected 'Gentlemen officers' from being given commissions – and even commands – through nothing more substantial than their friendships, or family acquaintances, with high-ranking officials. The would-be lieutenant had to prove his knowledge of seamanship, navigation, and ship-handling. Even in war-time there were always plenty of candidates with the qualifications needed to apply for the examination, and many midshipmen and master's mates found themselves already at the top of their personal careers. Vancouver, however, trained under officers such as Cook and Clerke, walked away from the examining board with his passing certificate tucked safely in his pocket. All that remained was to inform the Admiralty that he was available for an appointment, and wait for the call.

He did not have to wait long. In December, 1780, a mere two months after his return, Vancouver was appointed 1st (and probably only) lieutenant of *HMS Martin*. Captained by Commander William Warlaw, the *Martin* was a nineteen year old 300 ton sloop carrying fourteen 6-lb cannon and a ship's company of 125 men. Being far too small to take their place in the line of battle, sloops usually undertook patrols and minor escort duties. So it was for the first thirteen months of Vancouver's time in her. Confined to the North Sea and the English Channel, the *Martin* found little to bring laurels to her name or prize money to her ship's company. Things changed abruptly, however, in February, 1782. With a new captain, Commander William Merrick, the sloop was sent to join the fleet now squaring up to the French fleet in the West Indies.

Once the French had entered the war on the side of the American colonists, the West Indies inevitably became a major theatre of war. Whatever the outcome between the British and the Americans, the valuable West Indian islands would stay in the possession of the European powers. Britain, France, Spain, and later the Netherlands, would all take part in the struggle for territory.

The French had started first by capturing Dominica from their base on Martinique. The British retaliated by taking the French island of St Lucia. The French then fended off an attack on Grenada before Admiral Sir George Bridges Rodney arrived on the scene in 1780, fresh from his 'Moonlight Battle' victory over the Spanish. Minor skirmishes between Rodney and the French admiral, de Guichen, led to a major battle off Martinique. Unfortunately, Rodney failed to explain his battle plan to his captains who treated the affair as the usual slogging match whereas Rodney had intended to pick off the French rear before the enemy van could come to its aid. As a result, the engagement proved inconclusive.

Much to the British alarm, the French were soon reinforced by a Spanish fleet, but sickness in all the fleets prevented any immediate battle taking place. The British next suffered, not at the hands of the enemy, but of the elements. A hurricane hit Rodney's fleet sinking twelve ships and damaging a further thirteen. In January, 1781, Rodney – on learning that the Netherlands had entered the war against Britain – took the Dutch-owned island of St Eustatius whilst his second-in-command, Rear Admiral Samuel Hood, fought to another draw against the French admiral, de Grasse, who, in turn, captured Tobago. 1782 had hardly begun before de Grasse mounted an attack on St Kitts, landing soldiers to besiege the British garrison. Hood, with twenty-two ships at Antigua, sailed immediately on hearing the news and arrived off St Kitts on 24th January. De Grasse promptly sailed out to meet him and, after overnight manoeuvring along the coast of nearby Nevis, Hood produced a master stroke by racing across the French line of battle and anchoring his fleet in the same harbour de Grasse had just vacated. Twice de Grasse tried to engage Hood's line but found himself facing the same difficulty as if he was facing a huge fort. The anchored ships directed their combined fire on each French ship as it approached, sending the enemy reeling back from the intense fire-power. Unfortunately, all Hood's work was to be in vain. The garrison surrendered making his continued resistance pointless. In the dead of night, Hood's fleet slipped their cables and departed for Antigua. This, was the situation when Vancouver arrived on board the *Martin* in March, 1782.

Commander Merrick's first task was to accompany the 74-gun *Invincible* in escorting a convoy to Jamaica. This was followed by instructions to carry supplies to a small British garrison on Swan Island, 400 miles to the west of Jamaica. On arrival, and much to their consternation, it was found that the Spanish had fallen in force on the island a month earlier. The garrison had been captured, its building destroyed, and its guns taken. Only one member of the garrison and a number of slaves had escaped by fleeing into the bush. Revenge, however, was to fall into the *Martin's* path.

On 19th April, on her way back to Jamaica, the *Martin* fell in with a Spanish ship of similar size to herself. Merrick closed with the enemy and 'desired him to shorten sail'. The Spanish captain agreed, but when the *Martin* came alongside, she was met by a broadside. The reply was immediate and, for most of the next four hours, the two ships blazed away at each other until darkness prevented the action continuing. The next morning, at first light, the Spaniard was still seen to be in sight and Merrick – no doubt following the old French saying that '*a Spaniard chased is a Spaniard taken*' – gave chase until she was within range of his guns. Once again the thunder of cannonading rolled out across the Caribbean Sea. This time, however, the heart had gone out of the Spanish vessel and, before long, she struck her colours. A prize crew was placed on board the defeated enemy and both ships headed for Jamaica. Before they arrived, the *Martin* fell in with the British fleet under Rodney. Merrick's reward for his action on the 19th was to be a promotion to captain. Vancouver was also to be rewarded. A month after the action he was appointed to the 74-gun *Fame* as 4th lieutenant – the first time he had served on a ship-of-the-line. Once again, however, Vancouver's fate was to prove fickle. A week before the *Martin's* action against the Spaniard, Rodney had fallen in with de Grasse and the French fleet between two of the southern Leeward Island, Guadeloupe and Dominica. Close to a group of islets named the Saintes, Rodney's tactics of breaking the French line, coupled with the introduction of flintlock firing mechanisms for the cannons and the first use of the devastating firepower from carronades, brought about complete victory. British control of the West Indies was assured; there were to be no more fleet actions in which Vancouver might have taken part in the *Fame*.

In July, the entire 37 ships of the British fleet sailed north to New York to avoid hurricanes and returned in October to keep a watchful eye on the remaining French possessions in the Leeward Islands. Six months later the peace treaty was signed and the *Fame* was ordered home. She arrived in June, 1783 and was de-commissioned the following month.

Vancouver now found himself in the worst of all situations for a lieutenant with modest seniority. He had no ship, there was no war, and he was ashore on half pay out of the sight and mind of his superiors. In common with hundreds of his contemporaries all he could hope for was that his applications for employment might pass the desk of someone with 'interest', someone prepared to put forward his case. He might even have resorted to that most desperate of measures, taking a seat in the Admiralty waiting room in the hope that a vacancy might occur that could be snapped up by the nearest unemployed officer. For some the wait was to be a lifetime. Others, in desperation, would accept appointments to semaphore signalling stations, the Impress Service, or to the Sea Fencibles. But for Vancouver, after fortune had played him along for eighteen months, the situation changed dramatically when he was offered an appointment as 3rd lieutenant in the West Indies Station flagship, the newly-built, 50-gun *Europa*. By February, 1785, Vancouver was back at Jamaica.

The much reduced squadron in the West Indies was little more than a 'fleet in being', a naval presence to assure anyone who was interested that Britain was serious about its possessions in the area. Patrols were made, trade was guarded against pirates, and smugglers deterred. Sickness and death kept the hopes of promotion up, and hurricanes had to be suffered as the newly created United States of America showed no sign of welcoming a British fleet in its northern harbours. In January, 1786, the commander-in-chief, Rear Admiral Innes, provided some variety to the dull routine by dying. He was replaced by the senior officer on the station, Captain Allan Gardner, who, on assuming the temporary rank of commodore, shifted his broad pennant into the *Europa*. Just as Gardner arrived, the *Europa*'s captain, Edward Marsh, died and was replaced by Captain James Vashon. At the same time, a new master was appointed to the ship – Joseph Whidbey. All three men, Gardner, Vashon, and Whidbey, were to play an important part in Vancouver's future.

A vital step in that future came about as a result of an Admiralty decision to have surveys carried out of all harbours visited by their ships. As Cook and others like him had demonstrated, maritime surveying had become a well-practised skill and much of the world's coastlines had been charted to a high degree of accuracy. But working from the deck of a ship sailing down a coast is not the same as the detailed work required in surveying a harbour, bay, or inlet. This required an expertise in handling small boats, patience, and perseverance in addition to the ability to take soundings, measure distances, read angles, estimate heights, and keep an accurate record. Vashon had at hand someone who had sailed with Cook, and a competent sailing-master. Accordingly, Vancouver and Whidbey were appointed to the task. The two men were clearly a good team and the resultant chart – dedicated to Gardner – when put to the test, proved 'to be very correct.'

In the unhealthy climate of the West Indies, it was probably not the result of his survey that saw Vancouver appointed as second lieutenant of the flagship. It was much more likely to be yellow fever, cholera, or dysentery that provided the vacancy. Such an advancement was not a promotion, but a chance to take more responsibility and to bring an individual's talent to the closer attention of his superiors. Within three months, in February, 1788, Vancouver stepped into another vacancy. This time he became the *Europa*'s first lieutenant – still a lieutenant who could be re-appointed to a lesser position in a larger ship, but who now found himself second-in-command of a flagship.

The *Europa* remained on station for the next eighteen months before being relieved and ordered home. This time, Vancouver had been in the West Indies for almost five years. The once 'quiet inoffensive young man' had become a competent officer, an able ship-handler, and a first rate maritime surveyor. He had earned the unstinting admiration of his superiors and his contemporaries. With his record of reliability, initiative and enterprise, Vancouver might have hoped for the prospect of early employment when the *Europa* was paid off in September, 1789, and he found himself, once again, on half pay.

Chapter Six

THE SPANISH ARMAMENT

*'receive from the Spanish officers such lands or buildings
as are to be restored to the British subjects.'*

As a result of the work done by Cook in the southern hemisphere, and with the loss of access to American whaling ports by British whalers, the whaling industry had turned its attention to the south. The industry had expanded rapidly, and it was soon found that bases were needed from which the whalers could operate. Therefore, the British government decided that the Admiralty should mount an expedition to explore and survey the region. Once that task had been completed, the ships would then head northwards to the north-west coast of America to make a more detailed survey of its multitude of inlets, rivers, bays, and channels than Cook's instructions had allowed him to do.

Accordingly, a newly-built sloop was purchased from the Rotherhithe builders, Randall & Brents, and put into commission as *HMS Discovery* (Cook's *Discovery* had been sold eight years earlier). The 337 ton, copper-sheathed, *Discovery* had a main deck of 96 feet and measured 27 feet at the beam. She was armed with ten four-pounder cannon and ten gunwale-mounted swivel guns and carried a complement of 100 men. Instead of providing a second ship as escort, it was decided that the *Discovery* would carry a smaller vessel – a shallop – in her hold for use in in-shore surveying work. However, when put into practice, it was found that the shallop took up so much space that an unacceptable amount of supplies had to be removed for it to be stowed. Consequently, a separate escort in the form of the brig, *HMS Chatham,* was provided. Built and purchased two years earlier,

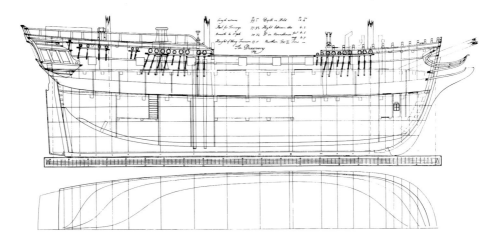

Naval architect's drawing of HMS *Discovery*

the 133 ton *Chatham* was serving as a tender at Deptford. With a complement of 45 men, she was armed with four three-pounder cannon and six swivels.

To command the expedition, their Lordships selected Lieutenant Henry Roberts – one of Cook's midshipmen on his second and third voyages. He was appointed as master and commander and entered the *Discovery* on 1st January, 1790. Although Roberts would have been in a position to select his own officers, it would have been a wise action on his part to consider those officers recommended to him by the Admiralty. As it was, there is little reason to suppose that he would have cavilled at the First Lord's suggestion as first lieutenant. Captain Alan Gardner – just about to take up his own appointment as an Admiralty Commissioner – had recommended to the First Lord that a suitable officer for the voyage would be Lieutenant George Vancouver, Roberts's former messmate. With Roberts's agreement, Vancouver (just five weeks junior to Roberts in seniority as a lieutenant) was offered the appointment as his second-in-command. He was delighted to accept, considering Roberts to be *'a fellow traveller for whose abilities I bore the greatest respect, and in whose friendship and good opinion I was proud to possess a place.'* The place of second lieutenant went to Richard Hergest – another of Cook's midshipmen. By the first week in January, 1790, all the *Discovery*'s officers were on board and preparations for the voyage begun. Events, however, far away on the other side of the world were to take a dramatic hand in the *Discovery*'s future.

Almost exactly three hundred years earlier, in 1493, the Spanish-born Pope, Alexander VI had issued a 'bull' dividing the world into two for the purpose of exploration and subsequent possession. Half went to Portugal, the other half to Spain. Not only was such a command preposterous but, in practice, it was recognized as being impossible to maintain the division against all-comers. The Spanish, however, were keen that the western coasts of both north and south America should remain solely their domain. It was, therefore, with alarm that the Spanish saw the threat of Russian expansion across the Bering Strait towards the coasts of north-west America. The Russians did not appear to have any grand colonial strategy in mind, and seemed only interested in the fur-trade possibilities in the area. But, as the Spanish knew well, trade led to trading-bases, and bases led easily to assumptions of possession.

In 1774 and 1775, the Spanish sent ships northwards from the west coast of Mexico in attempts to head off Russian activities. Both expeditions claimed to have visited a large bay on the coast and traded with the natives but, in neither case, was a landing made. Cook's arrival in Nootka Sound in 1778, provided evidence of the Spanish visits in the form of two silver spoons found hanging around the neck of one of the natives. There still remained, nevertheless, no evidence of a claim of possession having been made.

It was not the claiming of territory that attracted most attention amongst Cook's officers and seamen. During the voyage home, the *Resolution* and the *Discovery* had called at Canton where it was found that the Chinese had an almost overwhelming desire to own fur – especially the fur of the sea otter. Lieutenant John Mears took particular notice and, eight years later, he purchased two ships and set himself up in the north-west fur-trade. His second voyage in the region brought him to Nootka Sound where he established good relations with the natives and purchased from them 'a spot of ground' on which he built a house over which flew the British flag.

Leaving one of his ships, the *Iphigenia*, behind in company with the *North-west America* – a smaller vessel he had built in the sound, Mears sailed for China with a cargo of furs. In May, the following year (1789), whilst sharing Nootka Sound with two American fur-trading vessels, the ships were surprised to see two Spanish men-of-war sail into the sound. At first the Spaniards appeared to offer cordial relations but then the Spanish commander, Esteban Jose Martinez, announced that he had orders to seize all ships on the American coast. The captain of the *Iphigenia* – William Douglas – and all his crew were put in irons and his ship was ransacked by the Spanish. After the Spanish flag had been hoisted over Mears' property, Douglas was ordered to sign a document saying that Martinez had found him in 'great distress' and had supplied him with stores for a voyage to the Sandwich Islands. Furthermore, if it could be proved in a Spanish court that the two ships were legitimate prizes, Douglas and his owner (Mears) would pay suitable compensation to the Spanish. Douglas at first refused but, eventually, on seeing that it was his only means of escape, signed. The *Iphigenia* sailed on the last day of May, leaving the *North-west Passage* in the hands of the Spaniards.

Just over a month later, the fur-trader, *Argonaut* (in which Mears had a share), sailed into Nootka Sound and was seized by Martinez, an act causing her captain, James Colnett – formerly a midshipman with Cook – to become 'deranged'. A second British ship – the *Princess Royal* – was also taken when she appeared on the scene. Now with three British vessels to his credit, Martinez ordered them to sail for Mexico as his prizes, under escort of his men-of-war.

When he learned what had happened, Mears set off for England clutching a 'memorial' aimed at persuading the British government to recover the compensation from the Spanish which he *'and his associates have, as British subjects, a right to expect.'* Mears was, in fact, beaten to the government by a Mr Merry, the charge d'affairs in Madrid. In January, 1790, he wrote to the Foreign Secretary informing him that stories were emerging from Spanish sources that a British ship had been captured in Nootka Sound. A month later, the Spanish Ambassador wrote to the Foreign Secretary claiming that the two silver spoons found in the possession of a native at Nootka proved Spanish sovereignty over the area and that the British King should, therefore, 'punish' any attempt by British ships to interfere in the area. As he wrote, the Spanish began to build their naval strength – a fact brought to the British government's attention by Mr Merry. A second note from the Ambassador emphasised the *'incontestable rights to exclusive sovereignty, navigation, and commerce … including the right always exercised of capturing transgressors.'* The British ships, he announced, had been released and there the matter – as far as the Spanish were concerned – ended. However, just at that moment, a 'Memorial of John Mears, Lieutenant in His Majesty's Navy' landed at the government's feet. Within a week, the thirty year old Prime Minister, William Pitt, was demanding *'ample restitution to the individuals concerned, and full satisfaction to the nation for its insulted honour.'* A memorial from the king equally demanded *'an immediate and adequate satisfaction for the outrage committed by Monsieur de Martinez.'* The 'Spanish Armament' was under way.

It was neither the time, nor was there any enthusiasm, to continue with an expedition to the Pacific with rumours of an impending war flying about. Both the *Discovery* and the *Chatham* were re-deployed as 'receiving ships' – vessels used to hold both pressed men and volunteers prior to allocating them to ships in service. Vancouver received an appointment as third lieutenant to the *Courageux*, a 74-gun ship captured from the French in 1761. Vancouver's appointment was no accident. The *Courageux*' captain was Alan Gardner who had temporarily vacated his seat at the Admiralty in order to get involved with the possible action. Within six months, Vancouver had been advanced to first lieutenant.

It seems that the Spanish were looking for support from the French in their preparations to defend their position. But the French were in the throes of a bloody revolution and many of the senior French naval officers were having their heads removed for the entertainment of baying mobs. Neither did George Washington, the first President of the United States, feel like expressing any gratitude for the part played by Spain in his country's independence. Suddenly, in early November, just as it appeared that war was inevitable, if for no better reason than its own momentum, a dispatch arrived at the Foreign Secretary's office. An agreement had been negotiated between Great Britain and Spain. The 'Nootka Sound Convention' gave Britain most of what she had demanded. Reparations were to be paid to Mears and any claims of exclusive sovereignty over the north-west of America would be abandoned by Spain. Unfortunately, there proved to be a lack of clarity on certain points. The actual limit of Spanish sovereignty on the coast had not been established. In British minds it stopped at 40 degrees North – about two hundred miles north of the Spanish settlement of San Francisco. The Spanish, on the other hand, were considering a point on the Straits of Juan de Fuca, some 47 degrees North. Furthermore, it was not quite clear what Mears 'spot of ground' actually comprised before Martinez had taken it over. The only answer, especially to the latter difficulty, was, in accordance with the convention, to send a British representative to Nootka Sound actually to receive the 'buildings and tracts of land' in question from a representative of Spain.

Ten days after news of the convention had arrived at the Foreign Office, the Admiralty informed Deptford dockyard that it was *'to hasten the fitting of the Discovery and the Chatham tender as much as possible giving them the preference to all other Works.'* With the convention opening up the north-west coast of America to detailed exploration, the opportunity might be seized to carry out a survey in addition to the formal taking back of British property. Gardner, back at the Admiralty, began his manoeuvres by raising the possibility of an expedition to Africa and suggesting that the man for the job was Commander Henry Roberts. With that policy being pursued, and Roberts removed from the command of the expedition (actually to end up in the West Indies), the way lay open for a new commander.

On 17th November, 1790, Vancouver received instructions telling him to report to the Admiralty 'for the purpose of attending to the commands of the Board of Admiralty.' There he was offered command of a voyage to the north-west coast of America with a view to *'acquiring a more complete knowledge, than has yet been obtained.'* The area to be covered was *'between latitude 60 degrees north and 30 degrees north.'* He was to investigate a claim made by an American vessel, the *Lady Washington*, that it had passed through the Straits of Juan de Fuca and emerged north of Nootka. In order to avoid any loss of time, he was not to investigate any inlets or rivers further than they *'shall appear navigable by vessels of such burthen as might safely navigate in the Pacific Ocean'.* Nor was he to carry out a survey that was *'too minute and particular.'* Furthermore, he was to visit Nootka Sound to *'receive from the Spanish officers such lands or buildings as are to be restored to the British subjects.'* As continuing diplomacy was liable to change matters beyond Vancouver's knowledge, a final set of orders detailing how he was expected to carry out his diplomatic mission would be sent out to the Sandwich Islands in the transport *Daedalus* in time for his own arrival.

On accepting the command, Vancouver was appointed as Master and Commander on 15th December – he was thirty-two years old. His first task was to select his officers. He looked no further than the men he had served with in the *Europa*. As first lieutenant, Vancouver chose Zachary Mudge, a protegee of Rear Admiral Sir John Jervis who had put Mudge's name on the books of HMS *Foudroyant* when he was ten years old. Having passed his lieutenant's examination at the age of eighteen, Mudge was appointed first lieutenant of the *Discovery* when he was just twenty. Already serving in the *Discovery* having entered her as a masters mate was the newly-commissioned lieutenant, Peter Puget. Now aged twenty-five, Puget had served in the Royal Navy since he was thirteen. Four of those years had been served in the *Europa*. Also with service in the *Europa* was the *Discovery*'s third lieutenant, Joseph Baker. He had passed his lieutenant's examination just four days after Puget and was appointed to the ship in mid-December. Vancouver's final selection was one based on personal experience. Joseph Whidbey – the same warrant officer who had carried out the survey of Port Royal and Kingston harbours with Vancouver during his time in the *Europa*, was appointed as the ship's master. At thirty-five years old, he was one of the oldest men on board.

Command of the *Chatham* went to Lieutenant William Broughton, a twenty-eight year old who had seen considerable action against the French in the East Indies. During his time on the North America station he had been taken prisoner by the Americans after attempting to burn an American schooner that had been forced ashore on the coast of Massachusets. His first (and only) lieutenant was James Hanson whose seniority was one day less than Puget. The *Chatham*'s master, James Johnstone, had spent a considerable time on the north-west coast of America with the fur-traders – including Colnett. At some stage in his career he had managed to acquire considerable 'interest' and came to Vancouver, not only recommended for his knowledge of the region, but also with the recommendation of Lord Chatham, the First Lord of the Admiralty.

The surgeons appointed for the voyage were Alexander Cranstoun for the *Discovery*, and William Walker for the *Chatham*. With their appointment came the first of the dark clouds that were to cause Vancouver problems in the future. Archibald Menzies was an experienced naval surgeon who had served with Johnstone and the fur-traders on the north-west coast of America. He had used his spare time to collect seeds and plants which, on his return, he had sent to Sir Joseph Banks, now a baronet and President of the Royal Society. When it was learned that a voyage of discovery was about to be undertaken under the command of Henry Roberts, Banks used his influence to have Menzies appointed as the expedition's naturalist and botanist. The Spanish Armament had put an end to the appointment but, when Menzies found out that the expedition was to be re-organised, he applied for the position of surgeon in the *Discovery*. Vancouver, however, already had his own man, Cranstoun, but agreed to take Menzies as naturalist and botanist. At this point, Banks began to take a closer interest in the voyage to the extent that he demanded that certain upper deck fittings be erected including a twelve by eight feet glass frame on the *Discovery*'s quarterdeck. He had no doubt, due to his huge status and authority, that he would get his own way. His presidency of the Royal society had become autocratic, almost despotic. Even his friends recorded that *'It is possible that Sir Joseph Banks may have assumed a firm tone in the execution of his duty as president of the society, and may have been free in his rebukes where he apprehended that there was occasion for them.'*

Vancouver, however, seems to have been less than over-awed by the great man, and certainly resented his interference in the ship's and the voyage's affairs. At some stage, fully aware of the problems Banks had caused Cook by his proposed changes to the *Resolution*, Vancouver confronted him and brought an end to the alterations. Banks was outraged. More used to deference than challenge, he wrote to Menzies *'How Captain Vancouver will behave to you is more than I can guess unless I judge by his conduct towards me which was not such as I am used to receiving from Persons in his situation.'* For the great navigator, Captain Cook, to be unimpressed by Banks's wealth and influence was one thing, but for the youngest son of a petty official to oppose his views was another. With vengeance in mind, Banks suggested to Menzies that if Vancouver should be seen to be obstructing the naturalist in any way, he should record the matter – *'the instances whatever they are will of course appear as they happen in your Journal which as it will be a justification to you will afford ground for impeaching the Propriety of his conduct which for your sake I shall not Fail to make use of.'* The unpunctuated venom of Banks's letter gave Menzies a powerful weapon to be used against his own captain.

But an even more pressing problem for Vancouver loomed before him. Not surprisingly, when news of the forthcoming voyage spread, a large number of 'young gentlemen' were eager to take part. The official complement allowed Vancouver to carry six midshipmen and three master's mates. He ended up with fifteen. So many, in fact, that young Edward Roberts – recommended to Vancouver by William Wales, Cook's astronomer on his second voyage – was packed off to live on the main deck with the seamen.

Those successful in gaining a place in the midshipman's berth ranged from the son of an Earl and the friend of a Marquis, to two nephews of Alan Gardner and the son of Vancouver's Navy Agent (who looked after his financial affairs during his absence). The most seemingly illustrious of them all, however, a young man whose connections would have made any captain with the slightest ambition swell with pride, was The Honourable Thomas Pitt. The son of Baron Camelford, a cousin of the Prime Minister, and with a sister who was shortly to marry the First Lord of the Admiralty, Pitt was a well-built sixteen year old over six foot tall. He had already had an extraordinary experience that had nearly cost him his life. Whilst serving in *HMS Guardian* under the command of Lieutenant Edward Riou (one of Vancouver's messmates in the *Resolution*), the ship had collided with an iceberg. With the *Guardian* sinking beneath him, Riou allowed as many of his ship's company and passengers (convicts bound for Australia) to take to the ship's five boats as wished. He, however, stayed with the ship along with sixty-one other people including a Miss Schafer – a daughter of one of the Superintendents of Convicts – and Midshipman Pitt. So badly damaged was the hull of the *Guardian* that the ballast had all dropped out and there were sixteen feet of water in the hold. By sheer good fortune, however, a large number of casks had broken free and were bumping the underside of the lower gun-deck. It was almost certainly this unexpected aid to buoyancy that kept the ship from plunging to the bottom of the southern Indian Ocean. For nine weeks, under the barest threads of sails, the ship was nursed towards the Cape until, on the 21st February, 1790, land was sighted. After a hair-raising voyage of two thousand miles, the *Guardian* was run on to the beach where her destruction was completed by a gale. Only one of the crowded ship's boats had survived. Riou went on to become 'The gallant Riou', losing his life under Nelson's command at the Battle of Copenhagen whilst exclaiming *'What will Nelson think of us?'* Despite their time together in the *Guardian*, he had clearly not been impressed by the qualities of Midshipman Pitt. In refusing to grant Pitt a signed certificate of service (required for promotion to lieutenant), Riou had written that *'during the time he was under my Command his Conduct was such as not to entitle him to it.'*

The 'lower deck' of the *Discovery* and the *Chatham* was as varied as any ship of the time. A mixture of volunteers and pressed men, experienced and novices, they came from as far apart as Scotland and the Congo. One able seaman came from the West Indian island of Antigua, whilst another was 'John Ingram', a native of Hawaii. His real name was Towereroo and had asked to be taken home after a visit to the north-west coast. The ships also numbered a 'widow's man' on their books. An entirely fictitious entity, his wages would go towards funding pensions for the seamen's widows and orphans. Both ships carried a detachment of marines, each under a sergeant. Equally in common with other ships of the time, desertion was always a problem. Pressed men would always look for the opportunity to 'run' and even volunteers would keep an eye out for a better berth. There was little point in freezing off an American coast if a war broke out and there was the chance of prize money to be earned elsewhere.

Chapter Seven

SOUTHERN SURVEY

'Some body knows what.'

T
he ships sailed from Deptford on Friday, 7th January, 1791. Incredibly, the
Discovery had never been to sea before; she had never even had her sails bent
prior to that day and not a single sea-going trial had been carried out. Not
surprisingly, the voyage did not have a very auspicious beginning. The *Chatham*
was lagging behind as her master tried to improve her sailing qualities (he referred
to his ship as a 'dung barge'), and the *Discovery* lost a man overboard whilst making
her way down the Channel. She also had much of her ship's head (the structure
above the bows containing the seamen's lavatories or 'seats of ease') washed away.
By the time Falmouth was reached, the poor sailing qualities of the *Chatham* had
been clearly exposed and Vancouver was forced to transfer all his 'shot' (cannon
balls) to her as ballast. With extremely bad timing, whilst the two ships were at the
Cornish port, a proclamation was read offering bounties for seamen willing to enter
a number of ships about to be commissioned in the face of possible involvement
in Russo-Turkish war. By that night, sixteen men had deserted from the *Discovery*
and five from the *Chatham*. Another fifteen men were landed as unsuitable or sick.
With the loss of the man during the passage down the Channel, Vancouver had
to call on the resources of the Impress Service for the supply of thirty-seven men
before he could finally leave the shores of England.

The two ships, one with a bow structure that splintered apart with every modest
wave, the other so 'crank' that the best it could achieve was a sluggish wallow,
finally left those shore on 1st April (All Fool's Day) 1791. Neither of the captains
had ever held a command before, the first lieutenant of the *Discovery* was aged
twenty, the other two lieutenants holding passing certificates on which the ink was
still wet. The midshipmen varied between the totally ineffective and the potentially
rebellious. A civilian was carried who was eager to report every failing back to the
powerful President of the Royal Society whilst, below decks, the seamen nursed
grievances over missing the chance of prize money or of being victims of the press
gang. With this combination of inexperience, defective equipment, ill-will, and
ill-feeling, Commander George Vancouver was supposed to carry out a highly-
charged diplomatic mission, and to undertake the monotony and strain of an
extended coastal survey in a remote part of the world.

It was a rare opportunity for a commander to show his qualities of leadership,
to demonstrate his abilities to bring his officers and men together in the face of a
difficult, but achievable, challenge. Instead, with the best of intentions, Vancouver
instituted a health regime based on the issue of pickled cabbage and 'portable
broth'. Decks and bulkheads were washed down with vinegar as below decks the
seamen had to suffer the acrid effects of a mixture of gunpowder and vinegar being

burned to 'smoke' the decks clean. Yet more discomfort was added by the use of
fires as an aid to ventilation. Even Vancouver was moved to admit that *the smoke
and heat thence arising was considered as inconvenient and disagreeable.*

At Teneriffe, Vancouver allowed the seamen ashore for exercise as he,
Lieutenant Baker and Joseph Whidbey went to call on the Spanish Governor
General, Don Antonio Guitierres at his residence in Santa Cruz. So poor was this
distinguished official that he did not have enough gunpowder to return salutes
made in his honour, and was unable to offer Vancouver and his party dinner due
to the 'poverty of the country.' Instead, their meal took place at the house of an
Irish gentleman, Mr Rooney. Later that evening, as Vancouver and his party made
their way back to the ships, they found the wharf in a state of uproar.

Some of the midshipmen had been sent ashore to collect the seamen and
marines. The liberty-men having enjoyed the hospitality of the dock-side bars
were in no mood to ordered about and a fight had broken out between the
midshipmen and some of the *Chatham*'s seamen. Nearby Spanish sentries had tried
to break up the disturbance but the seamen (with 'an unalterable hatred for a
Spaniard') closed ranks and turned their attention on the soldiers. Some were
knocked down as another had his musket wrenched from his hands and thrown
into the sea. At this moment, Vancouver arrived and, after calming things down,
began to supervise getting the seamen into the ship's boats. Unfortunately, as this
was happening, Spanish reinforcements – accompanied by a mob – rushed to the
scene and started fighting with the seamen. To escape the melee, some of the
midshipmen, including Pitt, jumped into the harbour and swam to the waiting
boats. Baker – the only officer in uniform – was severely knocked about the head,
and Whidbey narrowly escaped injury or death as he side-stepped two lunging
bayonets which broke on the wall behind him. Close by, as he struggled with a
number of Spanish guards, Vancouver toppled over the harbour-wall and fell into
the water. Eventually, the officers and seamen managed to reach the boats lying
just off-shore and made it back to the ships. It had been an ugly and undignified
episode that enraged Vancouver. In the morning he wrote a letter of protest to the
Governor General, but Guitierres replied that, although disciplinary action would
be taken, the fault lay in the seamen for starting the fight and the officers for not
wearing uniform. No mention of the incident was made by Vancouver in his
reports to the Admiralty, an understandable omission that caused him great
embarrassment when letters from Menzies and others led to reports appearing in
the British press. Governor Guitierres was later to achieve his own small role in
history when, six years later, Santa Cruz was attacked by Nelson at the cost of his
right arm. The Governor was the first person to receive a letter – thanking him for
the way he had treated British wounded seamen – to be written by Nelson using
his left hand.

The voyage to the Cape was enlivened only by one of the *Chatham*'s seamen,
heavily fortified by rum during the Crossing the Line ceremony, falling overboard.
The ship was instantly brought into the wind, but no trace of the man could be
seen. Then someone looked over the ship's side and saw the man hanging from

a rope he had grabbed as he went over. Of far greater annoyance to Vancouver was the poor sailing speed of the *Chatham*. At last, in late May, he could take it no more and told Broughton that he intended to take the *Discovery* on ahead to the Cape. Broughton was to bring the *Chatham* as best he could. Much to his surprise – and, no doubt, annoyance – as Vancouver sailed into Simon's Bay, he found the *Chatham* already there and waiting for him.

Apart from obtaining provisions and testing the scientific instruments and chronometers, the most important task at the Cape was for the *Discovery*'s head to be put into order. The bowsprit was removed and 'fished' to give it greater strength and the head railings, head timbers, lace-piece, head frames, iron work, and 'seats of ease' all had to be replaced. It was as well that these basic sanitary requirements were attended to for, just as the ships were about to sail, their ships companies were hit by a severe bout of dysentery brought into the bay by a Dutch ship returning from Batavia.

Vancouver sailed on the 17th August in an effort to escape any further diseases brought in by the Dutchman. He had enough to contend with as a result of the dysentery which was affecting everyone. At first it seemed as if the surgeon, Cranstoun, was suffering the most when his illness brought on a stroke but, three weeks out of the Cape, Private Neil Coyle of the marines, died. Vancouver was forced to ask Menzies to undertake the role of ship's surgeon – the same position he had forcibly opposed Menzies receiving before the ship had left England.

As they were about to leave the Cape, Vancouver informed Broughton of his plans and the nature of his instructions. A number of rendezvous were agreed in case of separation, the final one being at the Sandwich Islands. On passage down the Atlantic, Vancouver had decided to have a close look at the southern coast of New Holland (Australia), following it eastwards until Van Dieman's Land (Tasmania) was reached. There he hoped to establish whether or not the land was actually an island or was merely a southwards jutting promontory.

An attempt to search for shoals around St Paul and Amsterdam islands failed when the ships sailed between the island without sighting either. They met rough seas as they sailed eastwards towards the south-west corner of New Holland and, on the morning of the 20th August, a following sea stove in one of the stern windows of the *Chatham*. Water continued to pour in and, for a while it looked as if the ship itself was under threat of sinking. A distress signal was hoisted but the *Discovery* sailed on without seeing it and was soon out of sight. After an alarming hour or more, Broughton and Johnstone brought the inflow under control and had the breach sealed and the water pumped out. Johnstone was particularly annoyed at the *Discovery*'s failure to stop and noted that the *Chatham* would not have *'received any relief from that quarter.'*

Vancouver had deliberately chosen an eastward course that took him between the route taken by the English navigator and buccaneer, William Dampier, in 1699 – which had taken him to the west coast of New Holland, and from where he explored the north-west corner of the land – and that taken by Cook in 1776, well to the south of New Holland. As he had hoped, Vancouver sighted the land at the south-west corner of New Holland, a stretch of coast to which he gave the name 'New Cornwall'. Two days later a deep wide inlet opened out to the ships. Vancouver landed and took possession of the site in the name of his sovereign, naming the inlet 'King George the Third's Sound' (King George Sound). More names were bestowed on the numerous features in the area – 'Cape Chatham' (Chatham Island), 'Mount Gardner', 'Cape Howe', 'Princess Royal Harbour', 'Seal Island'.

Altogether, twelve days were spent at anchor in the sound. Evidence of 'the most miserable human habitation' was discovered, but no people were seen. Menzies, the botanist, rambled over the land collecting plants and seeds, black swans were sighted, and whales sported about the ships. Lieutenant Mudge noted that *'A dead Cangaroo was the only Quadruped I met with.'* Both wood and water were collected as men who were still suffering from dysentery were put ashore to recuperate. To mark his first experience of discovery whilst in command of his own expedition, Vancouver left bottles containing notes of his visit and the names he had given to the local features.

They gained the open sea on 11th October only to find that an easterly wind delayed their progress. Little of the land was seen as they struggled in the face of a head wind. 'Doubtful Island' was seen and named as was 'Point Hood' (Hood Point). But what land was seen proved to present *'a dreary aspect, destitute of wood, or herbage.'* After a voyage of just over 300 miles, a rocky islet was encountered. Vancouver named it 'Termination Island'. The delay caused by the contrary winds and the unprepossessing character of the land directed him to change his mind about further exploration along the coast, and to abandon his attempt to enquire into the insularity of Van Dieman's Land. Instead he decided to head straight for Dusky Bay. They had not gone far before the *Chatham* collided with a whale, but with little apparent damage to either ship or animal.

A storm off Dusky Bay caused the ships to separate. The *Discovery* found a safe anchorage in which to anchor from the gale after suffering some damage to her sails and rigging. The *Chatham*, however, was forced to anchor in a much more exposed spot and was lucky to avoid being driven onshore. A lull the following day allowed the *Chatham* to be taken to Facile Bay on the north-east shore of the sound. Both vessels found themselves to be fortunate in their final choice of anchorage as 'Anchorage Island Harbour' and Facile Bay provided ample fresh water, wood, and spruce trees for the brewing of spruce beer (used as an antiscorbutic). The chief losers by this arrangement of widely separate anchorages were the midshipmen who looked forward to the frequent social occasions mounted by the two midshipmen's messes when the ships were berthed in company.

Cook's survey of Dusky Sound had missed out an area at the head of Breaksea Sound and he had marked the place on his chart with the words *'No body knows what'*. Vancouver decided to have a look for himself taking Broughton and Johnstone with him. They found that a promontory split the waters into two arms. Both inlets were surveyed and Vancouver was able to amend Cook's comment to read *'Some body knows what.'* The tip of the promontory was later named 'Chatham Point' and the arms 'Vancouver' and 'Broughton' after their surveyors.

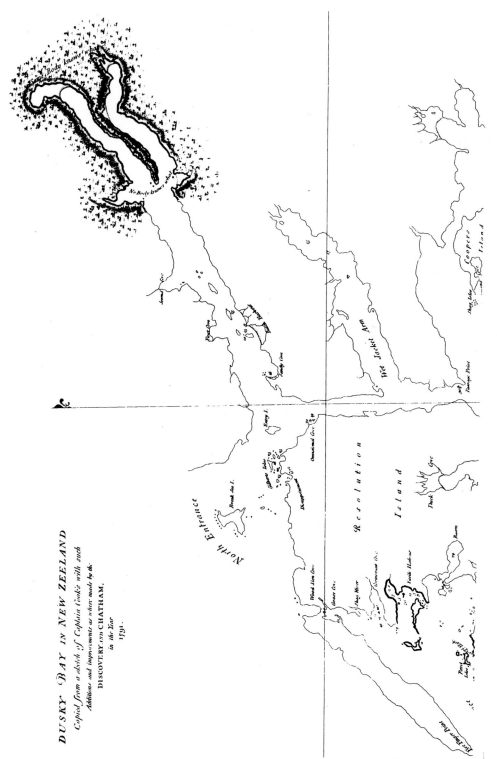

DUSKY BAY IN NEW ZEELAND

Copied from a sketch of Captain Cook's with such
Additions and improvements as where made by the
DISCOVERY and CHATHAM,
in the Year
1791.

Based on Cook's chart, Vancouver extends a corner of Dusky Bay from 'No body knows what' to 'Some body knows what'

Without having seen any local people, they left Dusky Bay on 22 November. Gales from the north-west caused the two ships to separate in the dark and Vancouver was greatly concerned that the *Chatham* had run foul of a group of dangerous, low-lying rocks he named 'The Snares'. A search revealed no sign of his consort so Vancouver headed for Tahiti, the next rendezvous.

The *Discovery* had not reached far out into the Pacific when Vancouver found himself up against a severe measure of indiscipline from the young gentlemen of the midshipman's mess. One of the midshipmen, who had the important responsibility of keeping the chronometers wound, failed to do so and felt the rough edge of one of the lieutenant's tongues. In a fit of pique, the midshipman then refused to carry on with the responsibility. In consequence of this action, Vancouver called Edward Roberts aft from his berth with the seamen. Roberts was a well-educated young man who had been recommended to Vancouver by William Wales, Cook's astronomer, but had been unable to find him a place in the midshipman's mess. Now Vancouver decided that Roberts, who was quite capable of taking responsibility for the chronometers, should be allowed 'quarterdeck privileges' – ie be allowed to live with the other young gentlemen. The midshipmen and their messmates had, however, other ideas and refused to admit Roberts to their mess. Vancouver's response was to tear down the canvas screen separating the midshipmen from the seamen. In a small vessel, where any shred of privacy would have been highly valued, Vancouver's act must have seemed outrageous. An important privilege and symbol of status had been swept aside and many in the midshipman's mess swiftly adjusted the respect they felt for their captain.

A month out of Dusky Bay, the jagged peaks of a mountainous land broke the horizon. It was a new island *'at a considerable distance from the tracks of former navigators.'* Keeping off its steep shores, the *Discovery* was soon met by canoes filled with natives who quickly overcame their timidity and began to scramble up the ship's sides. Although clearly friendly, the natives had no compunction about attempting to steal whatever could be taken away. Iron, in particular, attracted their attention; ring bolts, belaying pins, and tackle hooks were all grabbed, *'others tried to carry the guns from their carriages while others dragg'd at the Anchors with the utmost fury, expressing their rage they could not move them.'* Instead, they were given fishing hooks, mirrors and beads. Another strange sight for the islanders came in the shape

The ISLAND of OPARO in Lat.^{de} 27° 36′ 8th Long.^{de} 215° 19′ E.^t Var.^{on} 5° 40′ Easterly distant 7 Miles.

Island of Oparo discovered by Vancouver

of a Newfoundland dog belonging to one of the ship's company. At first the natives viewed the animal with some trepidation, but when it was seen to *'fetch and carry ... their gestures and Acclamations were unbounded.'* The Sandwich islander, Towereroo, could not understand the language of the natives, but Vancouver came to understand that the island was called 'Oparo' (Rapa Island). The natives had constantly urged Vancouver to land, but he refused, probably out of concern for the *Chatham*. Rumours, however, were spread that, on seeing some fortress-like structures on the island, he believed they might have been built by mutineers from *HMS Bounty* and, out of fear of a possible battle, did not want to land. In fact, the mutineers were on Pitcairn Island – a mere eight hundred miles to the north-east.

Matavai Bay was reached on 27th December. Much to everyone's relief, the *Chatham* was seen secure and at anchor. Broughton had been greatly concerned that the *Discovery* had not been there in his arrival for, with her far greater sailing qualities, he had expected to find Vancouver's ship waiting for him. The discovery of a new island could not be used as an adequate reason for the delay as Broughton had discovered an island of his own. Eight hundred miles east of New Zealand's south island, the *Chatham* came across an unknown island. An attempt to establish cordial relations with the natives went sour and a fight broke out in which, much to Broughton's distress, one of the islanders was killed. Before leaving its shores, Broughton took possession of the place and named it 'Chatham Island' after the First Lord of the Admiralty.

The stay at Tahiti began well with old friendships being re-established, but an outbreak of theft, especially of an iron axe and a large amount of clothing, led to a deterioration in the relationship between the natives and the visitors. Towereroo had also deserted and taken to the hills with a local chief's daughter. The young woman was of no concern to Vancouver, but his instructions were to take the native back to the Sandwich Island. If left on Tahiti, his knowledge of firearms could cause an imbalance in the local tribal structure. The effect on Vancouver surprised his officers. The once-affable – even amiable – man, threatened to burn down the house of the chief he believed had the missing axe and put a rope around the neck of a native whom he thought was involved in the theft of clothing. When this did not have the desired effect, he caused the area to be evacuated by threatening to *'desolate the whole district & destroy all their canoes.'* Towereroo was located and returned, but the clothing (including twelve shirts belonging to Broughton) failed to re-appear.

It was not only the natives who tested Vancouver's patience. Following the experience of his former shipmate, William Bligh, in the *Bounty*, Vancouver refused to allow anyone ashore unless they were on duty. This played particularly hard on both the young gentlemen and the young seamen. The attractions of the south sea islands with its tales of their beautiful, willing, and available women had been one of the promises of the voyage. Now it was to be denied them. It is not at all unlikely that several young men took every opportunity to try and circumvent Vancouver's restrictions. One who certainly did was The Honourable Thomas

Pitt – by now serving as a master's mate. In Dusky Bay the midshipman's mess had taken the iron grill from an old hen coop and made it into a griddle, or barbecue, for use on the beach. Now trapped on board, Pitt found himself being offered the favours of the young woman who had come alongside in a canoe. All she required in exchange was a small gift. The young man grabbed the griddle and handed it over, but his reward was not to be, for his action had been witnessed. Pitt soon found himself facing the captain. Vancouver, as he had shown on a number of occasions, had no hesitation about flogging men who disobeyed orders. But young gentlemen could not be triced up to a grating and flogged with a cat-of-nine-tails. Instead he ordered Pitt to suffer the punishment known as 'kissing the gunner's daughter.' This entailed being tied down over a cannon in the great cabin and being caned in front of the other young gentlemen. Pitt had been awarded twenty-four strokes and, after twelve had been delivered, Lieutenant Mudge stepped forward and offered to speak to the captain on Pitt's behalf if he promised to behave better in the future. The future Lord Camelford, in a fury at the indignity being inflicted upon the son of a peer of the realm, refused to be 'begged off' and took the final twelve strokes. Among those forced to watch the caning was Midshipman The Honourable Charles Stuart, the son of the Earl of Bute. Stuart – and who had probably never seen such an effrontery against a member of the aristocracy – later got drunk and approached Vancouver. Taking a cut-throat razor from his pocket, Stuart waved it under the captain's nose with the words, *'If Sir, you ever flog me, I will not survive the disgrace. I have this ready to cut my throat with.'* Vancouver, unimpressed by this display of lordly petulance, sent Stuart to the masthead and took every opportunity to repeat the punishment for every trifling offence Stuart committed whilst he remained on board.

Some of the young gentlemen, including Pitt, did manage to get ashore at one stage and returned with six pigs with which they had been presented. All thoughts, however, of a number of splendid meals to be held in the midshipman's mess were soon dashed when Vancouver confiscated the animals and had them served up to the entire ship's company in lieu of a day's official rations (Vancouver, in addition to being the captain, was also the ship's purser).

There were good reasons for Vancouver wanting to avoid the problems that had afflicted Bligh, and the actions of the natives were more than a simple annoyance. Moreover, he had not even started on the main reason for his presence in the Pacific, yet he had already found irrelevant distractions and sullen behaviour impeding his progress. His isolation and the responsibility and strain of command were beginning to affect his personality.

The only answer to the problem was to leave Tahiti and the ships sailed on 24 January, 1792, for Hawaii where they anchored in Kealakekua Bay – the site of Cook's death – six weeks later. There had been some unwelcome changes in Hawaii since Vancouver's last visit. Chief amongst these was the proliferation of fire-arms among the natives. These weapons had mainly come from the fur-traders – even Colnett had supplied them with a three-pounder swivel gun, muskets and blunderbusses. Two years before, in 1790, the natives had attacked an

American schooner, killing all on board. The days of willing native assistance and advantageous trade had gone.

The ships moved around to Whymea Bay on Kauai where Cook had first landed. There, Vancouver demonstrated the irrational behaviour to which he seemed to be becoming prone. During a walk for exercise along a beach, Vancouver noticed a number of large fires burning on the slopes of the surrounding hills. A rapid questioning of a number of natives failed to elicit a convincing reason for the flames and Vancouver took to the belief that the fires marked the beginning of an intended attack. Both Johnstone and Menzies, who were ashore at the same time, tried to calm him down by explaining that the fire were simply a means of clearing dead grass. Vancouver, however, would have none of such explanations and, according to one account *'behaved like a Madman raged and swore which terrified the Indians.'* He then demanded to be taken back on board despite the heavy surf then running. The *Discovery*'s pinnace was off shore so a native canoe had to be used to get him out to it. Two midshipmen clambered into the canoe and began to make for the boat only to have the fragile vessel overturned by the force of the waves. The two young men – both non-swimmers – clung to the upturned craft but Vancouver, claiming the accident to be an attempt on his life, struck out for the pinnace. To have placed people's lives in danger un-necessarily would not have been the action of a rationally-thinking Vancouver. What had brought on the bout of paranoia cannot be known, but it may not be stretching things too far to suggest that the death of Cook – and Vancouver's own narrow escape from death – on those same islands, had made such an impression that, keeping his irrational fears well-hidden for most of the visit, he finally succumbed to them. In addition, his feelings of tension could not have been helped by the fact that the supply-vessel *Daedalus*, which was supposed to bringing out extra supplies and an up-to-date set of instructions for the diplomatic mission, had failed to appear.

Five days later, loaded down with several tons of yams, the *Discovery* and the *Chatham* left the shores of the Sandwich Islands and turned their bows towards North America.

Chapter Eight

NEW ALBION

'no small degree of mortification.'

The Sandwich Islands were still above the horizon when a gale and some 'trifling squalls' revealed that the *Discovery*'s mainmast had a serious defect and required to be strengthened. To do this, and to relieve the pressure on the mast, the top-gallant mast had to be brought down. This, in turn, affected the *Discovery*'s speed, but not to the extent that she could not still out-sail the *Chatham* whose sails were beginning to fall apart with mildew. With the mainmast 'fished' (ie. strengthened with lengths of timber along the point of weakness) Vancouver's patience was further tested the following day when the foretop-gallant yard failed and required replacing. The ship's carpenter, Henry Phillips, by now probably exhausted from his work on the mainmast, was ordered to fashion a replacement. He did so, but when Vancouver inspected the new yard, he found it not to be 'agreeable' and told Phillips so in no uncertain terms. Instead of bearing the brunt of the captain's complaint about his workmanship, Phillips replied in like manner. Vancouver, in no mood to suffer contempt from one of his warrant officers, had the carpenter confined to his cabin and appointed the carpenter's mate, Thomas Laithwood, in his place.

With particularly bad timing, Midshipman the Honourable Thomas Pitt, then chose to indulge in a bout of horse-play with another of the midshipmen. As a result of his 'romping', the glass protecting the binnacle compass was broken. Vancouver had him whipped over a cannon for the second time. Pitt proved to be a slow learner for later, in response to an unrecorded incident, he was to earn a third humiliating thrashing from a boatswain's mate's rope in front of the assembled midshipmen. Even worse was to come. During a night watch on the forecastle shared with Master's Mate John Sykes, Pitt decided to lie down on his great-coat and go to sleep. Sometime later, Sykes clambered on to the forechains, threw the log over the side, and set about determining the ship's rate through the water. As he was doing this, the officer of the watch, stationed on the quarterdeck, called out for Pitt. Getting no reply, and with Sykes busy in the chains, the officer of the watch, called out once again. This time, Pitt answered and made his way aft. When he arrived on the quarterdeck, the officer accused him of being asleep on watch. Pitt denied the charge but, despite being backed up by Sykes, was hauled in front of Vancouver. By now, thoroughly disenchanted with the young aristocrat's behaviour and attitude, Vancouver did the almost unthinkable to a person of Pitt's social rank – he had him confined in the 'common bilboes'. Seated on the deck in full public view with his ankles secured to a metal bar, and with a seaman on either side of him (also under punishment), the future Lord Camelford had ample time to review his behaviour, or to consider the circumstances he was placed in by the son of a mere Customs officer. Later events would show that he chose to dwell upon the latter.

As the coast of America approached, the temperature fell and the ship's companies brought out their warm clothing. Albatrosses and giant petrels soared overhead as sperm whales breached and spouted around the ships. Soon ducks and puffins were seen. These, along with green vegetation floating on the sea, could only mean that the shore was not far off.

On 17th April, 1792, just over a year out of England, Vancouver saw land to the east. His landfall was close to 39 degrees, 20'N, about 115 miles north of San Francisco Bay – the 'New Albion' of Sir Francis Drake with its surf-washed shores and green-clad mountains. Hauling clear for the night, Vancouver returned the next day and with Puget, Whidbey and others took a total of eighty-five lunar distances to determine his longitude. In combination with his chronometer, he calculated that his longitude at noon was '236 degrees, 25' E' (123 degrees, 35' W, a calculation approximately 29' – 29 nautical miles – to the west of his true position). With his base calculations determined, the survey had begun.

Passing north along the coast, Vancouver soon began to bestow names upon features where he felt it was merited. On St George's Day (23rd April) he named 'Point St George' and 'Dragon Rocks' (St George Reef). The following day 'Cape Orford' (Cape Blanco) received its name. Anchoring close by the cape, both ships found themselves under the attention of a number of native canoes which had put out from the nearby shore on their arrival. Going alongside 'without any sort of invitation', the natives (Tututni Indians) proved to be 'pleasing and courteous' and 'scrupulously honest'. So honest, in fact, that when they were presented with trinkets, they tried to give items of their clothing in return.

Over the following days the coastline changed from low shores and sandy beaches to rugged cliffs rising straight from the sea backed by far-off mountains. Vancouver had now reached a stretch of the coast surveyed by Meares – the instigator of the 'Spanish Armament' – four years earlier. On the chart he had produced, Meares showed a promontory and a bay. Cook's former lieutenant had investigated the bay, but its steeply shoaling water and a line of breakers extending across the bay, forced him to haul off. An earlier Spanish expedition had encountered the same features and had come to the opinion that a 'great river' opened out to the coast at that point. Meares, however, was convinced that he could 'with safety assert, that there is no such river'. He named the promontory 'Cape Disappointment' and the wide inlet 'Deception Bay'. Although Vancouver found that the 'sea had now changed from its natural, to river coloured water' he considered the change to be a result of 'some stream falling into the bay'. Then, *'Not considering this opening worthy of more attention'*, Vancouver continued along the coast as it trended to the north-west. Before leaving the area, Menzies had climbed to the mast-head and thought that he could make out the entrance to 'a river or inlet' to the south of Cape Disappointment. Thomas Manby, a member of the midshipman's mess, at the time serving as an able seaman, felt that the line of breakers 'may be from a river … admissible at certain times.'

On 29th April, as the mountainous shore began to increase in height, and after naming a coastal feature as 'Point Grenville' (in honour of Lord Grenville, the soon-to-be brother-in-law of the *Discovery*'s troublesome Midshipman Thomas Pitt), Vancouver encountered 'a very great novelty' – the first sailing ship seen for eight months. The stranger proved to be the *Columbia*, a trader nineteen months out of Boston. Her captain was none other than Robert Gray, the same captain of the *Lady Washington* who had told Meares that he had entered the Straits of Juan de Fuca and had emerged from an outlet to the north (thus suggesting that Nootka Sound was on an island).

On completion of the normal hailing courtesies, Vancouver sent Lieutenant Puget and Menzies across to the *Columbia* '*to acquire such information as might be serviceable to our future operations.*' Their return saw them bring back a surprising admission. Gray was now claiming that he had never followed the course as suggested by Meares. He had done no more than enter the Straits of Juan de Fuca for about fifty miles and, finding little trade in sea-otter pelts, had returned the way he had entered. Soon afterwards he had come across Meares who had proceeded to boast about the large cargo of furs that he had been able to obtain. In retaliation, Gray '*knowing the North West passage to be the Hobby horse of his opponent in commerce, reports his discovery of it ... dressed up in language with a chart ... that points out the track of the Vessel with fanciful precision.*' So Meares had been taken in and fooled by the 'cunning Yankee'. Gray had not found an inner passage that had brought him out to the north of Nootka Sound. He had, however, been into Deception Bay and intended to take another, closer, look on separating from the *Discovery* and the *Chatham*. Before the two officers had left the *Columbia*, Gray had warned them to be very wary of the Indians. One of the trader's crew, a native of Hawaii, had made an agreement with the Indians to dampen the gun-powder in loaded fire-arms kept ready in case of native attack. The plan, however, had been discovered, an intended assault was foiled, and Gray had the Indian village burnt to total destruction. Although he must have been aware of recent Spanish incursions into the Straits of Juan de Fuca (Manuel Quimper in 1790 and Francisco de Eliza the following year), Gray did not mention them to Puget and Menzies.

On the separation of the ships (although Gray followed Vancouver from a distance to see if he was about to start fur trading), the next few hours were spent in passing a dangerous rocky shore before, at noon, the coast opened out into a wide passage. They were at Cape Flattery, the southern entrance to the Straits of Juan de Fuca. Vancouver had now searched the coast from his first contact near Cape Mendichino to Cape Flattery. He had found no harbour worthy of the name and noted that, if anyone else should carry out the same search they would '*experience like myself no small degree of mortification.*' His survey, however, had been done from off-shore; a method carrying the risk – as Cook had found – of darkness and contrary weather causing the surveyor to miss the very features that he was searching for. This had happened to Vancouver. Coos Bay, Willapa Bay, and Grays Harbour had all been missed (the latter passed in the dark). The possibilities of Deception Bay, on the other hand, would be heard of again.

Having hauled to the east to take up the line of the strait's southern shore, the ships were visited briefly by Indians (of the Makah tribe) whose villages could be seen along the shore. Vancouver was not averse to native visits but was keen to press on through the rain which had begun to fall heavily from a grey sky.

The following day the ships anchored off a low sandy spit which was given the name 'New Dungeness' from its appearance being similar to Dungeness in the English Channel. During the afternoon, the rain lifted enough for Lieutenant Joseph Baker of the *Discovery* to see a large (10,750 feet) mountain to the north east. Vancouver rewarded him by giving it the name, 'Mount Baker'.

Whidbey was sent off in the *Discovery*'s cutter to carry out soundings and to find water. He was astonished to find the local natives (Clallam Indians of the Coast Salish peoples) paid no heed to his appearance – a strong indication that Europeans had already passed that way. On his return, Whidbey was joined by Vancouver and, taking three boats, they set off to examine some nearby openings in the coast. One of these turned out to be a passage between the mainland and an island ('Protection island'). From its green pine-clustered heights, Vancouver saw an inlet to the south-east and set off to investigate. Surrounded by snow-covered mountains and with green meadows and forests sweeping down to the steep shores, once water had been found it was clear that the inlet would provide a perfect base for extended surveying operations. On 2nd May, the ships were brought round from New Dungeness and anchored five miles up the inlet and a quarter mile off the shore. Vancouver named the place 'Port Discovery' (Discovery Bay).

The site and the onset of fine weather gave the first opportunity to carry out repairs and replenishment since leaving the Sandwich Island. Casks were brought out of the hold and inspected for leaks, gun-powder was spread out to dry, sails were repaired, wood collected, and spruce beer brewed. Shingle was brought on board for ballast and the standing and running rigging given a thorough inspection. The bows of the *Discovery* and the sides of the *Chatham* were given a badly-needed re-caulking to improve their watertight qualities. After four days of strenuous effort, Vancouver gave his ship's companies their first day's 'holiday' since leaving the Cape of Good Hope and permitted them to exercise ashore.

That day, a number of local Indians, willing to trade, approached the ship. They brought with them fish and venison. The food was considered 'extremely good, and very acceptable', particularly as the transport *Daedalus* had not been met at the Sandwich Islands, and Vancouver had already put his ships on two-thirds bread allowance. Much to the surprise and abhorrence of everyone, the Indians also brought along two children, aged about six or seven, with which they were willing to trade for muskets or copper sheeting (unknown to Vancouver, the Spanish always took the children in the belief that they were rescuing them from slavery, or from cannibalism).

Possibly for the first time since he had left England, Vancouver must have felt that at last things were beginning to work out right. With the stress he had felt at the Sandwich Islands behind him, he had reached the area to which he had been sent by the Admiralty, his ships were in good condition, the summer lay ahead, and the view from Protection Island had revealed a wealth of inlets and waterways to be explored. There had been some problems with the ship's companies. The *Discovery*'s carpenter was still confined to his cabin, and some of the midshipmen – led by the Honourable Thomas Pitt – had proved to be difficult. Others of the 'young gentlemen', however, including the former forecastleman, Edward Roberts, the keen Thomas Manby, and even the razor-waving Honourable Charles Stuart, had begun to show promise. Menzies, now practically the ship's full-time surgeon due to Cranstoun's failure to recover from his illness picked up at the Cape, continued to write his notes with an eye to the approval of Sir Joseph Banks. The surgeon's first mate, George Hewett – probably infected by Menzies antipathy towards Vancouver – resorted to writing notes that verged almost on a hatred of his captain. The ship's companies were clearly capable of the tasks they had been set and seem to have been no more afflicted with human failings than any other set of men closeted within wooden walls. There had been punishments in the form of flogging, but no more than would have been expected from a ship of the time. A number of the men were punished frequently, suggesting a habit of bad behaviour amongst a few and, in the main, the punishments were for theft, neglect of duty, and drunkenness – misdemeanours as unpopular among the lower deck as they were with the officers. The occasional bouts of insolence – when not connected with drunkenness – probably reflected the strains of an arduous and difficult enterprise rather than a direct challenge to authority.

Whatever the problems found with his ship's companies, within the shelter of the cliff-lined refuge of Port Discovery, Vancouver could have looked forward to succeeding in his mission, both as a surveyor of an unknown coast, and as an emissary of his government. He had the skills, he had the means – all he needed was good fortune.

Chapter Nine

NEW GEORGIA

'The most lovely country that can be imagined.'

The use of the ships boats to sound the area around Possession Island had demonstrated to Vancouver that, at least for the next part of his survey, they would have to be used again. Accordingly, he gave orders that the *Discovery*'s pinnace and launch, along with the *Chatham*'s cutter, should be made ready for the early morning of the following day, 7th May, 1792. The boats were fitted out with supplies for five days and armed with swivel guns and muskets. At five-o-clock the next morning, leaving Broughton in charge of both ships and with Whidbey responsible for the completion of the survey of Port Discovery, Vancouver and Menzies set off in the pinnace, Puget took the launch, and Johnstone, the cutter. They had not travelled far when the morning fog lifted to reveal a wide passage ('Admiralty Inlet') leading to the south. At its western entrance a smaller inlet was explored and was given the name 'Port Townshend' (Port Townsend) after the Marquis Townshend, one of General Wolfe's officers at the Battle of Quebec. Thomas Manby, a friend of the Marquis's family, landed to carve on a pine-tree – 'Anne Marie Townshend. TM. 1792'.

Passing south through Admiralty Inlet, they landed on the western shore to have a meal and to dry their clothing. Before long, a group of Indians (from the Chimakum tribe) approached 'with the utmost confidence' and without weapons. A line was drawn in the sand over which no side would cross without invitation and Vancouver found them to be 'fair and honest' in their trading of skins and furs in exchange for trinkets. To the north-east, a snow-capped mountain was named after Captain Peter Rainier, an officer who had served with Vancouver in the Channel Fleet.

Their southern journey was interupted by a headland ('Foulweather Bluff') dividing the inlet into two arms. Deciding to keep to the western shore, Vancouver entered a narrow opening that extended first south and then turned to a more westerly direction. In a strange, almost eerie, silence, the boats passed down between the rocky, fir-clad, shores. The only sounds to be heard came from the occasional *'croaking of a raven, the breathing of a seal, or the scream of an eagle.'* With their rations being stretched beyond the intended five days, and 'at the expense of a little hunger', Vancouver pressed on until the waterway turned suddenly to the north-east. The waters then appeared to terminate about three miles further on (actually they continued for about another thirteen miles) and it was decided to return to the ships after trading for some fish, cockles and clams from some Indians. The narrow fifty-mile stretch of water up which they had rowed and sailed was honoured by the name 'Hood Canal', after Vice-Admiral Sir Samuel Hood, one of Vancouver's senior officers when he was on the West Indies Station and a signatory to his sailing instructions.

Alexander del: from a Sketch taken on the Spot by J. Sykes.

J. Heath Sculp.

FOUR ... ... BOATS ... in PORT TOWNSEND, GULPH of GEORGIA

They reached the ships after an absence of eight days. Just three days were spent in getting the ships ready for sea before anchors were weighed and the vessels stood to the north out of Discovery Bay. Broughton and the *Chatham* were sent to the north to examine a group of islands that could clearly be seen on the horizon (the San Juan Islands) as Vancouver returned to Admiralty Inlet. This time, taking the *Discovery* to the east of Foulweather Bluff, Vancouver continued almost directly south past shores which he found delightful to behold: –

> *'The serenity of the climate, the innumerable pleasing landscapes, and the abundant fertility that unassisted nature puts forth, require only to be enriched by the industry of man with villages, mansions, cottages, and other buildings, to render it the most lovely country that can be imagined; whilst the labour of the inhabitants would be amply rewarded, in the bounties with which natures seems ready to bestow on cultivation.'*

From the masthead, Vancouver could see the mountains (the Cascade Range) to the east ending in 'another high round mountain covered with snow' (Mount St. Helens). To the west, more snow covered mountains (the Olympic Range) bounded an horizon from which reared Mount Olympus itself.

The *Discovery* dropped anchor to a salute of seventeen guns off a projection of land on the eastern side of the passage. It was 19th May – the anniversay of King Charles II's landing in England in 1660 and the restoration of the monarchy. On the shore of 'Restoration Point', Suquamish Indians gathered to watch the strange, noisy, vessel as Vancouver sent Puget in the launch and Whidbey in the cutter to press on southwards to examine a passage that could be seen to the south-west. The following day, as the carpenters replaced the topsail yards, Vancouver went ashore to meet the natives. He found them 'not wanting in offers of friendship and hospitality' and keen to offer bulbs of wild hyacinth which their women had dug up for food. The next two days were spent in returning the hospitality as several canoes were paddled out to the ship. On the 25th the Indians brought out to the vessel a very welcome gift in the shape of a deer which had just been killed. Another welcome sight was the mastheads of the *Chatham* as she hove into sight to join the *Discovery* at anchor.

Broughton, following Vancouver's instructions, had arrived off the islands on 19th May. He was unaware that two Spanish expeditions had already visited the area and had named the islands 'Archipielago de San Juan'. Their charts, however, showed the islands to be a single land mass with, to the west, Canal de Lopez de Haro (Haro Strait) and, to the east, Canal de Fidalgo (Rosario Strait).

Broughton had probed the bays and inlets of the group and had found them to consist of three main islands (San Juan, Lopez, and Orcas). Emerging to the north of the group, Broughton had seen *'a spacious sound containing several islands and openings in all directions'* before running aground as her boats tried to pull her clear against a strong current. No damage ensued, however, and the *Chatham* was pushed off by a turning tide. The master, Johnstone, and Lieutenant James Hanson, both carried out surveys from small boats. One Indian village was found and venison was traded for trinkets when the natives came out to the ship in their canoes.

Once Broughton had shown Vancouver the results of his survey of the islands, Vancouver: *'became thoroughly convinced, that our boats alone could enable us to acquire any correct or satisfactory information respecting this broken country; and although the execution of such a service in open boats would necessarily be extremely labourious, and expose those so employed to numberless dangers and unpleasant situations, that might occasionaly produce great fatigue, and protract their return to the ships; yet that mode was undoubtedly the most accurate, the most ready, and indeed the only one in our power to pursue for ascertaining the continental boundary.'*

Not averse – and even eager – to take his share of the 'dangers' and 'fatigue', Vancouver joined Johnstone in the pinnace, and with Lieutenant Baker in the yawl, set off for a passage that could be seen to the south-east. Broughton had been ordered, on Whidbey's return, to take the *Chatham* northwards to examine an opening that had been seen to the east.

Vancouver's south-eastern destination opened out into a large bay where he encountered a group of Indians. Inviting the natives to join his party at dinner – with the Indians still remaining on one side of a line drawn in the sand – Vancouver allowed two of the natives to cross the line and taste some of the food he and his men were eating. The fish and bread were accepted eagerly but, when they were offered venison pie, their attitude changed abruptly. By their angry gestures it became clear that the Indians believed that they had been offered cooked human flesh to eat. Vancouver shook his head and pointed to the deer-skins that the Indians were wearing, but the natives replied by pointing to each other with expressions of great disgust before throwing the meat to the ground. Desperate to put an end to this false accusation (which could have led to conflict and worse), Vancouver sent to one of the boats for a haunch of deer. On its arrival he was able to convince the Indians that they were not eating human flesh to the extent that *'some of them ate the remainder of the pye with a good appetite.'* The incident also went some way to convincing Vancouver that not all the Indians were cannibals. Captain James Cook, with dramatic experience of cannibalism amongst the south sea islanders and the Maoris, had come to believe that all the Pacific peoples were cannibals. The Spanish and the fur-traders continued the belief as a means of keeping their men disciplined through fear of the natives. The evidence for such a practice amongst the tribes of the north-west coast of America remained, nevertheless, at worst, sparse, and at best, non-existent. Perhaps the most peculiar aspect of the whole affair, however, is the puzzle as to why people wearing deer-skin clothing and clearly used to eating venison, should suddenly fail to recognise it – unless it was an unkind reflection on naval cooking of the period.

A number of bays and inlets around the southern end of the waterway were examined beneath torrential rain before Vancouver came to the conclusion that he was likely to be surveying the same area that would have been covered by Puget and Whidbey. He decided to return to the *Discovery* and headed for a passage that appeared to offer a course northwards only to find it to be a dead end (Case Inlet). His disappointment was somewhat relieved when Master's Mate William LeMesurier used his musket to bring down a deer which *'afforded our people a good fresh meal.'*

Vancouver arrived on board his ship on the evening of the 29th having discovered that the land which divided the passage to the south was an island. To this, 'the most extensive island we have yet met' he gave the name 'Vashon's Island' (Vashon Island) after his captain in the *Europa*.

Puget and Whidbey had returned two days earlier (the latter having left with the *Chatham* on the 28th). In his instructions to Puget, Vancouver had stressed that, although Puget was the senior man, he was to 'follow in such points as appertain to the Surveying' the directions given by Whidbey. No difficulties had arisen from this order and the two men had carried out a successful survey to the bottom of the sound that had linked up with Vancouver's own work (at one stage Puget saw Vancouver's camp fire, but took it to be Indians). They had not been many days from the ship, when they came up against the threat of Indian opposition. They were having a meal ashore with a number of men guarding the boats when three canoes (whose occupants had already been given gifts) were seen to be silently approaching. On their being discovered, the Indians – in company with a fourth canoe – landed close by and began to string their bows. At first, Puget had difficulty with the situation facing him: –

'This reduced me to a most awkward predicament, for unwilling to fire on these poor People, who might have been unacquainted with the advantage we had over them, & not wishing to run the Risk of having the People (ie. his own men) wounded by their first discharge of their Arrows I absolutely felt at a Loss how to Act.' He then proceeded to make a tactical error by firing one of his swivel guns, loaded with grape-shot, in a direction away from the Indians. To his surprise and 'contrary to our Expectations they did not express any Astonishment or fear at the Report of the Effect of the Shot.' By humanely firing the gun without causing any casualties among the natives, they had become instantly convinced that the weapon held no threat. However, the noise of the discharge did have another effect. It brought the rest of Puget's men running to see what the commotion was all about. Faced now by a much larger party, the Indians unstrung their bows and 'solicited our Friendship by the most abject submission.'

With all his surveying parties safely back on board, Vancouver would have been justified in feeling some sense of achievement in his first extended survey by boat. His boats crews had performed well beneath open skies and soaking downpours, and they had put up with mosquitos and food shortages (Puget's men had been forced to resort to crows to supplement their diet). For the most part, the natives had proved to be friendly, and not a man had been lost. 'Thus by our joint efforts', he wrote, 'we had completely explored every turning of this extensive inlet; and to commemorate Mr. Puget's exertions, the south extremity of it I named Puget's Sound.' (Puget Sound – the name later extending as far north as Admiralty Inlet).

On 30th May, with a southerly breeze in their favour, the *Discovery* sailed from Restoration Point to join the *Chatham*. Entering the inlet to which he had directed his consort, Vancouver could find no trace of the ship until that evening when, on firing a cannon, he received an answering report from behind a point of land on the eastern shore. Guided by a lantern hoisted in the *Chatham*'s rigging, the *Discovery* dropped her anchor close alongside.

Broughton had sent Whidbey and Hanson northwards to investigate an opening to the east of a long projection of land dividing the passage. If that failed to provide an opening to the north, they were to return to the *Chatham* before continuing to explore the opening to the west. Vancouver decided to take both ships to the eastern opening in the belief that, as Whidbey and Hanson had already been absent for three days, they must have found on open passage. After delays caused by the weather and contrary tides the ships entered the two-mile wide strait only for Vancouver to find that he was in, what appeared to be, yet another inlet with a rapidly shoaling bottom. A signal was made to the *Chatham* to 'bring up', a signal quickly rendered pointless as a reply informed Vancouver that the *Chatham* had run aground. David Dorman, a seaman frequently in trouble for neglect of duty, had been given the task of taking soundings by the use of the lead. For some unaccountable reason he had *'announced false soundings'*, the *Chatham* had buried her bows in a mud bank, and Dorman had earned himself three dozen lashes at the grating.

There was no great risk to the *Chatham* and all that could be done immediately was to lay out anchors and wait for the turn of the tide to lift her off. Vancouver took the opportunity to take the *Discovery*'s pinnace to the north to examine the shore for any passage out of the inlet and came to the conclusion that 'it was not impossible a channel might exist' (one did exist, but the shoals would have prevented his passage). Midnight brought the tide that lifted the *Chatham* clear and Vancouver stood to the south to leave the inlet after naming the area 'Port Susan' in honour of the wife of his supporter and Commissioner at the Admiralty, Captain Alan Gardner.

In a secure anchorage at the entrance to Port Susan, the sound of a gun being fired brought the welcome news that Whidbey and Hanson's boats were in the offing. The *Discovery*'s master had surveyed Port Susan and, taking the advantage of a southerly wind, had gone up the western branch (Saratoga Passage). The boats had not gone far when it was decided to land on the western shore for a meal. As they closed with the beach they found it to be occupied by a large number of Indians (members of the Skagit tribe). This made them make for the eastern shore only to find yet more of the natives in large numbers. Whidbey, keen to get ashore to take surveying angles, decided to risk the temper of the natives and landed. Much to his relief the Indians turned out to be both friendly and co-operative. The following day they met more peaceful natives including a chief who was wearing two 'hangars' (short, curved swords used at sea), one Spanish, the other English. The Indians stood and watched with deep interest as Whidbey took the angles he needed. They were also keen to know why he had painted his hands and face white. When he unbuttoned his waistcoat to demonstrate that he was white all over, *'their astonishment was inexpressible.'* Later, as they sailed past another village, they were invited ashore and into the people's huts. When the invitation was politely turned down, the native women, in particular, *'expressed much chagrin and mortification that their offers of civility were declined.'*

After reaching a wide shallow area of open water (Skagit Bay) Whidbey decided to make his way back. The reception from the natives was as before with food being brought out to Whidbey's party and some of the Indians enjoying short passages in the boats. The land to the west impressed all the party with its 'delightful prospect, consisting chiefly of spacious meadows, elegantly adorned with clumps of trees.' There was, in fact, much to recommend the entire country that had been seen since their arrival off the coast of north-western America. The natives had showed little belligerence, there was enormous potential for settlement and subsequent trade, and – probably the most important factor of all – there was enough of the best type of timber to supply the Royal Navy's wants for centuries to come. Consequently, the expedition's leader was moved to an action for which he had no offical authority other than his own. On 4th June, 1792, Vancouver, Broughton, and some of the other officers, landed and 'took formal possession of all the countries we had lately been employed in exploring, in the name of, and for His Britannic Majesty, his heirs and successors.' To the rolling echoes of a gunnery salute from the ships, and ignoring any previous Spanish claims to the territory, Vancouver claimed on behalf of his sovereign:

'the coast, from that part of New Albion, in the latitude of 30 degrees 20' north, and longitude 236 degrees 26', to the entrance of this inlet of the sea, said to be the supposed straits of Juan de Fuca; as likewise all the coast islands &c. within the said straits, as well on the northern as on the southern shores; together with those situated in the interior sea we had discovered, extending from the said straits, in various directions, between the north-west, north, east, and southern quarters.'

The 'interior sea' (by which Vancouver intended all the waters to the east of the Straits of Juan de Fuca) was to be named 'The Gulph of Georgia' (Strait of Georgia), and the entire area already surveyed was given the name 'New Georgia' (a name now defunct). The waterway on which the momentous ceremony took place was honoured with the name 'Possession Sound.'

Three days later the vessels passed north through Admiralty Inlet and once again reached the eastern waters of the Straits of Juan de Fuca. There they met unusually calm weather and were forced to anchor to avoid drifting. With the season now advancing and immediate progress impossible, Vancouver sent Puget in the launch and Whidbey in the cutter to survey the eastern coast towards an opening that could be seen some twelve miles to the north-east. Over the next two days, the ships were pushed northwards by occasional breezes and managed to reach 'Strawberry Bay', first visited and named by Broughton during his examination of the San Juan Islands. The Discovery managed to anchor safely, but the Chatham was gripped by a strong current and forced towards a nearby island. Broughton ordered the stream anchor to be dropped only to discover that the rocky bottom had cut through the anchor cable. The bower anchor was then immediately dropped and took hold, enabling Broughton to start searching for his lost anchor. With no instant success, Broughton informed Vancouver of the incident. The loss of an anchor – especially in the case of the stream anchor where no spare was available – was a very serious matter and Vancouver was greatly annoyed. He ordered Broughton to search for the missing anchor only until the next slack tide. If it had not been found by then, he was to risk his bower anchor no longer and head out to open waters until he could re-enter the bay and anchor with safety. Two days later, the *Chatham* returned without the stream anchor and felt the force of Vancouver's displeasure when Broughton asked for some oil to complete the painting of his ship. Vancouver refused, and with one side of his ship painted yellow, Broughton was forced to paint the other side black. This novel colour scheme served to remind Broughton, and anybody else who was interested, that Vancouver was not impressed by – what he believed to be – bad seamanship.

That afternoon Puget and Whidbey returned from their survey. The inlet which they had been sent to examine had proved to be impassable for any vessels of even modest draught. Vancouver named it 'Deception Passage'. There had, however, been one interesting discovery. The land on which Whidbey had dealings with the friendly Indians had been proved to be an island. Accordingly, it received the name 'Whidbey's Island' (Whidbey Island) in honour of its first circumnavigator. There had also been one challenging incident. As the party were spending the night ashore, one of Puget's boat's crew – a marine – tripped over a skunk in the darkness –

'the intolerable stench it created absolutely awakened us in the Tent. The smell is too bad for a Description. This Man's Cloaths were afterwards so offensive that notwithstanding boiling, they still retained the Stench of the Animal & in the Next Expedition others were given him on Condition that those that retained the Smell should be thrown away & happy he was to comply with it.'

An early morning breeze enabled the ships to leave Strawberry Bay and thread their way through *'a cluster of numerous islands, rocks, and rocky islets'* as they sailed northwards. That evening, a bay was found ('Birch Bay') which offered a safe anchorage and a base for further boat journeys. With Broughton's survey of the San Juan Islands to the south of them, all the waters and shorelines ahead offered the glittering prospect of new discoveries.

Chapter Ten

JOHNSTONE'S STRAIT

'A region so truly desolate and inhospitable.'

With his ships safely anchored in six fathoms, and half a mile off the wooded shores of Birch Bay, Vancouver planned the next stage of his coastal survey. An examination of the shore had revealed a suitable site for setting up the observatory (the rate of the chronometers needed to be ascertained), and water was available both for the ship's supplies and for the brewing of spruce beer. There remained a section of the coast that had not been examined during the passage through the San Juan Islands and Whidbey was ordered to take two boats to complete the survey. Broughton was given instructions to take the *Discovery* and the *Chatham* to an anchorage closer to the observatory site and to oversee the routine maintenance of the ships and the observatory calculations.

At five-o-clock on the morning of 12th June, 1792, Vancouver in the pinnace and Puget in the launch set off to examine the coast to the north. A large opening to the east revealed two bays (Boundary and Semiahmoo bays) and a shoreline that swept around to end at a cliff-lined projection which Vancouver named 'Point Roberts' after Commander Henry Roberts – the first captain of the *Discovery*. On rounding the point , Vancouver found himself facing a difficulty for which *'we conceived our equipment very unequal'*. The low-lying shore continued out to sea in extensive shoals which prevented the boats from closing with the coast. The situation was particularly frustrating as the shore was broken in three places, each opening choked with *'logs of wood, and stumps of trees innumerable'*. Both the shoaling and the debris strongly suggested a watercourse of some magnitude (the Fraser River) was reaching the coast at that point. However, it was equally clear that there was no passage available for any substantial vessels and Vancouver came to the conclusion that the openings *'can only be navigable for canoes'*.

The following morning, after an uncomfortable night spent sleeping in the boats off an island in the west of the straits, Vancouver returned to the continental shore at a position he named 'Point Grey' after his friend, Commander the Honourable George Grey, the third son of the first Earl Grey. From there, an inlet ran south-east, its northern shores rearing up into high mountains. Some three miles into the inlet, at a point where it narrows abruptly, a large party of Suquamish Indians in canoes approached and offered cooked fish. Taking in some of the boat's sail, Vancouver allowed the natives to keep company with him for part of the way until, one after the other, the canoes broke off to return to their families with the gifts that had been given in return for the fish. Before the last of them left, one of the Indians was allowed to fire a musket – a courageous act which he carried out *'with much fear and trembling'*.

For most of the boats crews, that night was spent sleeping in the boats off the southern shore of the inlet. The steep, rocky, coast did not provide a suitable landing place, but some of the midshipmen decided that they would prefer to sleep on the rocks rather than suffer another night of discomfort in the boats. Unfortunately, they did not consider the tidal range of the inlet and 'found *themselves incommoded by the flood tide, of which they were not apprized until they were nearly afloat.*' One of the young gentlemen slept so soundly that *'he might have been conveyed to some distance, had he not been awakened by his companions.*'

Believing himself to be close to the end of the inlet (which actually veered to the north-east for another ten miles), Vancouver returned to the entrance after naming it 'Burrard's Channel' (Burrard Inlet) in honour of one of his *Europa* messmates, Commander Harry Burrard. The northern point of the entrance was named 'Point Atkinson' (after whom is not certain, the only contemporary naval candidate is Lieutenant John Anson Atkinson who died during Vancouver's absence).

A group of islands, two of them large (Bowen and Gambier islands), crowded into the entrance to the next inlet to be surveyed. Now surrounded by magnificent vistas provided by mountains that rose straight from the water (which he thought to offer a '*dreary prospect*'), Vancouver named the waterway 'Howe's Sound' (Howe Sound) after Admiral the Earl ('Black Dick') Howe who, two years later, was to crush the French fleet at the Battle of the Glorious First of June.

Fifteen miles to the north the strait was divided by a long, narrow, island (Texada Island). Keeping to the continental side (through Malaspina Strait) another mountain-fringed inlet was discovered and searched until, fifty miles from its entrance, it ran out into low swampy ground. They were now a hundred and fourteen miles from the ships and Vancouver decided it was time to return. It was already six days since they left Birch Bay and, apart from the occasional bird being brought down by the midshipmen's muskets and the supply of fish by the natives, there had been little opportunity to extend the seven days rations with which they had started out. The inlet was named 'Jervis's Channel' (Jervis Inlet) after Admiral Sir John Jervis who, five years later, would destroy the Spanish fleet at the Battle of Cape St. Vincent.

Where possible, the boats' voyage had been under sail, but much time had been spent – by officers as well as ratings – pulling at the oars. They had slept either in their boats or on rocks. Puget described the conditions during one such night: '*..it was not until 11 at night we landed, after a most disagreeable & laborious Row, the Boats and their Furniture were all wet nor was there a Spot to shelter from the Inclemency of the Weather, & as it was equally uncomfortable either remaining in the Water afloat or on Shore most of us preferred the Ground & Fire for the Remainder of the Night; from which however we experienced little or no Inconvenience except the being under the Necessity of laying down in wet Cloaths.*'

Where there was inconvenience, it was shared by all, including Vancouver, who also suffered under the pressures of direct command, responsibility for his men, and of being absent from his ships. Exhausted by his efforts, and facing the prospect of hauling into a southerly gale, Vancouver would have received no cheer from the news that his accompanying boat – the launch, under the temporary command of Master's Mate Thomas Manby whilst Puget had joined the pinnace – had gone missing. The boats had separated near the entrance to the Jervis Inlet. Manby, convinced that Vancouver would have left by the same route as he had entered, followed that course as Vancouver chose another. The launch had no compass, no provisions, and only the leadership of a young man to keep the crew together. Without food – apart from what came into range of his musket – and constantly pulling into the wind, it took Manby and his crew three days to reach Birch Bay. One night spent ashore had nearly caused the death of them all: 'My Boats Crew suffered every hardship fatigue and hunger could inflict, in a small cove I passed a Night that abounded with Muscles. A fire soon cooked us sufficient to make a voracious Meal of. In the course of an hour, the whole of us were taken violently ill, and experienced every agony a poisoned set of beings *could feel, I gorged them all, with hot water, which had the desired effect, by clearing the Stomach from this dangerous food, it threw one man into a fever, the rest fortunately recovered.'* The effects of the consumption of mussels was to appear again later in Vancouver's voyage.

On the morning of 22nd June (Vancouver's thirty-fifth birthday), two days after leaving Jervis Inlet, Vancouver's boat was being rowed towards Point Grey, where it was intended to take breakfast, when he came across a most disturbing sight. Two vessels (which he took at first to be the *Discovery* and the *Chatham*) were seen off the point. On closing with them they turned out to be two Spanish 46-ton schooners (one rigged as a brig). The *Sutil* and the *Mexicana*, commanded by Dionisio Galiano and Cayetano Valdes, had been sent to complete a survey first carried out by Alejandro Malaspina the previous year. Malaspina had reached further north than Vancouver and had believed that a great river flowed into the straits from the east. He had come to the conclusion that Burrard Inlet was the estuary of the river and had sent the two Spanish vessels to make a survey in the summer of 1792. Able to assure the Spaniards that no great river flowed into the inlet, Vancouver *'experienced no small degree of mortification'* to learn that the Spanish had already been along the coast and had reached *'four leagues further than had been seen by us.'* He also learned that the Spanish official involved in the hand-over of the land at Nootka Sound was waiting for his arrival. In an attempt to rescue his expedition and its achievements from being overtaken by Spanish exploration, Vancouver then invited the Spaniards to join him as he continued north. At first the two captains were reluctant but Vancouver managed to persuade them *'in such terms that not only were we obliged to agree but we comprehended that if we did not it would be discreditable, not only as far as we were concerned, but even for the public credit of the nation.'* At the same time they *'might discern their views relative to these countries and the true object of the explorations in them, gaining at the same time an idea of their methods of service and mode of working.'* Birch Bay was reached on the morning of 23rd June. Even the news that Whidbey had successfully surveyed the unknown coast to the south could not assuage the bitter disappointment that Vancouver was feeling after the arrival of the Spanish ships. His anger found release on the head of the unfortunate Manby, still recovering from his boat journey and the effects of the mussels. So violently did Manby feel Vancouver's wrath that he wrote; '*his salutation I can never forget, and his language I will never forgive, unless he withdraws his words by a satisfactory apology.*'

The following day the ships were joined by the Spaniards. After a polite bout of cheering the flotilla made its way northwards through Malaspina Straits to a mountainous eastern inlet that Vancouver considered to be '*gloomy and dismal*' and to which he gave the name 'Desolation Sound'. The Spanish officers repaired on board the *Discovery* and a plan of action was worked out. Puget and Whidbey were to return for a short distance along the route of the ships to examine closely the shore before making their way northwards into a large inlet (Homfray Channel). The Spaniards agreed to go northwards between two islands, and Johnstone and Master's Mate Spelman Swaine would head to the north-west along the continental shore. Throughout, Vancouver insisted that the eastern shores would be surveyed by his men, never losing sight of his instructions to search all possible passages to the east.

On completion of their stretch of coastline, Puget and Whidbey found themselves at the entrance to a large inlet (Toba Inlet) and began its survey. They had not been working long before they met Spanish boats under Valdes on their way out of the inlet. The Spaniard informed Puget that he had been to the bottom of the channel and found it to be closed. To his immense irritation, however, Puget decided to continue up the opening: '*I had no Orders from Captain Vancouver respecting the Spanish Survey in case of meeting their boats; their Determination of this Inlet proved of no Service to us, for we were under the Necessity of following it up to its Source.*' On his return to the ships Valdes reported immediately to Vancouver telling him that '*the way to advance the surveys was to treat one another with perfect confidence.*' His wounded pride made little impression on Vancouver who told him that '*although he would always have the greatest confidence in our work, he did not think he would be free from responsibility if he did not see it all for himself, for he was expressly directed in his instructions to survey all the inlets on the coast.*'

Puget's continuation up the Toba Inlet brought its own retribution for disregarding the previous Spanish examination. Both boats landed at a deserted Indian village only to be faced by '*an unexpected numerous enemy*'. Menzies recorded the attack:

'*The narrow Lanes between the Houses were full of filth, nastiness & swarmed with myriad of Fleas which fixed themselves on our Shoes, Stockings & clothes in such incredible number that the whole party was obliged to quit the rock in great precipitation, leaving the remainder of these Assailants in full possession of the Garrison without the least desire of facing again such troublesome enemy. We no sooner got to the Water side than some immediately stripped themselves quite naked & immersed their Clothes, others plunged themselves wholly into the Sea in expectation of drowning their adherents, but to little or no purpose, for after being submerged for some time they leaped about as frisky as ever; in short we towd some of the Clothes astern of the Boats, but nothing would clear them of this Vermin till in the evening we steeped them in boiling water.*'

To the north-west things seemed to be going much better. Johnstone and Swaine had made a spectacular survey in their boats. 'Bute Channel' (Bute Inlet) had been discovered and named after the Earl of Bute – the father of the razor-waving Midshipman Stuart of the *Discovery*.. They had then come across the fast-flowing waters of the Arran Rapids which convinced Johnstone that *'this narrow passage had communications with some very extensive inlet of the sea.'* After a visit to the ships for more provisions, they returned to extend their survey. Pushing first westwards, then in a more southerly direction, they found an inlet ('Loughborough Channel' – now Loughborough Inlet) before making their way to a passage ('Johnstone Strait') that clearly led to Queen Charlotte Strait and the sea. Johnstone had become the first of the explorers to confirm the insularity of the land with Nootka Sound on its western coast. The time needed to reach a view of the ocean had seriously depleted their provisions and they *'therefore hastened night & day to join the Ships which they did about two in the morning on the 12th of July harassed with hunger & fatigue being for the last two days upon a single scanty meal & without any rest or out of the Boats for the last 24 hours.'*

Puget had also found, what seemed to be, a passage to the same sea. Lieutenant Zachary Mudge, the *Discovery's* first lieutenant, had climbed a mountain and seen a south-trending promontory to the west. Beyond it – between the main shore and the promontory – an inlet could be made out. Vancouver named the southern tip of the promontory 'Point Mudge' and sent Puget and Whidbey to examine the opening. In crossing to the west, Puget had met Indians but *'stopped for breakfast on the SE point of the Island to be clear of the Inhabitants whose Company on these Occasions is particularly offensive from the Intolerable Stench of the Whale Oil in general use among all the tribes we have seen.'* Like Vancouver, however, Puget was appreciative of most of the qualities displayed by the natives. Apart from the threatened attack in Puget Sound *'it would be doing* them an injustice not to mention that in all our Dealings, since we began the *Examination of the Continental Shores of America we have found the Inhabitants conducting themselves with strictest Honesty & Friendship towards us.'*

On entering the inlet seen by Mudge, Puget found himself pulling hard against a strong current; *'For the first time since our Entrance into the Streights we perceived the Water flowing by the Shore & the Stream running at the Rate of five Knots from the Northward. This certainly was the most favorable prospect we had had of finding a passage to the Northward for the Ships & most gladly did we pursue the Inlet which trended in a Nd 11 Wd Direction & was little better than a mile in Breadth.'* A pull of ten miles up the inlet failed to reveal a termination and both Puget and Whidbey felt able to *'flatter ourselves that by the Branch we should find a Communication with a Passage leading to the Sea; with this Intelligence I thought it necessary to join the Discovery as soon as possible.'*

Although Johnstone had actually penetrated far enough to obtain a clear view of the ocean (his passage being named 'Johnstone's Strait' by Vancouver in his honour) Vancouver elected to attempt the wider passage found by Puget. The Spanish, on the other hand, chose to follow Johnstone's route. With the *'general satisfaction that prevailed on leaving a region so truly desolate and inhospitable'* the two nations parted on the morning of 13 July *'after an intercourse, not only harmonious, but of the closest friendship.'* Thirteen years later both the Spanish officers were to face Nelson at the Battle of Trafalgar – Valdes, commanding the *Neptune*, survived the encounter, but Galiano ('El Inclito' – 'the brilliant') was killed during the action whilst in command of the *Bahama*. The *Discovery* and the *Chatham* anchored off Point Mudge to await an ebb tide to help them through the passage (Discovery Passage). To learn more about the native peoples and to gain some exercise, Vancouver, Menzies and some of the other officers, went ashore to the Kwakiutl Indian village that dominated the steep cliffs of the point. They were received with great courtesy and several Indians accompanied them as they walked through the forest picking berries from the trees and presenting them to the visitors on green leaves.

The ships sailed at three o'clock on the morning of the 14th aided by an ebb tide and with Puget and Whidbey ahead in the ship's boats to check for any obstructions. Two days later they felt the roll of an ocean swell beneath their feet. There was, however, to be no dash for the open seas. The shore to the south of Johnston Strait provided little indentation but, to the north, lay a region of broken shore coasts and scattered islands. Numerous inlets presented themselves for examination and Vancouver, using Broughton and the shallow-draughted *Chatham* where possible, probed every likely opening. As usual, it was back-breaking toil when the enclosed waters prevented the sails from being hoisted. It was also dangerous when the newly-encountered fogs prevented safe navigation. There were, nevertheless, some slight advantages to be gained away from the comfort and security of the ships. On one occasion, as Vancouver, Broughton, Puget, and Whidbey met in Kingcome Inlet, a deer was seen, apparently trapped on a nearby cliff face. Instantly, *'a platoon of muskets was discharged at the defenceless animal by the whole party without effect.'* A seaman then jumped ashore and, with the aid of a boat-hook, managed to force the deer to a lower ledge. This time *'Upwards of twenty muskets ... were fired, seven of which hit him, but no one mortally; or wounded him in such a manner as to have prevented his escaping, had not the over-hanging precipices of the rocks rendered it impossible. Venison had long with us been a scarce commodity; our buck proved excellent, and afforded us all one or two excellent fresh meals.'*

In the wider – but still treacherous – waters of Queen Charlotte Strait, Vancouver was standing to the northern shore when, on the late afternoon of 6th August, and with an ebbing tide, the *Discovery* ran aground on submerged rocks. It was immediately clear to all that they were in a desperate situation. The ship remained upright as she settled on the jagged bottom, her bows lifting higher and higher as the water receded. An anchor was sent out in an attempt to haul the ship off but, when the heaving began, the anchor *'came home'* having failed to grip. All that then could be done was to reduce the ship's top hamper by bringing down the topmasts and yards, and by reducing her weight elsewhere by discharging all her water, and by throwing overboard as much as possible of her ballast and all the timber carried for fuel. Vancouver proved to be right in his alarm at their situation, and in the actions he took. Half an hour after she had struck, whilst the yards and topmasts were being ranged along her side to act as shores, the *Discovery* toppled over with a *'terrible crash'* on to her starboard side. The ship's company were forced

W. Alexander del. from a Sketch taken on the Spot by Z. Mudge.

Engraved by B T Pouncy

The DISCOVERY on the ROCKS in QUEEN CHARLOTTE'S SOUND.

to cling on to the ship's larboard side as boats from the *Chatham* (anchored close by) laid out an anchor and three cables in readiness for the returning tide. Less than an hour had passed when the ship suddenly swung round and heeled over even further. It seemed as if the ship would be lost, but something, possibly a large rock under the starboard bilge, brought the fearful movement to a halt. For the next seven hours the men clung on, in what Vancouver called a *'very irksome and unpleasant situation'*, until, just after midnight, the tide began to return. By two-o-clock in the morning, to the relief of all, the ship was almost upright. Shortly afterwards, the stern cable was sent out and the ship was hauled off; the only damage being to the top-gallant top-rope; the only injury being a broken arm. Later that day, the *Chatham* ran aground with the added refinement of a heavy swell which repeatedly lifted her up and brought her crashing down on to the submerged rocks. Two spare top-masts put out as shores both cracked under the pressure and the situation was only saved by the providential arrival of a long tree-trunk which drifted by just at the right time. Her anchor, however, had held and she was able to haul herself off without any great injury. It had been a difficult time for Vancouver for, having survived his own grounding, he could not see what was happening to the *Chatham* due to thick fog obscuring his view. He had known nothing of his consort's escape until she appeared under sail out of the mist.

It was not just the opportunity for further surveys that caused Vancouver to delay his arrival at Nootka and his meeting with the Spanish Commissioner. He had expected to meet the supply ship *Daedalus* at the Sandwich Islands, but she had failed to materialise. Not having found him there, the *Daedalus* was expected to make her way to Nootka and Vancouver wanted to give her every chance of being there on his own arrival. Nor was it just her provisions that he was keen to see. She was also expected to be carrying the latest orders associated with the hand-over of the British property by the Spaniards, and Vancouver did not want to begin negotiations without being fully aware of any possible changes to the procedure he was to follow. Extra time could be gained by a close look at the already roughly charted and named coasts to the north of Queen Charlotte Strait.

Intending to use Port Safety on the eastern side of the mountainous Calvert Island as his base, Vancouver sent the *Chatham* to look into Smith Inlet (Smith Sound) but recalled her when a scatter of rocks was seen at the entrance and soundings proved to be irregular. Instead, both vessels set off for Calvert Island along a high, mountainous, and thickly wooded, coast. Port Safety was found with little difficulty and proved to be a safe anchorage where the ships could be refitted after their narrow escapes. No time was lost in setting up surveying parties. Puget and Whidbey were sent to the south to cover the coast from the northern entrance of Queen Charlotte Sound to a point almost directly north of Port Safety – the start of the shores being examined by Vancouver and Johnstone.

The northern party, under Vancouver's direction, entered the Burke Channel beneath incessant rain before Vancouver turned back. He arranged a rendezvous at the entrance to the channel where he would direct the ships to meet Johnstone in five days time. The *Chatham*'s master was to continue to examine the continental shore along the steep-sided waterway through country described by Vancouver as *'desolate and inhospitable a country as the most melancholy creature could be desirous of inhabiting.'* Eagles, ravens, and even crows, were not to be seen, the area seemed to be *'devoted intirely to the amphibious race; seal and sea-otters, particularly the latter, were seen in great numbers.'*

On his return to Port Safety, Vancouver found that the ships had nearly completed their watering and had been supplied with fuel and timber to replace that lost during the grounding. He had hoped that the *Chatham* could have been moved to a position where she could have been left to settle on the bottom by the retreating tide. This would have provided an opportunity to examine her hull to see if there had been any damage caused by her running aground. The muddy bottom of the bay, however, had prevented this being carried out. The next day, much to the surprise of everyone, a ship wearing a British flag, hove to at the entrance to the bay. The stranger turned out to be the *Venus*, a fur-trader looking for a supply of sea-otter pelts. She had recently left Nootka and brought the news that the *Daedelus* had arrived and that the Spanish Commissioner was waiting with increasing impatience for Vancouver's arrival. The captain of the *Venus* also brought news of a personally distressing nature to Vancouver. The captain of the *Daedalus*, Lieutenant Richard Hergest, an old friend of Vancouver's, had been murdered at the Sandwich Island whilst landing with a watering party. Also killed at the same time was the astronomer, William Gooch, who had been sent out to join the *Discovery*, and one of the *Daedalus*'s seamen.

The following day, Puget and Whidbey's boats entered the bay. They had explored the full length of Smith Inlet. Some Indians had been met who *'made signs too unequivocal to be misunderstood, that the female part of their society would be very happy in the pleasure of their company. Having no leisure to comply with these repeated solicitations, the civil offers of the Indians were declined.'* Having stoically forgone the delights of female company, Puget and his men then entered another extended and much-branched inlet to which Vancouver gave the name 'River's Channel' (Rivers Inlet) after George Pitt, Baron Rivers (a relative of the recalcitrant Midshipman Thomas Pitt). They had not reached the point where Johnstone's survey had taken over and had to return when their provisions ran out. Not that it mattered greatly as there was clearly no passage to the east on the unsurveyed part of the coast.

The ships left the anchorage on the 19th August after Vancouver had decided to rename it 'Safety Cove' as its description did not fit that of the Port Safety shown on the charts he had been given. A few hours later Johnstone and his party were safely on board. He had examined Burke Channel to a position ('Point Menzies') where it divided into three broad arms. But, with their provisions low, Johnstone had little choice but to return and leave the three branches unexplored.

With his boats crews safely back on board, Vancouver ordered the ships to sail for Nootka – to duties of a quite different nature.

Entrance to Nootka Sound

Chapter Eleven

NOOTKA SOUND

'I named that Country the Island of Quadra and Vancouver.'

B efore the incidents that led to the Spanish Armament had become known in Madrid, the King of Spain had decided that the coasts of North-west America should be explored and surveyed to establish Spanish priority. British activity along that coast from Cook's visit in 1778 to the increasing activities of the fur-traders placed Spanish enterprise at risk and had, where possible, to be forestalled. Only by establishing legitimate claims of sovereignty, gained through Spanish exploration, could Spain lay claim to the region. The Government decided to send a new viceroy to Mexico and appointed the heroically-named Juan Vicente de Guemes Pacheco de Padilla Horcasitas y Aguayo, conde de Revilla Gigedo. He was to take with him a number of senior naval officers who could be depended upon to advance the Spanish claims. Chief amongst these men was Captain Juan Francisco de la Bodega y Quadra. Born in Peru in 1743, Quadra had previously served at the Pacific naval base at San Blas and had made his name through a voyage in a tiny vessel along the north-west coast to between 58 and 59 degrees North. During the voyage, seven of his men were murdered by Indians. This demonstration of leadership and initiative, combined with proven administrative skills, led to his promotion to captain in 1785 and an appointment in Spain. Now he was to lead the naval effort in securing the north-west coast for the Spanish crown.

On his arrival in Mexico, and with the Nootka Sound controversy having been brought to his attention, Revilla Gigedo ordered Quadra to reoccupy 'Puerto de San Lorenzo' (Nootka Sound) and to use it as a base for the exploration of the coast as far north as 'Principe Guillermo' (Prince William Sound). The resulting expeditions reached as far north as Cook Inlet, probed the Straits of Juan de Fuca, and reached past the San Juan Islands as far north as Texada Island. A separate expedition under the command of Alejandro Malespina was also in the region in the search for the mythical Strait of Anian which had been claimed to have been penetrated in 1609.

The news of the Nootka Sound Convention had caused some changes to be made to the Spanish plans, but they did not include the cessation of exploration in the area – a policy resulting in Vancouver's encounter with the *Sutil* and the *Mexicana*. Action in accordance with the Convention could, however, not be avoided, and so Revilla Gigedo appointed the experienced Quadra as Spanish Commissioner at Nootka. There, on the 28th August, Vancouver – the first man to circumnavigate the great island lying off the north-west coast – arrived to represent his country.

After a Spanish pilot had guided the *Discovery* to an anchorage in Friendly Cove, Vancouver sent Puget ashore to meet Quadra and offer him a thirteen gun salute on the understanding that the Spanish Commissioner would reply in like manner. Quadra agreed, and the first of many salutes to visiting officers and far off sovereigns thundered and echoed around the bay. Menzies was singularly unimpressed and remarked; *'that there was scarcely a day past without puffings of this kind from some Vessel or another, & we too followed the example, & puffed it away as well as any of them, till at last we were become so scarce of ammunition to defend ourselves from the treacherous Indians, that we were obliged to get supplies of Powder from both the Spaniards & Traders before we left the coast.'*

When invited ashore to sample Quadra's hospitality, the British officers were amazed and deeply impressed by the extent of the Spanish work that had been carried out over the recent months. Quadra lived in a balconied, two-storey, house and entertained his guests to lavish meals with silver tableware. A barracks, storehouse and hospital had been erected, and vegetables flourished in well-stocked gardens. Poultry, cattle, sheep and goats roamed freely as blacksmiths and carpenters built more houses and worked on the ships. The hospitality did not extend just to those allowed ashore. On their arrival, each ship was sent two sheep and a supply of cabbages along with a cask of rum. Milk, hot rolls, and vegetables were supplied every morning.

The Spanish had established very good relations with the local Indians under their chief, Maquinna. Vancouver, equally keen to remain on the best of terms with the Indians, found himself with a difficult problem when Maquinna turned up uninvited on the deck of the *Discovery*. The duty officer and the marine sentry promptly ejected him from the vessel with little ceremony and much to his outrage. It took all the diplomacy of Quadra (and a large number of gifts from Vancouver) to restore the situation. Not everyone believed that the natives should be treated with such deference. The *Chatham*'s clerk, Edward Bell, after noting the courtesy and kindness extended to the Indians by Quadra, thought *'such goodness is thrown away on these wretches, they were possessed of no affection, nor gratitude and the man that would profess himself your warm friend today would cut your throat & dine off you tomorrow.'*

Almost immediately on his arrival, Vancouver had ordered the establishment of an observatory ashore, bringing into use for the first time the astronomical instruments the Board of Longitude had sent out with the unfortunate astronomer, William Gooch. The situation in the *Daedalus* brought about by the death of Lieutenant Hergest had to be attended to and Vancouver appointed the second lieutenant of the *Chatham*, James Hanson, as her 'Agent' (ie. captain). In his place, Vancouver appointed the master, Johnstone, as acting lieutenant, and sent Master's Mate Spelman Swain to replace Johnstone as master. With extraordinary lack of foresight, the Admiralty had sent Vancouver on a diplomatic mission without a Spanish interpreter. During his earlier dealings with the *Sutil* and *Mexicana* he had been fortunate enough to find that Galiano spoke a little English but, even though that officer had now arrived at Nootka, his skills would not be enough to handle the diplomatic negotiations. However, to his good fortune, Vancouver found that Thomas Dobson, a 21 year old midshipman in the *Daedalus*, had a good enough command of Spanish to act as translator. To Vancouver's surprise and possible disappointment, The *Daedalus* had brought out no further instructions that were of any use in effecting the hand-over of the British claims. All that came was a copy of a letter from Count Florida Blanca – the Spanish Prime Minister – to Quadra ordering him '*to cause such Officer as may be appointed on the part of His Britannic Majesty to be put into possession of the Buildings & Districts or Parcels of Land therein described which were occupied by His Majestys subjects in the month of April 1789 agreeable to the first article of the late Convention &c &c.*' There was no mention in the letter of a dividing point to separate the Spanish from the combined British/Spanish coasts (the Spanish had already decided to establish a presence on the Juan de Fuca Strait which would give them control of the strait itself).

The situation was then further complicated by the arrival of Captain Gray and the *Columbia*. Gray had been present at the taking of the British ships by Martinez and – according to Mears – had assisted the Spaniards in making restraining irons to hold the British prisoners. Now he was eager to acquaint Quadra of his opinions regarding the limited extent of the British holdings at Nootka. He did, nevertheless, find time to inform Vancouver that the *Columbia* had penetrated the shoals off the entrance to the suspected river near Cape Disappointment and discovered beyond them a great river – which he had named after his ship – leading to the interior.

For Vancouver, however, nothing had changed from his original instructions that he was to accept the return of the land and the buildings that had been put up by Mears (including land at Port Cox, some fifty miles to the south) prior to their seizure by Estevan Martinez in May, 1789, and to provide a British presence off the disputed territories north of San Francisco. Quadra, in the meantime, had other ideas. In his first letter to Vancouver, thereby opening the negotiations, he wrote: '*The sovereigns of Spain and England not being well satisfied of the reality of the things which has passed in places so distant from Europe, and animated with the most sincere desire to terminate their differences, they have agreed to leave the examination to the direction of two Commissionaries of the different Courts.*'

This made no sense to Vancouver. He was not a diplomat and had no authority to examine the problem and arrive at a diplomatic conclusion. Even to have discussed the possibility of an unauthorised change to his instructions would have placed him in severe – and accountable – difficulties. Quadra's letter went on to remove all blame from Martinez, and to claim that the accusations by Mears amounted to '*injuries, prejudices, and usurpations*' against Spain. The building claimed by Mears amounted to nothing more than a '*small hut*' (gone by the time of Martinez's arrival) which had been built on land that had not been purchased from the Indians. Consequently, '*it is clear that Spain has nothing to deliver, nor the smallest damage to make good.*' Quadra was prepared, however, '*without prejudice to our legitimate right, nor that of the Courts better instructed resolve, generously to cede to England the houses, Offices, and gardens which has with so much labour been cultivated; and retire to Fuca.*' After this apparent act of generosity, there was a sting in the tail: '*and there* (the Juan de Fuca Strait) *to fix the dividing point: and from thence to the Northward to be common the free entrance, use, and commerce conformable to the 5th Article of the Convention: and that no others may be able to form themselves without the permission of the respective Courts: neither for the English to pass to the South of Fuca.*' Not only were the land and buildings being returned as an act of generosity – rather than in accordance with the agreement – but the Spanish were grabbing five hundred miles of the American coastline.

In his reply, Vancouver pointed out that much of Quadra's letter '*doth not at present come within the limits of my commission to enter into any retrospective discussion.*' Having established his inability to amend the Convention, Vancouver then reminded Quadra of what the 5th Article actually said:

'*It is agreed, that as well as the places which are to be restored to the British Subjects by virtue of the first article, as in all other parts of the Western Coast of North America or Islands adjacent, situated to the North of the parts of the said Coasts already occupied by the Spaniards* (ie. south from San Francisco), *wherever the subjects of the two powers shall have made settlements since the month of April 1789, the subjects of the other shall have free access and carry on their trade without disturbance or molestation.*'

Quadra remained unmoved and responded by confirming that: '*I am only to restore to His Britannic Majesty, the Edifices, districts, or portions of land, which in April 1789 were taken from his subjects. I have been able to justify that the small hut they had did not exist on the arrival of Martinez, nor is our establishment in the place where they had theirs.*' Sensing an impasse, Quadra decided that both sides should seek advice from their respective authorities '*You say that you do not consider yourself authorised to agree upon those points which exist in my commission. Each of us will lay before our respective Courts what we think most just, that from thence they may be able to resolve.*' In the meantime: '*you from hence to be in possession of what Mears occupied; and at your command the houses, gardens, and offices, which we have, and I shall retire till the decision which ought to result after clear and authentic information.*'

It seemed clearly the best that Vancouver was going to get. He had no other option but to seek advice from his superiors. To obtain such guidance he decided that Lieutenant Zachary Mudge would take passage to China in a Portuguese brig which had arrived off Nootka. Once there, Mudge should would be able to find an East India Company ship to take him back to England. In case Mudge encountered difficulties, Vancouver also decided to send Broughton and the *Chatham* to England via Cape Horn. He had already planned to spend the summer surveying along the western coast of America – a decision strengthened by Gray's claim to have entered the Columbia River.

The loss of Mudge required Vancouver to make some adjustments amongst his officers. Puget was appointed first lieutenant of the *Discovery* and Baker moved to be second. Spelman Swain was promoted to acting lieutenant and returned from his short spell as master of the *Chatham*. He was replaced by Thomas Manby, still smarting from his tongue-lashing from Vancouver over the separation of the boats in Jervis Inlet.

Despite the differences between them, both sides got on well together and frequently entertained each other both afloat and ashore. On one occasion, the Spanish and British officers accepted a combined invitation to visit to Maquinna's village. Four boat-loads of guests set off and were greeted by Maquinna at the entrance to his 'big-house'. Approached via a number of highly decorated totem-poles, the covered area of the building was ninety feet long, eighteen feet wide and twelve feet high. More totem-poles carried huge timbers which ran the entire length of the building and, in turn, supported the roof. Several families lived inside the house, each with their own fireplace, the smoke being allowed to escape by pushing aside the roofing plank immediately overhead. The more important the family, the further inside the house they were placed – the most important of all being furthest from the entrance.

The visitors were entertained to a variety of performances with dancers wearing grotesque masks and imitating the hunting of animals. This was followed by songs to the beat of weapons and ending in a war-like yell intended to terrify enemies. The main performance, however, came from Maquinna himself who danced 'dressed in a very rich garment of Otter skins with a round Black Hat, and a Mask on, and with a fanciful petticoat or apron, around which was suspended hollow tubes of Copper and Brass and which as he danced, by striking against each other made a wonderful tingling noise. After dancing thus some time in the course of which he play'd some dextrous Pantomimical tricks with his Hat & Mask, he retired.'

Quadra had arranged to bring food for the occasion (and impressed the British officers by also providing a cook, steward, and a complete set of tableware), and Vancouver brought the drink. Maquinna and his family joined the visitors as the rest of the house dined on 'a large Tunny & a porpus cut up in small pieces entrails & all into a large Trough with a Mixture of Water blood & fish Oil, & the whole stewed by throwing heated Stones into it.'

On their return journey, Quadra repeated a request he had made previously. The Spanish captain wanted Vancouver to name some feature in the area after himself. To an Englishman, such an idea would be seen as somewhat embarrassing. It was all very well to name features after kings, politicians, friends, and even family, but to aggrandise one's self in such a way seemed somehow inappropriate. Vancouver, however, came up with a splendid compromise:

'Conceiving no spot so proper for this denomination as the place where we had first met, which was nearly in the centre of a tract of land that had first been circumnavigated by us, forming the south-western sides of the gulph of Georgia, and the southern sides of Johnstone's straits and Queen Charlotte's sound, I named that country the island of Quadra and Vancouver' (Vancouver Island).

Relationships with the Indians deteriorated rapidly after the grievously mutilated body of a fifteen year old boy from Quadra's ship was found. The suspects were a black man 'of most infamous character' who deserted from Quadra's ship at the same time the boy disappeared, and the natives. Puget thought differently. He thought it possible that the boy had gone off with a native woman to 'obey the Dictates of Nature', but had been murdered by the Indians 'in the very height of his happiness'. However, he thought it more probable that the Spaniards had murdered the boy with the intent of blaming it on the Indians. Whatever the reason, a demand from Quadra to Maquinna that the boy's murderer should be surrendered led to the flight of the natives, thus giving *'a strong presumptive proof of their delinquency.'*

Quadra left Nootka on 22nd September as the final repairs were being carried out on the *Discovery* and the *Chatham*. Stores were transferred from the *Daedalus* and found to be in a very poor state due to incorrect stowage. A number of invalids were sent across to the storeship including the surgeon Alexander Cranstoun and William House, the *Discovery*'s boatswain. They were joined by Phillips, the carpenter who was sent home to face charges of neglect of duty and insolence.

The loss of Cranstoun caused Vancouver some difficulty as Menzies – qualified in every respect to serve as the *Discovery*'s surgeon – was reluctant to take the post. Equally, Vancouver was not authorised supply the warrant required for the official appointment of Menzies as ship's surgeon. Faced with Menzies' reluctance, Vancouver countered by asking him to provide a written refusal. Menzies was trapped – *'as I did not know how far this might operate against my interest at the Navy Office, I with considerable hesitation accepted of the appointment.'*

Vancouver left Nootka on 13th October and headed for the river claimed to have been entered by the American, Gray. On passage, the ships passed another harbour surveyed by Gray (Grays Harbour) and Vancouver sent Whidbey in the *Daedalus* to test Gray's chart. On completion the *Daedalus* was to rendezvous with the other ships at Monteray.

The mouth of the Columbia River once again presented a mass of broken waters as breakers foamed over the submerged reefs forming the bar. With a rapidly shoaling bottom beneath his keel, Vancouver approached the river estuary only to be driven back by the threat of imminent grounding. The *Chatham*, with her more shallow draft, managed to find a passage through at the cost of one of her boats being smashed by the surf. Much to his surprise, Broughton found another ship inside the bar. She was the 78-ton *Jenny*, a Bristol ship he had already met at Nootka. Despite her tiny size, the captain was still forced to wait for an opportunity to sail out through the breakers, the threat of bad weather keeping him within the safety of the bar.

The *Chatham* passed Gray's furthest point some twenty miles beyond the coast, but Broughton was still not convinced that he was actually in the river itself, a belief supported by the fact that he was still sailing through salt water. It took another ten miles before fresh water was reached. At that point Broughton and Johnstone took to the ship's boats and, rowing constantly against a strong stream, rowed for a hundred miles. There they named 'Point Vancouver' and took possession of the country in the name of King George III at 'Possession Point'. Broughton, unaware that the river continued for another thousand miles, believed that he was close to its source and began his return journey.

With the estuary achieved, Broughton found the *Jenny* still waiting for a chance to reach the open sea. It took another four days before such an opportunity arose – four days spent in replenishing the ship's provisions with an abundant supply of wildfowl and salmon. On the chart he produced as a result of his examination – rather than accept Gray's naming of the river – Broughton used the original name, 'River Oregon'.

With the *Chatham* on its way towards the river, Vancouver paused only to name a 'high round snowy mountain' – actually a volcano – 'in honor of His Britannic Majesty's ambassador (Baron St Helens) at the court of Madrid', before setting off south. After a voyage delayed by poor weather the *Discovery* reached San Francisco three weeks later. Much more to his concern than the slow passage, however, were the cases of scurvy that appeared in the ship as he approached the port. Fortunately, his training under Cook, and the stores brought on board by the surgeon, Cranstoun, meant that he knew the value of such anti-scorbutics such as orange and lemon juice. The application of these, (along with the less effective 'essence of malt'), soon restored the situation.

Ten days were spent at San Francisco. Thanks to Quadra's instructions to the commandant of the Presidio, Vancouver and his ship's company were treated with great hospitality. The seamen were allowed to rest from their arduous labours of the past months and the officers were given horses to explore the surrounding country. A misunderstanding led to a considerable number of aching bones and muscles when an invitation to visit the Santa Clara Mission on horseback – assumed to be a journey of eighteen miles – turned out to be eighteen leagues (fifty-four miles). The work done by the Franciscan monks amongst the Indians, however, received the unstinting admiration of Vancouver and the other officers. Three days after the arrival of the *Chatham* on 22nd November, the ships sailed for Monteray with gifts of fresh beef and vegetables: '*a matter that gave the Jacks no small satisfaction*'.

Quadra himself was found waiting for them at Monteray. The Spanish captain, unimpressed by the Acting-Governor of the province, had put himself in command until the arrival of a replacement Governor. This temporary assumption of power worked to Vancouver's advantage as Quadra proved to be a generous host, paying for much of the hospitality out of his own pocket. He also had important news. In his capacity as commander of the Spanish naval forces in the region, he had been instructed to arrest every foreign trading vessel found off the coast of America north of San Francisco – an order leading both Quadra and Vancouver '*to believe that our respective sovereigns had adjusted, and finally concluded, every arrangement with respect to the territories at Nootka*'. Again, Vancouver found himself without advice or instructions in how to respond to the supposed final conclusion. Vancouver had originally intended to send the *Chatham* back to England via Cape Horn but (much to the disappointment of the *Chatham*'s ship's company) he now accepted Quadra's offer to send Lieutenant Broughton overland to the Atlantic coast. From there he could pick up transport for England, deliver Vancouver's dispatches, and seek instructions before returning via the quickest route. possible. Amongst the letters taken by Broughton was one from Vancouver to the Under Secretary of State, Evan Nepean. In it, Vancouver, angered that he had been left alone and un-instructed in how to deal with the Spaniards, complained bitterly that he had '*felt no small degree of disappointment in not receiving a single line either officially or privately from your Office or from yourself*'. Without such advice, he felt that to have accepted the conditions laid out by the Spanish would '*have proved myself a most consumate fool or a traitor*'. Again, his '*embarrassment*' was stressed when he was *'left totally in the dark what measures to pursue'*. Finally, he returned to re-emphasise his failure to find any instructions on board the storeship: *'You my good Sir may easily figure to yourself the disappointment at finding nothing to that effect on joining the Daedalus at Nootka.* In a post-script Vancouver took the opportunity to indicate that not all his problems had been caused through lack of communication with England: *'Nor can I at last avoid saying that the Conduct of Mr. T. Pitt has been too bad for me to represent in any one respect.'*

There were plenty of means of taking Vancouver's mind off his diplomatic problems. The ships had to be re-caulked and replenished and there was much to do ashore. A visit to a Franciscan mission was followed by a dance given by Quadra. Menzies was not in the least impressed by the *'Spanish exhilarating dance the 'Fandango', a performance which requires no little elasticity of limbs as well as nimbleness of capers & gestures. It is performed by two persons of different sex who dance either to the Guittar alone or accompanied by the voice; they traverse the room with such nimble evolutions, wheeling about, changing sides & smacking with their fingers at every motion; sometimes they dance close to each other, then retire, then approach again, with such wanton attitudes & motions, such leering looks, sparkling eyes & trembling limbs, as would decompose the gravity of a Stoic.'* Manby was equally un-impressed by another Spanish pastime: *'after dinner, a Bull is dragged into the Presidio square, and there cruelly tormented for an hour, till the poor Animal becomes perfectly mad, All Spaniards expressed a partiality for this barbarous sport.'*

The *Daedalus* – which had arrived at Monteray before Vancouver own arrival – was fitted out to take a large number of cattle and sheep for *'His Majesty's infant colony in New South Wales.'* The animals had been offered by Quadra and Vancouver thought that Australia, already an expanding convict destination, would make good use of such a supply. More pigs and poultry were to be collected from Tahiti in addition to a number of British seamen whose ship had been wrecked on a nearby reef. The Governor of New South Wales was requested to see that the storeship was resupplied with a year's provisions before her return to Nootka. Vancouver sailed from Monteray on 14th January, 1793, minus the *Discovery's* armourer and one of the marines. Manby was convinced that the Spanish had *'inticed'* the men away despite their claims to have searched high and low for them. Another would-be deserter was rewarded for his attempt to flee the ships by being given one-hundred and forty-four lashes in two sessions separated by fourteen days. It was the most severe punishment awarded by Vancouver and demonstrated his determination to persuade his men that desertion – an expression of disloyalty to a man's shipmates – should not be considered lightly.

With the departure of Broughton, the *Discovery's* first lieutenant, Puget, was made commander of the *Chatham* until she was rejoined by Broughton. On taking up his new appointment, Puget began a new volume of his personal journal. In it he noted that, between the time he had left England and time he had taken command of the *Chatham*, he had sailed or rowed 30,704.8 miles.

Hawaii was sighted on 12th February and Vancouver sent Puget to survey the western shore as he covered the eastern and northern coasts. The two ships met

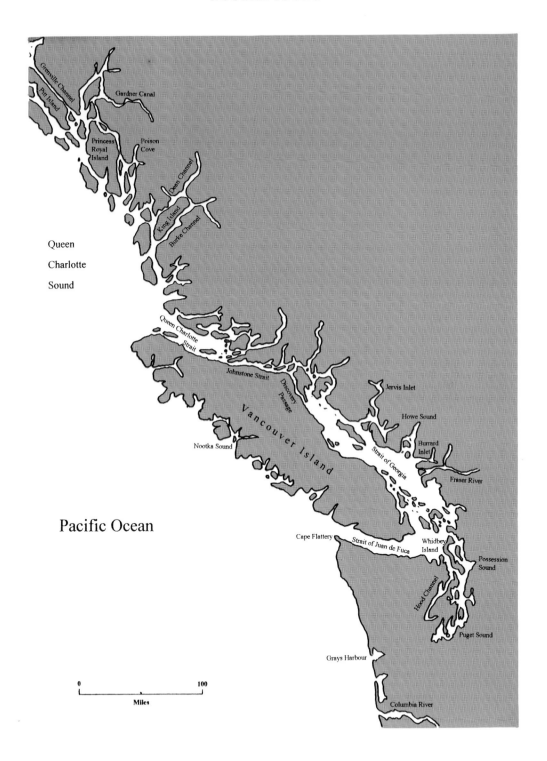

Coastline of North West America, Map 1

off the north coast and made their way to Kealakekua Bay where they were met by huge crowds of natives. Puget claimed that there were over four thousand people in and on the water, and Edward Bell, the *Chatham*'s clerk, noted that the canoes were so closely packed around the ships that he *'might have walked over from the Chatham to the Discovery.'* The king, Kamehameha, gave Vancouver a magnificent cloak of bright yellow feathers to be presented to *'King George in Britannee.'*

To his grave disappointment, Vancouver discovered that the natives had not only been supplied with firearms, but had become proficient in their use. There were several requests for such weapons during trading, but he always forbade such items being used for trade Instead he managed to counter their demands for weapons by saying that the guns were the property of the king, and by supplying them with status-enhancing lengths of red cloth.

The survey of the islands and the chance to spend time in warmer climes were not the only reasons that Vancouver wanted to be in the Sandwich Islands. Whilst on Hawaii he tried to persuade the king that it would be in the interest of both himself and his people if he put himself under the *'dominion of the King of Great Britain.'* Kamehameha was not averse to the idea, but insisted that his agreement depended upon Vancouver leaving one of his ships behind. Such an agreement being impossible, the idea was dropped.

Vancouver was also very keen that the murders of his friend Richard Hergest; the Astronomer, William Gooch; and the seaman from the *Daedalus*; were avenged. Not only had he known Hergest well but, he felt that no visiting ships would be safe from attack if he allowed the deaths to go unpunished. Leaving Hawaii for Maui, the site of the murders, Vancouver was eventually presented with three men who, it was claimed, had been involved. An enquiry by Vancouver seemed to lead to the same conclusion, and the three men were executed by the island's chiefs.

Once again the stress of lone command under difficult circumstances began to affect Vancouver. Kahekili, the king of Maui, was visiting the *Discovery* when a length of ribbon went missing. On learning of this, Vancouver exploded in a rage and (according to Menzies): *'in endeavouring to recover this trifle put himself into such a passion & threatened the Chiefs with such menacing threats that he terrified some of them out of the ship with great precipitation; The King in particular came running into my Cabin before I knew anything of the business & instantly jumping into his Canoe through the port hole, paddled hastily to the shore & we saw no more of him.'* Even bearing in mind Menzies' antipathy towards Vancouver, such a display at a time when calm negotiation would have been a better inducement towards good relations with the natives, suggests that Vancouver was suffering from the strain of isolation. Matters were not improved when it was discovered that the *Chatham* had suffered damage from submerged rocks when leaving Nootka Sound the previous October: *'all the False keel abaft the Main Chains was entirely torn off, the Gripe a good deal shatter'd and much plank and Copper beat off different parts of her.'* With the range of tides at the Sandwich Island too small to allow the ship to be beached, Vancouver decided to send her to Nootka Sound for repair. She sailed on March 15th.

Nine days later, whilst surveying the coast of Oahu, the *Discovery* came to anchor off a lagoon known by the natives as 'O-poo-ro-ah' (Pearl Harbour). Whidbey was sent with two boats to carry out a survey of the area and came back with a generally favourable report marred only by a sandy bar across the entrance. This led Vancouver to the opinion that the lagoon was *'a very snug and convenient little port'* but, *'the bar outside renders it fit only for the reception of very small craft.'* Another opening, which the natives called 'Honoonoono' (Honolulu), was ignored altogether.

A week later, with her water replenished, and with a surprisingly small amount of fresh provisions, the *Discovery* sailed from the Sandwich Islands towards the shores of western America, once again to take up her surveying duties off the north-west coast.

Chapter Twelve

SALMON COVE

'those under my command, whose zeal and laborious exertions
had justly intitled them to my best thanks.'

The *Chatham* had made a fast passage from the Sandwich Islands and arrived north of Nootka Sound on 8th April, 1793. Seeking to avoid a gale, Puget took his ship into – what he thought was Bahia de Buena Esperanza (Esperanza Inlet) – but he had actually entered another inlet just to the south (Nuchatlitz Inlet). Consulting a chart given to Vancouver by Quadra, Puget decided to press on up the inlet to reach an arm of Nootka Sound which would provide a sheltered, inside, passage to Friendly Cove. Still under the impression that he was in Bahia de Buena Esparanza he sailed on until he reached what looked like an impossibly narrow opening. Whilst attempting to bring the ship about, Puget was horrified to find that he had been caught in the grip of a strong tidal flow which forced the *Chatham* towards the gap. Already beyond the point where an anchor could have held them, Puget and his ship's company could only watch with fear as the vessel was swept through the narrows with her starboard main yard-arm wrenching branches off the trees. Indians from a nearby village ran along the shore shouting for the ship to go back, but it was too late, the *Chatham* had been driven into a closed basin like a cork forced into a bottle. Twice Puget attempted to get his ship back through the narrows and was repulsed by the tide. At last, after three days, a period of slack water allowed him to escape at the cost of a lost bower anchor.

They reached Nootka Sound on the 15th and Puget found that Quadra had left Captain Salvador Fidalgo in charge during the winter months. The Spanish had had a very poor time of it. They had been subject to incessant rain, violent storms and even an earthquake. Much of their provisions had been destroyed by damp and scurvy had taken a firm hold. Using the *Chatham*'s supplies, Puget helped out where he could and was rewarded by Spanish assistance in carrying out repairs to his ship. Whilst this was being carried out, an Indian came alongside the ship and was seen holding a beautiful humming-bird secured by a human hair tied around its leg. Considerable interest was shown in the creature and, after much hard bargaining, one of the ship's company obtained it. Two hours later the ship was surrounded by every canoe in the district packed with Indians and *'every Man, Woman and Child, had three or four Live humming-birds, to dispose of, which in a few Minutes so overstocked the Market, that a brass button was willingly received for two.'* A month after his arrival, with no sign of the *Discovery*, Puget opened sealed orders from Vancouver which instructed him to resume the survey from Detention Cove in Burke Channel where it had been left off the year before.

Less than a week after Puget's departure Vancouver sailed into Nootka Sound. His voyage had been a difficult one. The ship's jib-boom and foretop-gallant-mast were carried away in bad weather and a serious leak at the bows meant that the pumps had to be in operation the whole time. Some surveying north of Cape Mendichino had been carried out and Whidbey made an examination of Porto de la Trinidad (Trinidad Bay). On his arrival at Nootka, Vancouver noted that Fidalgo, despite the weather conditions, had managed to build a fort on one of the sound's islands and armed it with eleven nine-pounder cannon.

The *Discovery* remained in the sound for just three days before Vancouver took her out to catch up with Puget. The *Chatham* was found eight miles up the Burke Channel near mid-day on the 25th. Apart from the repairs needed by the *Discovery*, both ships and their ship's companies were in good condition, ready to face the next four months of cold, wet, and hardship.

The ships moved up the inlet to 'Restoration Cove' (Restoration Bay) – named for the same reason as Puget Sound's 'Restoration Point'. The leak at the bows of the *Discovery* was stopped, she was caulked and had her sails repaired. Spare and replacement spars were obtained from the many tall trees lining the shore. The ships' boats were lowered and prepared for the coming surveys. Experience the previous year and experiments carried out whilst in the Sandwich Island had produced protective awnings for each of the boats, a waterproof groundsheet, a tent, and waterproof bags for each seaman's belongings. Extra food was allocated so that two hot meals a day could be served, and additional rum was provided, to be issued at the officer's discretion.

First to leave was Johnstone, ordered to follow up the inlet's two eastern arms that he had been unable to survey the previous season. Vancouver and Lieutenant Swaine followed the next day and entered a wide inlet heading north from the entrance to the Burke Channel. The eastern side of the entrance was named 'Point Walker' after the surgeon of the *Chatham* and the western side 'Point Edmund' after the politician, Edmund Burke (the same individual whose name was given to the Burke Channel). The rocky, fir-lined, inlet itself was named 'Fisher Channel' after a Wiltshire vicar.

Keeping to the starboard shore, the boats arrived at a point where Johnstone's party had already been. The discovery could only mean one thing – that the mountainous land to the east was an island. Vancouver named it after his previous captain in Cook's *Discovery*, James King. An extended inlet to the north-east was named 'Dean's Channel' after King's father, the Dean of Raphoe.

Returning the same way, but now looking at the northern shore, an inlet was found containing a number of waterfalls that fell from its precipitous cliffs. 'Cascade Channel' (Cascade Inlet) was followed by a much shallower inlet (Elcho Harbour) where they met a number of friendly Indians who traded trinkets for fish. The date of Vancouver's visit was 5th June. Six weeks and five days later the same spot was reached by Alexander MacKenzie, the first man to cross North America north of Mexico. The Indians told MacKenzie that *'a large canoe had lately been in this bay, with people like me'*. One of those people had been called *'Macubah'*. History was thus narrowly deprived of a meeting that would have earned a noted place in its records.

The ships were reached on the 8th and Vancouver learned that Johnstone had explored the two eastern arms and found no easterly trending waterways capable of navigation. The following day, Vancouver sent him northwards to probe other inlets as the ships were taken to a new anchorage.

In the course of all the boat expeditions, numerous Indians were met. All had proved to be hospitable and keen to invite the visitors to their villages. The enormous communal houses, raised clear of the ground on tree trunks, greatly impressed them with their colourful totem poles and grotesque carvings. Once again, the native women indicated that they *'would have no objection to our company'* whilst the men of the tribe collected cockles and pounded the inner bark of the spruce tree into edible cakes. Among the Heiltsuk Indians, the women had adopted the labret as a facial ornament. This wooden, plate-like, insertion into the upper lip gave Edward Bell the opportunity to express his general view of women: *'As may readily be supposed, this beauteous ornament affects their Speech - or rather their articulation in a very great degree, and it is droll to observe this enormous Trencher wagging up and down at every word the wearer says, and this it does with a most extravagant motion very often, for the Women in this* part of the world, like many other parts, wear the breeches, and are not only *great scolds, but great orators, and the vehemence and violence with which they speak, gives ample play to the Trencher.'*

The ships anchored in Fisher Channel where they were joined by Johnstone five days later. He had suffered a tragedy whilst examining the far reaches of one of the inlets he had probed. Despite the experience of Manby the previous year, some of his men had collected mussels to eat for breakfast. Several of them had been affected by sickness and had to be given warm water to make them reject the shellfish. One man, however, John Carter, died and was buried in a nearby bay. Vancouver had the spot where the mussels were picked named as 'Poison Cove'. The inlet leading to it was named 'Muscle Channel' (Mussel Inlet) and the unfortunate Carter gave his name to the bay in which he lies buried.

The two ships continued to edge their way northwards from anchorage to anchorage as Johnstone and Whidbey led boat parties in surveying the coast. 'Gardner Channel', Douglas Channel, 'Hawkesbury Island' and the entrance to the Skeena River were all examined. After four separate attempts to enter the river beyond its rock-bound entrance, Whidbey decided it was clearly un-navigable and returned to the ships via 'Grenville's Channel' to join them as they passed through Nepean Sound and the Principe Channel before reaching Chatham Sound.

On the morning of 20th July, with Stephens Island now in their wake, Queen Charlotte Island to the west was soon lost in a mist driven by an increasing easterly wind. Even worse were *'the innumerable rocky islets and rocks'* that could be seen ahead. *'These dangers, the gloominess of the weather, and the impending gale from the S.E., combined to give this unexplored channel an appearance so forlorn, as scarcely to admit the idea of its being navigable.'*

Vancouver gently felt his way northwards towards the rocks in the hope of finding an anchorage but, as he advanced *'our prospects became less flattering. The lucid intervals of the mist only exhibited our situation to be more intricate and dangerous.'* Then to his *'no small degree of relief'* (and, no doubt, astonishment) a whale-boat was spotted pulling out of the mist and heading towards them. The ships were brought to immediately and one of the boat's crew climbed on board the *Discovery*. The small craft belonged to the London trader *Butterworth* which, in company with the *Jackal* and the *Prince Le Boo*, were anchored. The man from the whaler – one of the *Butterworth*'s officers – volunteered to pilot the *Discovery* and the *Chatham* through the rocks to the anchorage. They arrived safely that evening to a salute of seven guns from the *Butterworth*. Her captain, William Brown, was welcomed on board the *Discovery* where he informed Vancouver that he had been told by the natives of an inland navigation existing to the north-east, its probable entrance being a wide opening that Brown had visited some twenty-seven miles in that direction. The inlet could have been the supposed passage to the east claimed to have been discovered in 1640 by Bartholomew de Fonte and laid down on Spanish charts as Estrecho del Almirante Fontes. Brown had also entered a southern arm of the inlet where the *'improper conduct'* of the Indians had led to a number of them being killed by musket-fire from the ship.

The day after his arrival at the anchorage, Vancouver set sail for the suggested inlet as Whidbey took the cutter and returned to the coast where he had left off his earlier survey. Guided by the *Prince Le Boo*, the ships headed northwards along a much broken coast backed by tall, snow-covered mountains and fringed by rocky islands covered with fir trees.

The wide inlet was reached with little difficulty and Vancouver named the south-eastern point of the entrance 'Point Maskelyne' after the Astronomer Royal whose *Nautical Almanac* had proved to be an invaluable tool to navigators since its introduction in 1766. With a fair wind behind them the inlet was penetrated until a night anchorage was obtained six miles from Point Maskelyne. Whidbey arrived with the cutter having completed his survey without finding any significant openings. The following morning, the *Prince Le Boo* returned to join Captain Brown and the *Butterworth*.

Avoiding temptation to follow a branch leading off to the north and continuing along a north-eastern arm, Vancouver found an anchorage in a cove on the western shore. The site ('Salmon Cove') proved to have salmon in abundance and so many could be caught in the nets that they almost broke under the strain. However, they were *'of an inferior kind, and partaking in no degree of the flavor of European salmon.'* Whidbey was sent with the American-born midshipman, Robert Barrie, to return to Point Maskelyne and continue the survey of the coast northwards. An observatory was set up ashore under the direction of Whidbey, and the other officers were ordered to take frequent observations in an attempt to find their exact location. Vancouver had not taken part in any of the surveying since his voyage up the Fisher Channel two months earlier. For a man who was intent on leading by example, and who expected others to always give of their best efforts in the same way he did, only the probability of illness can account for such inactivity. What the illness was can only be guessed at as Vancouver leaves no clue in his account of the voyage. Menzies – at the time of his reluctant acceptance of the surgeon's appointment ten month's earlier – had noted that he had *'constantly prescribed for Capt. Vancouver himself since leaving England'*. Assuming that his illness had remained the same over the twenty-seven months, it is also reasonable to assume that Menzies' prescriptions were not having much effect. Furthermore, it would have been easy for the hostile Menzies – supported by the equally antagonistic surgeon's mate, George Hewett – to have been somewhat less than benevolent in the medication he was supplying to Vancouver. However, whatever the illness was, it clearly had a physical effect, and might also account for the frustration suggested by the occasional outbreaks of raging intolerance to which Vancouver seemed to have been increasingly prone.

In company with Puget, Swaine and Menzies, Vancouver set off on 24th July with the pinnace and the launch and continued up 'Observatory Inlet' to where it divided into two arms. Both branches were examined to their terminations before Vancouver returned to the ships to replenish his provisions. South of Salmon Cove a north-trending inlet led to a more easterly waterway ('Portland Canal') which terminated in low, marshy land some seventy miles from the sea. *'Mortified with having devoted so much time to so little purpose'* the party returned the way it had entered and continued on to reach the coast. Passing to the north through the Revillagigedo Channel they reached a wide opening heading generally in a northern direction ('Behm Channel' after Major Behm who looked after Cook's ships during their visit to Kamchatka in 1779). Once through the 'Behm Narrows' the passage turns abruptly towards the south-west. On 12th August, the boats were heading for the shore to fix their position when they were met by three canoes. The Indians (from the Tlingit tribe), heavily armed with firearms in addition to spears and knives, followed the boats ashore. Whilst Vancouver was taking a sighting, the natives began to behave in a hostile manner by attempting to steal anything they could get their hands on. Puget fended them off until Vancouver returned and ordered the boats back on to the water. Two more canoes joined and the Indians surrounded Swaine and Menzies in the launch. At first it seemed as if they wanted to trade otter skins for trinkets, but then the largest canoe, seemingly commanded from the stern by an old woman with a large lip ornament, cut across Swaine's bows in an attempt to stop him. At this, Swaine ordered one of the seamen to raise his musket and the canoes veered off.

The Indians – by now numbering about fifty – then made their way over to the pinnace, some distance from the launch. There they grabbed hold of the boat's gunwales as, once again, the old woman steered her canoe across the pinnaces's bows. As the two vessels closed, the old woman grabbed the lead line and used it to lash the canoe and boat together. At the same time one of the natives from her canoe jumped into the pinnace and put on a wolf mask (the Tlingit traditionally divided themselves into 'wolves' or 'ravens'). At this another attacker reached into the pinnace and stole a musket. Vancouver, carrying a musket went forward in an attempt to speak to the wolf-masked Indian but only succeeded in causing all the natives to produce spears and knives with which they threatened the boat's occupants. The masked boarder jumped back into the canoe and waved at

Vancouver suggesting that, if he lay his weapon down, the Indians would do the same. Vancouver complied, followed by the natives. For a second or two it seemed as if peace had been restored, but the old woman began to shout orders to the canoes closest to the pinnace's stern. Suddenly, the boat's oars were grabbed and spears began to be thrust from all directions. At the same time the natives began to grab whatever they could from inside the boat. Looking up, Vancouver could see that the launch was closing and was now within pistol shot. Returning to the scuffle going on around him, he was presented with the fearful sight of an Indian aiming a musket directly at him. The native pulled the trigger, but the lock merely snapped in the pan. Faced with the possibility of the attackers resorting to fire-arms, Vancouver ordered his men to open fire. The crack of swivel guns and the rattle of muskets echoed across the water from the surrounding mountains. The effect was immediate. The canoes raced for the shore as Vancouver prepared to follow them with the intention of destroying the native craft. The boats had not gone far when Vancouver learned that two of his men had been injured in the fracas. A Scottish seaman, Robert Betton, whilst defending the arms chest, had been lunged at with a spear. The point had penetrated but Betton had grabbed the spear only to have it pulled from his hand and thrust into his thigh. George Bridgeman, a seaman who had voluntarily entered the *Discovery* from one of the fur trading ships that had been at Nootka the previous May, had also been speared in the thigh as he prevented a native from unshipping one of the swivels. Rather than pursue the Indians, Vancouver gave Menzies time to tend to the wounded as the attackers made their escape. It was not known how many of the natives had been killed or wounded, but estimates from the witnesses average at about nine. The site of the attack was named 'Traitor's Cove'.

True to his accustomed desire to see justice done, Vancouver immediately held an enquiry into the cause behind the native attack. At first he suspected that some form of insult had been committed when the Indians first landed alongside the boats. Assured that this was not the case, Vancouver then came to the conclusion that the Indians had been trading with fur-traders and – as was often the case – had been supplied with defective weapons which had exploded in the hands of their users. This, he felt, could have led to their desire to obtain replacement firearms from other traders – of which, they might have assumed, he was one. Finally, he blamed himself, for: *'that attentive wariness which had been the first object of my concern on coming amongst these rude nations, had latterly been much neglected.'*

The surgeon's mate, George Hewett, following his leader, Menzies, in his hostility towards Vancouver, took a different view of the attack and its outcome. According to his version, George Bridgeman had informed Vancouver that he believed the Indians were about to attack and that they should prepare their weapons. Vancouver's response was to tell him *'to hold his tongue and mind his own business'*. The arms were to remain in the arms chest until he decided when they should be taken out (thus earning the subsequent sneer from the surgeon's mate of *'here behold the God Almighty'*). As a result – according to Hewett – the only weapons available when the attack came were two pocket pistols and Vancouver's shot-gun.

The following day, salt water and the Spanish charts revealed them to be back at an arm of the Pacific Ocean. The land around which they had sailed could only be an island. Vancouver name it 'Island of Revill Gigedo' (Revillagigedo Island) after the Viceroy of Mexico.

From the northern entrance to the Behm Channel, Vancouver headed south-east past Gravina Island – named by the Spanish after Don Frederico Gravina, commander the Spanish Fleet at Trafalgar in 1805. Revillagigedo Channel was regained and a favourable wind allowed the sails to be hoisted for the first time since leaving the ships.

Salmon Cove was reached on 16th August. Vancouver's party had examined seven hundred miles of coast, an effort that had advanced them a mere sixty miles from the ships: '*Such were the perplexing, tedious, and laborious means by which alone we were enabled by degrees to trace the north-western limits of the American continent.*' Most of the time had been spent at the oars, and the precipitous mountains that rose directly from the waters provided little shelter ashore leaving most nights to be spent in the uncomfortable boats. They had taken food for a fortnight but had been away for twenty-three days. On the day before they reached the ships, all that remained was '*half a pint of peas*'.

Johnstone had returned to the ships two weeks earlier. He had briefly examined the estuary of a river (Nass River) to the south of Observatory Inlet but had found it to be barely deep enough for their own boats – much to Menzies' annoyance who was convinced the river led to inland lakes and an eventual route across North America. Another opening was entered (Work Channel) and Johnstone made sure that each of his men were armed with a musket, bayonet, pistol, cutlass and tomahawk and that his half-pounder swivel guns were ready for action. The inlet had been the scene of cannon-fire against the natives by Captain Brown of the *Butterworth* and Johnstone had no intention of allowing his party to become a focus of revenge. The natives, however, had fled, abandoning their villages, leaving the houses pierced by Brown's cannon. With his survey completed, Johnstone returned to Salmon Cove.

Leaving Observatory Inlet on 17th August, the ships made their way back to Chatham Sound and entered 'The Duke of Clarence's Strait' (Clarence Strait – after Prince William Henry) and found an anchorage on the west coast ('Port Stewart', named after the Master's Mate sent to survey its coastline). To the east lay the entrance to the Behm Canal with Traitor's cove about four miles off on its eastern shore. The Clarence Strait continued on its way to the north-west. Two survey expeditions were immediately set under way. Whidbey was to re-enter the Behm Canal and examine a number of inlets along the continental shore that Vancouver had not been able to enter. Johnstone was to cross over to the eastern shore of Clarence Strait and work his way northwards until he reached the open sea.

The ships were visited a number of times by Tlingit Indians (the same tribe who had mounted the attack at Traitor's Cove). Vancouver considered them to be '*good folk*' as they traded furs with a cheerful honesty. One was so impressed by what he saw on board that he begged Vancouver to take him to England. The apparent admiration for all that they had seen, however, came to an abrupt halt when the natives witnessed a punishment flogging. They immediately took to their canoes and left the anchorage. Among them was one Indian who had suddenly lost his desire to take passage to England with the ship.

Whidbey returned shortly after the Indian's departure. Apart from an accurate laying down of the continental coast of the Behm Canal, nothing of note had been discovered.

The earlier disappearance of one group of Indians did not prevent another group from arriving and enjoying the bread and molasses served to them by Vancouver. He was less taken by their response – a bladder of whale oil which he was expected drink as a delicacy: *'it was not without much difficulty, that I was able to excuse myself from partaking of their nauseous meal, which they seem to relish in the highest degree'.* Events then took an unpleasant, and surprising turn. Another flotilla of canoes arrived in the bay and made their way over to the *Discovery.* This led to a great amount of haranguing from both groups of Indians. Spears were jabbed in each other's direction, threats were made, and fire-arms produced before a peaceful outcome was negotiated. The Indians were of the Kaigani-Haida tribe, noted both for their long canoe journeys and their war-like behaviour. Their fire-arms had been supplied by American fur-traders. Puget, outraged by such a trade wrote: *'I sincerely hope, if ever they are used in an hostile Manner, it may be against those people who supplied the Indians with them.'*

On the 2nd September, both ships were moved to the harbour entrance to await the return of Johnstone and his party. Some alarm was felt for their safety now that it was known that the Indians had fire-arms but, two days after the move, Johnstone arrive safely on board to report to Vancouver. A large inlet to the east ('Prince Ernest's Sound' – Ernest Sound) had been examined before an eastern passage round a number of islands saw the coastline curve first to the west, then the south-west (Sumner Strait). 'Bradfield Channel', to the north-east of Ernest Sound had been surveyed in pouring rain. The bad weather continued along, what Johnstone took to be, an unbroken coast. In fact, beyond a series of mud-flats and shoals, lay the entrance to the Stikine River and a strait leading to the north-west. Johnstone had not reached the open sea during his survey and so Vancouver took the ships into the Sumner Strait and found an anchorage near the northern point of Prince of Wales Island. The harbour had not been found a moment too soon for, as the anchors were being dropped, a gale blew up that would have placed the ships in great danger had they been caught in the rock-bound strait. *'Grateful for such an asylum'*, Vancouver named the place 'Port Protection'. Johnstone was sent to complete his survey of the northern shore. He was away for only one night having looked into two bays before reaching a position opposite to Port Protection. Both bays were studded with rocks, many just below the surface and dangerous in the extreme. By keeping clear of these hazards, Johnstone managed to miss a passage (Keku Strait) which flowed northwards out of the second bay. The point of Johnstone's return was the same as Whidbey's start. Ordered by Vancouver to

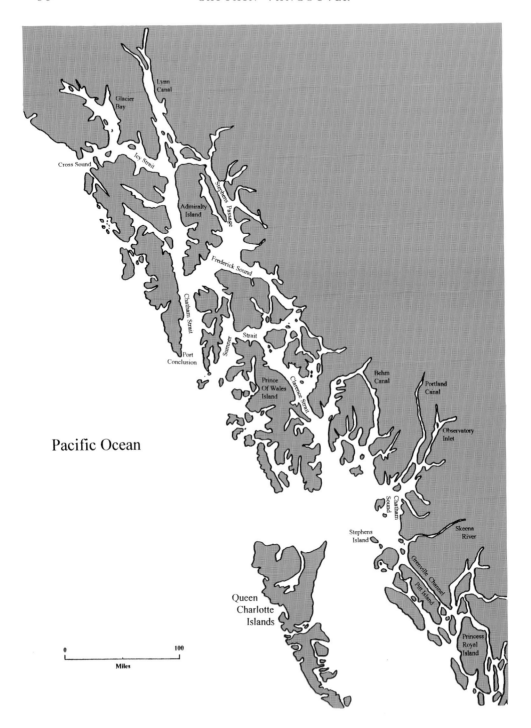

Coastline of North West America, Map 2

continue the survey to the sea, Whidbey had an unfortunate start when his rudder and part of the stern-post was broken off in a collision with a submerged rock. The coast was followed into a succession of bays and inlets until gales drove them for shelter in a secluded cove. Whilst waiting for the winds to subside they carried out repairs to the boats. A wide inlet ('Affleck's Channel' after Rear Admiral Phillip Affleck) was entered and found to terminate in flat, stream-laced country. Pestered by fog and rain, Johnstone continued to follow the coast to the south where, subjected to the rolling of an ocean swell, he found the coast turned sharply to the north. From there he returned to the ships at Port Protection.

For Vancouver, the *'boisterous state of the weather, the advanced season of the year, and the approach of long and dreary nights'* could only mean one thing. It had become *'highly expedient that the vessels should retire to some milder region, where refreshment might be obtained; and where such relaxation and ease as now became necessary might be given to those under my command, whose zeal and laborious exertions, during the summer, had justly intitled them to my best thanks and highest commendation.'* As the *'extent of the discoveries of De Fuca, De Fonte, and other pretenders to a prior knowledge of these regions, must necessarily be decided'* he named the southern point reached by Johnstone 'Cape Decision'.

They reached Nootka Sound after a journey down the west coasts of the islands in order to compare and improve earlier British and Spanish charts. Foul weather had made the voyage difficult, especially for the *Chatham* who suffered considerable damage to her sails and rigging in trying to keep up with the *Discovery*. Only three days were spent in the sound, mainly in repairs to both vessels and in paying respects to the Spanish commandant, Ramon Saavadra, who had replaced Fidalgo. There had been little activity at the port since their last visit, the chief interest having been a French ship whose mutinous crew seemed intent in carrying the principles of the revolution to sea. The lack of activity was actually an indication of a decline in Spanish interest in Nootka. Rumours that the British had ideas of establishing a base north of San Francisco had led to a Spanish survey from the Golden Gate northwards to the Juan de Fuca Strait. The Columbia River had been entered, but left shortly afterwards as the ship ran aground and was threatened by war-like Indians. Another rumour was to reflect directly upon Vancouver. Fidlago had returned to the south with a tale that Vancouver was considering an attack on Monteray and San Diego. Although the Spanish settlements were very poorly defended, the probability of such an assault was unlikely in the extreme. The combined fire-power of Vancouver's ships amounted to no more than ten 4-pounder and three 3-pounder cannons, he had less than two-hundred men, and no support for thousands of miles. Nevertheless, the Spanish Viceroy gave orders that all British ships were to be treated with the greatest suspicion and not to be welcomed in the Spanish ports.

Chapter Thirteen

THE CEDING OF HAWAII

*'unanimously ceded the said island of Owyhee to his
Britannic Majesty and acknowledged themselves to be
subjects of Great Britain.'*

The first inkling that Vancouver had that not all was well came on his arrival at San Francisco. Instead of the usual exchange of salutes and other courtesies, an unannounced boat came alongside bearing the commandant, Heamegildo Sal. The amiable Spaniard offered provisions and hospitality as if the situation was normal, and gave the news from Europe up until the previous February. After supper, Sal returned ashore – again without ceremony. The reason for the almost clandestine visit became clear to Vancouver the next day when two official letters arrived from the commandant. From them Vancouver learned that, not only was his length of stay to be reported immediately to the Provincial Governor, but also that, apart from himself, one other officer, and fuel and water parties, no-one else was allowed ashore.

Vancouver's reaction to the restrictions was to try and be diplomatic. He was aware that they did not come from Sal, but from Jose Joaquin Arrillaga, the acting Governor of Alta California. A dinner was arranged on board for the commandant and his wife at which an increase in the numbers of officers allowed ashore was agreed. In accepting the invitation, Sal announced that he would be bringing his guards with him. Vancouver replied that it would be unacceptable to have armed foreigners on board a British vessel, but *'if he was desirous of being attended by these Men, they might go on board as Visitors & being military men would be allowed to wear their side arms'*. Edward Bell, the clerk of the *Chatham*, however, reflected other views of the restrictions when he wrote that:

> *'Captn. V. condescended to act below his dignity and consequence as Commander of a British Man of War … he should have demanded what refreshments he wanted in the name of the King of Great Britain, watered his Ships and proceeded to Monterey … and expostulate with the very Officer from whom these orders sprung.'*

Despite the restrictions he had found at San Francisco, Vancouver sailed for Monterey in the *'hopes of meeting a reception worthy of our situation'*. The ships had not long left the port when a most welcome sight hove into view. It was the *Daedalus*, bringing them stores and provisions from the colony at New South Wales. They reached Monterey on 1st November and Vancouver went ashore to pay his compliments to the Governor, Arrillaga. He had prepared a statement outlining his reason for being off the coast of Spanish America and for calling into the ports along that coast but, before he could begin, the governor demanded that all communications should be in writing. That afternoon, two letters arrived at the *Discovery* with contents of the same tenor as those received at San Francisco. The stay of the British vessels was to be as short as possible consistent with the transfer of stores from the *Daedalus* and the obtaining of wood and water. In accordance with one of the demands, Vancouver was required once again to state his purpose for being in the area. He replied that he '*had been intrusted by his Britannic Majesty with a voyage of discovery, and for the exploring of various countries in the Pacific Ocean; of which the north-west coast of America was one of the principal objects.*' He further explained that he could not understand why, despite his previously good relationships with the Spanish, he was now being treated in such an unfriendly manner. In reply, Arrillaga, pointed out that he had no instructions to give Vancouver any special treatment. He would, however, allow a warehouse to be used in the transfer of goods from the *Daedalus* in an effort to speed things up. An observatory could be erected ashore, but only '*in the day time*' (therefore severely restricting its utility). No-one would be allowed ashore during the hours of darkness, and, apart from provisioning parties, only officers during the daytime. Such self-imposed treatment by a mere captain in the Spanish infantry against ships of the Royal Navy tested Vancouver's patience severely. In a despatch to the Admiralty Secretary, referring to Arrillaga's '*incommodius assistance*', he explained that the Governor's letter '*was in such a sneering, forbidding and ungracious stile, I considered it far too degrading and humiliating to the character and situation in which I am placed to accept such offers*'. Rather than agree to the restrictions, he would sail for the Sandwich Islands on completion of his survey of the coast to the south of Monterey. He would, however, still call at those Spanish ports on the way to 30 degrees south – the southern limit of his survey. Four days out of Monterey, Vancouver found himself sailing through waters the like of which he, nor anyone else on board, had never seen before:

The surface of the sea, which was perfectly smooth and tranquil, was covered with a thick slimy substance, which, when separated, or disturbed by any little agitation, became very luminous, whilst the light breeze that came principally from the shore, brought a very strong smell of burning tar, or of some such resinous substance. The next morning, Sunday the 10th, the sea had the appearance of dissolved tar floating upon its surface, which covered the ocean in all directions within the limits of our view and indicated that in this neighbourhood it was not subject to much agitation.'

Unknown to him, or to anyone else for the next hundred years, Vancouver was sailing over the under-sea portion of the vast Southern Californian oil field. Its natural leakage of unrefined oil was calming the surface waters and filling the air with its smell of '*burning tar*'

The ships' visit to Santa Barbara was made in complete contrast to that at Monteray. The commandant – Lieutenant Feliupe de Goycoechea – proved to have a '*noble and generous mind*' and strongly recommended that Vancouver obtain as much wood and water from the port as possible as such commodities were in short supply further to the south. His only restriction was to ask that no-one be allowed ashore at night. Food, both meat and vegetables, was provided willingly and a supply of soap and candles was given by the commandant when he learned that the ship's stocks of such items were low. San Diego was reached on 27th

November. Unfortunately, the commandant, a cavalry lieutenant named Antonio Grajero, had received a letter only four days earlier from Arrillaga ordering him to apply the same restrictions to Vancouver as he had at Monteray. Grajero, a hard-drinking man to whom hospitality came naturally, could do little more than try to ease things for his visitors. Before his recent appointment to the port, Grajero had met Quadra and had been asked to treat Vancouver and his expedition to all courtesies. Although now strictly limited in what he could provide, the commandant agreed wherever possible with Quadra's request. When the ships were ready to leave, Vancouver and his officers invited Grajero and Captain Zuniga – the Governor of Tucson – on board for dinner. During the meal they learned that their guests *'regretted with much sincerity the ridiculous & unmerited restrictions we lay under, which dampd all their proferred friendship & hospitality towards us, & which they were confident was contrary to the wishes of the Viceroy & the Spanish Court.'*

In revenge for the treatment that had been meted out to him by some of the Spaniards, Vancouver, in completing his voyage south to 30 degrees North (a distance of 1700 miles from his furthest north at 56 degrees North), named prominent coastal features after those Spanish officer who had shown him kindness and support. 'Point Sal', 'Point Zuniga', 'Port Juan Francisco' (now Bodega Bay) after Quadra, and 'Point Grajero' (Cabo Punta Banda), all appeared on Vancouver's chart. Nothing was named after Captain Arrillaga.

With the southern end of his survey completed, Vancouver set sail for the Sandwich Islands *'where I had little doubt that the uneducated inhabitants of Owhyhee, or its neighbouring isles, would cheerfully afford us that accommodation which had been unkindly denied us at St. Francisco and Monterrey.'*

Anchors were dropped in Kealakekua Bay on 12th January, 1794. The King of Hawaii, Kamehameha (or 'Tamaahmaah' as Vancouver spelt his name), had been picked up further along the coast and had arranged for the ships to be supplied with pigs, vegetables and water. Close to the *Discovery* lay the American fur-trader *Lady Washington*. Her captain, John Kendrick – much to Vancouver's disapproval – had been supplying the natives with *'Swivels, Muskets, and Gunpowder'* to the advantage of the king's war aims against the island of Maui. Fate was to mete out her own justice eleven months later when Kendrick was in Honolulu. A fellow trader – the *Jackal* – fired her cannons in a ceremonial salute to the *Lady Washington* and killed him with an accidentally loaded shot. The balance of power in the islands, however, were of considerable importance to Vancouver. The supply of fire-arms had confirmed Kamehameha as the strongest of the island kings. It was he who would have to be persuaded – if Vancouver's plan was to succeed – to use his influence with the Hawaiian chiefs and enable the island to be ceded to Great Britain.

As Puget went to watch the natives *'amusing themselves in the Surf on Swimming Boards'*, and Menzies led an expedition to climb a nearby volcano, Vancouver set about obtaining the island for his sovereign. His first move was to provide the king with a vessel worthy of his station. Three Englishmen, who were employed by the king to assist his trade with foreign ships, had begun to build a thirty-six foot yacht, but had found that its completion was beyond their skills. Vancouver promptly sent over his carpenters to assist in the work and the king watched with joy as the *Britannia* began to take shape on the shores of Kealakekua Bay.

Before negotiation had got under way, the stores from the *Daedalus* had to be transferred. With the help of the islanders the work was quickly accomplished and the storeship was ready to sail on 8th February. With her went three of the young gentlemen. Midshipman Thomas Clarke of the *Discovery* had been flogged for misbehaviour. The *Chatham*'s Midshipman Augustus Boyd Grant had also been flogged but, even worse, had taken up with *'one of the foremast people with whom he lived, & whose habits he had contracted in a most shameful Manner'*. Consequently *'excluded from the Society of Gentlemen'*, Grant was sent home. To no one's surprise, the third midshipman was The Honourable Thomas Pitt. Instead of proving to be the aristocratic passport to the higher reaches of society all naval officers aspired to, Pitt had turned out to be a rebellious, oafish, thug without a single moral bone in his body. Having tolerated his behaviour for too long, Vancouver was glad to see the back of him as he was rowed across to the *Daedalus*. However, as time would show, Vancouver had not rid himself of Pitt, and neither of them knew that the midshipman – due to the death of his father – was now the Second Baron Camelford.

Before he could attempt to pursue his aim of accepting the island for his country, Vancouver found himself faced with a royal domestic difficulty. The king, having found that his wife had committed adultery, had (despite his own frequent acts of infidelity) banished her from his court. Now he wanted her back, not just for her company, but also to restore the loss of status and dignity he suffered from for being a king without a queen. The problem was, that if he went to one of the island's chiefs to ask for help, that in itself would mean a loss of status, even to the extent of threatening his throne. Vancouver offered to help *'not only in his domestic comforts, but in his political situation by receiving again and reinstating his consort in her former rank and consequence.'* A plan was hatched with the king to effect a reconciliation. Kamehameha was anxious not to appear *'that he had been privy to the business'* and marked two pieces of paper which he left with Vancouver, one *'was to indicate that the result of my enquiries was agreeable to his wishes and the other that it was to the contrary.'* The queen, her family and friends, were invited on board the *Discovery*: *'for the purpose of presenting them with some trivial matters, as tokens of my friendship and regard.'* During the social conversation, Vancouver managed to discover that the queen was as keen to get back with her husband as he was with her. He then suggested that a joke could be played upon the king by sending him a message telling him that Vancouver was giving gifts to a number of his Hawaiian friends and he had not been forgotten. The message would be on a piece of (markd) paper wrapped up as if it were a gift. The queen and her friends thought this a splendid idea and the message was sent by canoe to the shore where, unknown to the queen, the king was waiting. Within minutes the king arrived on board where, after some awkwardness on both sides, Vancouver brought the couple together by taking the king's hand and joining it to the queen's. A tearful reconciliation followed marred only by the queen's insistence that Vancouver go with them to the king's house to ensure that he did not beat her. That accomplished, Vancouver then turned his mind to obtaining Hawaii for the British Crown.

Apart from Kamehameha's approval, support for the idea had to be obtained from the island's six district chiefs. And therein lay a difficulty for Vancouver. Four of the chiefs were friendly, but one had been found guilty of stealing from the ships, and another was believed to have been involved in the massacre of the *Fair American*'s crew. The former could be dealt with easily by simply ignoring the offence. The murders, however, could not be disregarded so lightly and put Vancouver to a lot of soul-searching before he came to a decision. Despite *'not being ambitious to have much acquaintance'* with the assumed murderer, he decided that *'the adoption of conciliatory measures … was most consistent with my duty as a man, and with the station I then filled.'* Not everyone agreed. Bell felt that *'Here then is an instance of a Pirate, and a murderer, suffered to commit these acts with impunity … Surely Captain Vancouver's lenity has been carried to too great a length. Here was an opportunity of giving these people an idea, in what light we looked upon such atrocious crimes.'* Not surprisingly, Menzies also disapproved: *'We cannot defend the policy of thus countenancing & soliciting either the acquaintance or friendship of such a notorious villain.'* Under normal circumstances, Vancouver would not have disagreed, but he could not gain the cession without the approval of *all* the chiefs. When the alleged murderer (Kameeiamoku) arrived at the tent erected for the treaty discussion, Bell recorded that he *'entered the marquee pale and trembling expecting momentary death, every conviction of his former barbarous conduct seem'd at that moment to have taken possession of him, he seem'd Struck with remorse & shame, and I may add terror too, for his own life, and his appearance and manner altogether displayed a great want of resolution and Fortitude.'* Vancouver's reaction was to go up to him and shake his hand *'as a token of my forgiveness and reconciliation.'*

Before the treaty could be discussed in detail a great amount of feasting and entertaining had to be endured. Hula dancers repeatedly performed to men beating out the rhythm on their spears. If they were slow in getting started, the native men making up the audience would shout 'Hula Hula pouliuli! *'signifying that it would be dark and black night before the performance would begin'*. Plays were performed by native women, and Vancouver replied with a show of fireworks.

The discussions did not go as smoothly as Vancouver had hoped. At the last minute it was decided that the priests of the island would have to be consulted. This meant a delay of several days before the king and the chiefs assembled once again in the *Discovery*'s great cabin. On the morning of Tuesday, February 25th, 1794, Vancouver, Baker, Swaine, Whidbey and Menzies heard Kamehameha state his main reason for ceding his country to Great Britain. Since Cook's arrival on the island, many foreign ships had arrived and many more were likely to visit. This increasing activity could lead to the inhabitants being ill-treated, and possibly subjugated, by the foreigners with their superior fire-power. Inevitably, they would have to look for help from outside their own society. The other foreigners, mainly Americans and the Spanish, had not treated the people of Hawaii with respect, and had supplied their enemies with fire-arms. Therefore, it was to King George of Great Britain that he would look for protection. The chiefs then expressed their opinions. One wanted the British to attack the neighbouring island of Maui as he had ambitions to take over as king. Another, stated that, as Hawaii had been attacked four times by the natives of Maui, and they had only made one attack in return, they should be allowed three further assaults before any outside authority imposed restrictions upon their warlike activities. One chief was concerned that foreign ships would arrive claiming they were British. How would the Hawaiians know the difference? Following considerable discussion, the king rose and formally proposed that the island should be ceded to Great Britain. The decision was unanimous, each of the chiefs stating that they were no longer "*Tanata no Owhyhee*" ("People of Hawaii"), but *"Tanata no Britannee"* ("People of Britain"). The cry was taken up by hundreds of natives surrounding the ships in canoes and by hundreds more thronging the beach. Vancouver promptly sent Puget ashore with a Union flag to take formal possession of the island in the name of King George III and his descendants as gun salutes were fired from the *Discovery* and the *Chatham*. Copper plates recording the event were displayed at the site and at the Kings house. On them were the words: '*On the 25th of February, 1794, Tamaahmaah king of Owhyhee, in council with the principal chiefs of the island, assembled on board His Britannic Majesty's sloop Discovery in Karakakooa bay, and in the presence of George Vancouver, commander of the said sloop; Lieutenant Peter Puget, commander of his said Majesty's armed tender the Chatham; and the other officers of the Discovery; after due consideration, unanimously ceded the said island of Owhyhee to his Britannic Majesty, and acknowledged themselves to be subjects of Great Britain.*'

Without instructions, and entirely on his own initiative, Vancouver had acquired for his sovereign a country that, just sixteen years earlier, had been unknown to all but its natives. Although almost as far from the Government in Whitehall as it is possible to get, and remote even from its closest continental shores, Hawaii had the potential to become the main mid-Pacific staging-post between Asia and America. In commercial terms the island could not have been better situated and, for a nation which had just given up one empire and was about to start on the acquisition of a second, Hawaii's strategic position was a bonus that would be widely welcomed in England – or so it seemed to Vancouver.

With the treaty of cession completed, there was little to hold the ships at Hawaii. They sailed from Kealakekua Bay the following day with the king and several chiefs remaining on board until they were put ashore at Kawaihae Bay. Almost a hundred pigs were taken on board as gifts of the king along with a large amount of fresh vegetables and fruit, but – according to Menzies – Vancouver repaid this kindness by refusing the king a short length of red cotton fabric with which to make a loin-cloth. The king had then abruptly left the *Discovery* with hurt feelings and had gone across to the *Chatham* where Puget gave him the desired length of cloth. Menzies, who claimed that the '*refusal of a trifle of this kind, on such an occasion, cannot be viewed in a favourable light*' was choosing not to link the denial of the gift to a bout of serious theft carried out by the chiefs as the ships had passed down the coast. Finally, the last contact with the people of Hawaii came as a canoe was sent from the shore to collect the king's 'spitting box'.

To complete his survey of the islands, Vancouver charted the coasts of Woahoo (Oahu), Attowai (Kauai), Oneehow (Niihau), and Moka Manu (Nihoa) until, with their work at the Sandwich Islands then at an end, the ships were steered to the north-east, their jib-booms pointing towards Cook's River on the bleak north-west coast of America.

Chapter Fourteen

COOK'S RIVER AND PRINCE WILLIAM SOUND

'several of our people were frost bit in performing their duty.'

To avoid passing along the same coast twice, Vancouver decided that he would start his final season on the north-west coast at the most northerly limit indicated by his Admiralty instructions – 60 degrees north. That position happily coincided with what Vancouver considered to be the best opportunity to find a passage to the east. Cook's River, discovered by Cook in 1778 (with Midshipman Vancouver on board the *Resolution*), trended to the north-east for about two hundred miles before dividing into two arms, either of which could have been supplied by a navigable river fed by inland lakes. Cook's orders had prevented him from a detailed examination as he was required to penetrate Bering's Straits. Consequently, it fell to Vancouver to carry out a full survey and to see if the river continued on to *'any extensive navigation easterly'*.

Shortly after leaving the Sandwich Islands the two ships were separated. The *Chatham*, leaking badly and with over four feet of water in her hold, reached Kodiak Island (to the south of Cook's River) on 10th April, and made her way towards Cape Douglas. From there Puget intended to follow his instructions and explore northward along the western shore of the river. Off Point Banks, on the northern tip of Shuyak Island, a boat came out to the ship carrying two Russians. They told Puget that no ship had been seen entering the river (once again the sluggish *Chatham* had managed to out-sail Vancouver's vessel) and that Russian trading posts had been established on the island, on the shores of the Cook River, and at Prince William Sound. An eight-gun sloop under the command of the local fur-trading manager – Aleksander Baranof – was at Point Banks and the captain would be happy to pay a courtesy call upon the visiting ship. Puget, however, concerned about the threat of deteriorating weather, decided to continue to Cape Elizabeth, the most southerly point of the Kenai Peninsula. From there, the western coast of the peninsula formed the eastern shores of the river.

Ice still clung to the banks of the wide waterway, and floes drifted out of the river's mouth as the *Chatham* struggled to make her way to Cape Elizabeth. At last, safe within the protection of a small inlet ('Port Chatham'), the ship was subjected to heavy snow falls, a bitter frost, and temperatures of 20 degrees (F). Outside the inlet, a gale blew so hard that Puget ordered a second anchor to be dropped for fear that the ship would be driven ashore. With no sign of the *Discovery*, Puget decided to stay where he was and carry out a number of urgently-needed repairs. The day after his arrival he was surprised to find an umiak – a large Eskimo boat – arriving alongside containing twenty-six natives keen to trade furs. They were followed by a number of Russian visitors, one of whom came – already in a state of intoxication – with a request for some rum (which Puget refused). Two weeks after her arrival, the *Chatham* left her anchorage and crossed the mouth of the river to begin the survey of the western shore, Puget was unaware that the *Discovery* had sailed past Port Chatham just two days after he had hauled into the inlet.

Vancouver had suffered from such low temperatures as he approached Cook's River that the ship's rigging was festooned in ice and her upper deck deep in snow. The country ahead of him seemed *'dreary and inhospitable... intirely destitute of trees or shrubs, or they were hidden beneath its winter garment of snow.'* Finding no beauty in the starkness of the country around him, matters were not to improve as he made his way up the river.

On 16th April, with the thermometer well below freezing, three natives (possibly Eskimos) came alongside and clambered on board with no sign of fear. Their bowing to all and sundry, coupled with a few words of Russian, showed that they had previously had contact with white men. With the exception of requests for tobacco and snuff, and the chance to share in the ship's company's meal, they asked for nothing more than passage up-river for themselves and their 'skin canoes'. The next day, the *Discovery* ran aground but, after swinging around, freed herself with a violent shudder. That evening, the ship ran aground for a second time but was lifted clear by a large wave. She had not gone far when – south of Kalgin Island – she struck bottom again and again. It was not simply 'touch and go' but a severe pounding as each lift of the approaching swell was followed by a juddering fall. For an hour and a half the ship rose and fell on to the rock-strewn bottom, at times striking so hard that it seemed as if the masts would go by the board. It was an *'unpleasant predicament'* that could have led to the ship's destruction. With no idea of a way out, Vancouver took his courage in both hands and decided to attempt to force his way across the obstruction and into the deeper waters of the river. The ship gathered weigh and surged forward towards the unseen obstacle only to sustain a massive crash which threw everyone to the deck. For a moment it seemed as if the worst had happened, that the *Discovery* had run aground with damaging violence. But she floated free again, this time on the deep side of the shoal.

In clear weather the following day, with the Iliamna Volcano on her larboard quarter issuing steam from its vents, the *Discovery* came into sight of three cliff-edged promontories that Vancouver named 'West', 'North', and 'East' Forelands as they had not been given names by Cook. The American first lieutenant of the *Resolution*, John Gore, had tried to persuade Cook to name the West Foreland after *'Nancy...a favourite Female Acquaintance'* – but his captain, with true Yorkshire distaste for fripperies, ignored him.

Off the West Foreland, *'our Indian friends'* asked to be put ashore as they were close to their village. Vancouver had been impressed by their behaviour and demeanour: *'if the conduct they exhibited during the time they passed with us, is to be received as their general national character, it indicates them to be a people unactuated by ambition, jealousy, or avarice; the passions which so strongly operate on the human species, to produce a constant dread and variance with each other, and stimulate to acts of oppression, violence and rapacity, as well on their nearest neighbours as the most distant strangers'*.

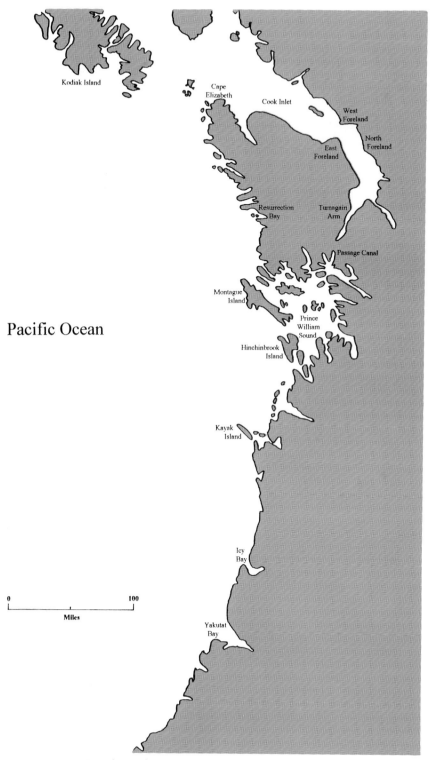

Kodiak Island

Cape
Elizabeth

Cook Inlet

West
Foreland

North
Foreland

East
Foreland

Resurrection
Bay

Turnagain
Arm

Passage Canal

Montague
Island

Prince
William
Sound

Pacific Ocean

Hinchinbrook
Island

Kayak
Island

Icy
Bay

0   100

Miles

Yakutat
Bay

Coastline of North West America, Map 3

Beyond the North Foreland the river took a pronounced turn to the east and, as Vancouver neared the point where the river divided, he was puzzled and alarmed by the sight of a shoal barring the entrance to the northern (Knik) arm. Such a barrier had not been there when he had been with Cook. With some of his ship's company already frost bitten and the lead emerging repeatedly from the water encased in ice, he was not prepared to risk another grounding. Whidbey was sent off in the cutter to investigate the rock-scattered shoal. He returned after a few hours with the news that the barrier was, in fact, a long stretch of ice. By mid-day *'our horizon was encompassed in most directions with floating ice, of various shapes, magnitudes, and colours.'*

With the temperature continuing to stay well below freezing point, Vancouver gave thought to searching for a place of shelter where he could wait for an improvement in the weather. Menzies explained why: *'Our sudden transition from the tropical regions to which our constitutions had been in some measure inured, but ill fitted us to withstand such harassing duty in this cold bleak & dreary country, we were therefore anxious to find some port, where we might take refuge & and remain comfortably till the season broke up & the rigour of the Climate so far abated that we could commence our operations, for the frost was now so very intense, that a little before we got under way, this morning the Thermometer was so low at 7 degrees. At eight it was at 13 degrees & at noon it rose no higher than 18 degrees - the effect of which was that several of our people were frost bit in performing their duty on this & the preceding day.'* However, no suitable bay, creek, or inlet could be found to where the ship could retreat and wait for better conditions. Unable to hide, the *Discovery* was subjected to a constant barrage of ice-floes crashing into her hull as the ebb and flow of the tide swept the ice back and forth over the anchorage.

Another grounding was made on shoals lining the northern shore, but the ship came off easily as Whidbey was sent up the eastern arm – Turnagain River – to see if there was a haven in that direction. He came back only with the news that he believed that the river terminated a few miles further on. Vancouver took a boat to see for himself, and came back with the same opinion. Nevertheless, only a complete and thorough survey could give a final answer and, as the ship was being watered and fuelled, Whidbey was sent off with two boats and ten days provisions to examine the river. If he found a termination, he was then to return and survey the coasts as far south as the West Foreland. The following day, ice carried away one of the *Discovery*'s bower cables and, with it, the anchor. This left her with just two anchors, both constantly under threat from the ice.

An umiak full of Eskimos paid a visit and was followed by a whaling-boat rowed by fourteen Indians (probably from the Athabascan tribe) and carrying ten Russians. The Russians had intended to spend the night on board but, after three hours, the shuddering caused by the constant collisions with the ice changed their minds and they left. Through sign language (no Russian interpreter had been supplied to Vancouver), it had been learned that the Russians claimed that Turnagain River ended just a few miles further on, and that an inlet from Prince William Sound lay just few miles beyond the termination.

Whidbey arrived at the ship on the 4th May. He had confirmed that no great river extended east of Turnagain River and had returned along its southern shore to Point Possession, the site of Cook's taking of the country for the British Crown. Rounding the point, Whidbey had proceeded to East Foreland before crossing over to West Foreland. North of that promontory lay Trading Bay, the site of a number of native villages. The people proved to be friendly and, whenever Whidbey found difficulty in approaching the shore to take sightings, they would run into the freezing water and carry him and his men ashore. At one point the party received an invitation to join a group of Russian traders for a meal in their single, large, house. Inside they were offered fish and cranberries but were unable to eat them due to the strong, offensive, smell which pervaded the building. On seeing their reluctance to eat, one of the Russians took the cranberries away and returned them covered in seal oil *'with the hope of their being rendered in this state more palatable.'* The Russians had clearly taken to living the native way *'differing from them in their exterior appearance only by the want of paint on their faces, and by their not wearing any of the Indian ornaments.'* Eventually, Whidbey and his men could stand it no longer and *'having sacrificed as much to politeness as their stomachs could bear, felt great relief in once more breathing the pure though cold air, and returned to their tents.'*

With Whidbey's return, Vancouver had some chart corrections to make. Turnagain River became 'Turnagain Arm' and Cook's River became 'Cook's Inlet' (Cook Inlet). Sadly, for someone who had always held Cook in the very highest regard, Vancouver found himself contributing to a diminishing of the great navigator's name. If only Cook had *'dedicated one more day to its further examination, he would have spared the theoretical navigators, who have followed him in their closets, the task of ingeniously ascribing to this arm of the ocean a channel, through which a north-west passage existing according to their doctrines, might ultimately be discovered'* and, of course, Vancouver himself would not have wasted time on the inlets survey. Menzies was even more scornful. Having climbed a hill from where he could see the extent of the inlet, he wrote:

'Our station at this time was little more than a league above where Capt Cooks boats returned, & had they come up thus far what a satisfactory view they would have had, of the termination of this great inlet, where they could behold the impossibility of navigating it higher up, & consequently prevented the indulging of those chimerical speculations concerning its spacious and unbounded extent.' It was, perhaps, unfortunate that Cook had not gone the little extra distance to prove the waterway to be nothing more than a large inlet, but both Vancouver and Menzies appear to have forgotten Cook's instructions which directed him *'not to lose any time in exploring rivers or inlets'* whilst on his way to 65 degrees north.

That evening, the boom of signal cannon announced the arrival of the *Chatham.* Puget had encountered natives and Russians during his voyage along the inlet's western shore but had managed to avoid grounding on its shoaling waters. Several of the natives had trinkets in their possession that could only have come from the *Discovery* and at one stage, natives were met who knew Vancouver's name and could point out to Puget where the ship had last been seen.

Much to his relief, Vancouver could at last weigh anchor and leave the icy waters of Turnagain Arm. His voyage up the inlet with its repeated groundings had damaged his ship and the drifting ice had cost him one of his anchors. He decided that there was little point in carrying out a close survey of the eastern shore of the inlet or, indeed of any part of the Kenai Peninsular. He would be better employed in taking the ship south out of the inlet to a Russian shipyard at Port Andrews (Resolution Bay) where repairs to the *Discovery* could be undertaken. Before leaving the inlet, Vancouver and Menzies responded to an invitation by landing at a Russian trading post. As if to support previous comments made by Puget and Whidbey, the visit was not to provide their most wholesome memory – the most vital attribute needed was a very strong stomach. To reach the Russian post they had to walk along a path' *'which was rendered more disagreeable by a most intolerable stench, the worst, excepting that of the skunk, I have ever had the inconvenience of experiencing; occasioned I believe by a deposit made during the winter of an immense collection of all kinds of filth, offal &c. that had now become a fluid mass of putrid matter.* After struggling to eat a meal of dried fish they were eventually able to take their leave and reach fresh air, bearing gifts from their hosts of a few skins and a halibut.

The *Discovery* and the *Chatham* left Cook's Inlet and reached the coastal waters on 14th May. They had not gone far when a gale forced them to take in sail to avoid being forced out to sea. A heavy sea sprung the bowsprit of the *Discovery* and temporary repairs had to be carried out in driving rain. The pitching and rolling of the vessel had, however, shown that, despite the hammering the hull had taken from the groundings in Cook's Inlet, no serious damage had been done. This important information caused Vancouver to change his mind and, instead of heading towards Port Andrew, he shaped his course for King William Sound and Montague Island. On the southeast shore of the island lay Port Chalmers, a harbour in which the ship could be careened (ie. laid on her side by the retreating tide, allowing her hull to be inspected). The decision almost led to disaster. Just as the ships were rounding the northern edge of King William Sound, the *Discovery* was struck by the full force of a squall. The rapid approach of the violent wind allowed time for just the topsails to be lowered. Most of the other sails were split and the masts bowed to such an extent that it seemed certain that they were to go by the board. To their immense good fortune, only the foreyard splintered and was left hanging from its rigging. Astern of the *Discovery*, the *Chatham* had a fraction more warning and managed to suffer just the loss of her jib boom. The ships entered Port Chalmers under rough-hewn jury rigs three days later.

Whilst the ships were being watered, and as the carpenters got to work on the damaged bowsprit and yards, arrangements were put in hand for the survey of the sound's coast. Whidbey was ordered to take two boats to the south-western entrance to the sound and survey the western and northern coasts to Snug Corner Cove, the site of Cook's anchorage in 1778. That point would be the start of Lieutenant Johnstone's survey. Johnstone – who had visited the area during a voyage with fur-traders in 1788 – was to follow the coast to the south-east as far as Kaye Island (Kayak Island) and Cape Suckling. Both parties left Port Chalmers on 26th May.

A violent storm hit the ships on the last day of the month. The *Discovery* lost her anchor and was driven aground but was floated off on the next tide. The anchor was recovered and re-secured to its cable as, much to Vancouver's surprise, Whidbey's boats were seen returning to the ship. It transpired that they were bringing an injured seaman back to get medical aid. A violent argument had broken out between two of the seamen and one of the officers had attempted to separate the quarrellers by using an Indian spear. Unfortunately, this action merely resulted in one of the men being stabbed through both fore-arms. Having found out who started the altercation, Vancouver rewarded him with forty-eight lashes at the grating.

Whidbey returned to his survey having replenished his provisions thus missing a days rest ordered by Vancouver – and supplemented with an extra ration of rum – on the 4th June in honour of the King's birthday. Four days later Johnstone returned to the ship.

On reaching Snug Corner Cove, Johnstone had camped on an island ('Bligh Island' – after Captain William Bligh, Cook's master in the *Resolution* and later of *Bounty* fame). He then explored a deep inlet ('Port Fidalgo') where his party were joined by four Indians as they spent the night on the shore. The following morning the Indians had gone, taking with them an axe. Whoever had been on guard during the night had clearly not been paying attention to their task and Johnstone *'took such measures as produced a very different conduct in the persons who had been thus inattentive to their duty.'* Puerto Gravina – the most northerly possession taken by the Spanish in America – was followed by Puerto Cordova, both inlets surveyed in constantly pouring rain. At one camp their supplies were supplemented by a bear cub which provided an excellent meal. At other stops, birds eggs were found to be plentiful and, at many places, wildfowl were brought down by the officer's muskets.

The coast-line led to an area of shallow flats (Orca Inlet). From there, Johnstone had hoped to continue along the coast as he had been ordered to do by Vancouver, but he found he was subject not only to deteriorating weather, but also the effect of an open sea being driven against the shore. Clearly, his open boats could not face such conditions and he was forced to turn about and begin his return to Port Chalmers. Landing on a small island, Johnstone met a group of Russians living under an up-turned Umiak. They were waiting to trade with the Indians, two hundred of whom were encamped close by. Johnstone viewed the situation with much concern as a trading party in small boats had been attacked in the same area six years earlier. His concern was not alleviated when another forty natives arrived in canoes. The Russians, however, assured him that they were at no risk, and an uninterrupted night proved them to be correct.

A large Russian trading post was found at Port Etches, on the western shore of Hinchinbrook Island. Made in the shape of a square with three sides of buildings and one of a seventy-ton vessel that had been hauled ashore, Fort Konstantin and Elena provided accommodation for a hundred men. The party were treated well by the inhabitants but had great difficulty settling down to eat a meal of seal meat on which remained the hair and skin. Johnstone helped matters by offering to contribute chocolate, beef and bread from his own provisions – a gesture much appreciated by the Russians. In further appreciation of the hospitality he and his men had been shown, Johnstone presented the fort's manager with half a gallon of rum. On receiving this gift, the manager promptly decided to put the spirit to immediate use and downed enough in a few deep gulps to bring him to the verge of collapse. Johnstone and the other officers were amazed at this reaction to a gift and: *'being greatly hurt that a foreigner, capable of conducting himself in a manner that bespoke him worthy of a superior station, should have so little esteem for himself, as to fall into the general error; especially as he was a man advanced in years, and whose previous deportment had very justly intitled him to their respect: he became an instant object of their pity, and they were under the necessity of taking their leave, whilst he was so intoxicated as to be nearly in a state of insensibility.'*

Johnstone arrived back at the ships on the 8th June and was followed by an umiak full of Russians from Port Etches. Amongst the information they brought with them was that the manager would be visiting the ships the following morning – a delay possibly caused through an excess of rum. In the meantime, Johnstone's return had left the coast south of his turning point unsurveyed. Clearly boats could not be used for the task, so Vancouver decided to sent Puget and the *Chatham* to complete the work as far as Kaye's Island and Cape Suckling. Then, instead of returning, Puget was to continue the survey south to Port Mulgrave. If he was not joined by the *Discovery* by the 1st July, he was to continue on to Cross Sound (both positions named by Cook in 1778). Puget sailed on the 11th June escorted by the Russians, their boat stocked with iron, copper, axes, provisions – and rum.

When Whidbey returned to the western shore of the sound he found numerous bays and inlets, many ending in glaciers that poured down from the surrounding mountains. Floating ice was still a hazard and it was some time before he found himself free of the effects of the ocean swell. A storm held the party trapped on a beach for some time and, as they crammed for shelter into a single small tent, they became aware of an increasingly thunderous roar that threatened to engulf them. Tumbling out of the tent, they watched spellbound as part of the mountain-side, trees, rocks, and snow, slid down to crash on to the beach less than a hundred yards from their encampment. None had ever seen an avalanche before.

By the 7th June Whidbey had reached the inlet that approached to within eleven miles of the end of Turnagain Arm and found the two connected by low country. Carrying their kayaks and umiaks with them, the route between the inlets was frequently used by both the natives and the Russians as a portage between Prince William Sound and Cook Inlet. Further on, inside another inlet (Barry Arm), a low projecting point was – with Vancouver's later approval – named 'Point Pakenham' after Captain the Honourable Sir Thomas Pakenham, one of Lord Longford's sons, with whom Whidbey had served in the West Indies.

The inlet itself was typical of the many fiord-like indentations along the coast. At its end a vast glacier swept down from high, dominating, mountains; its waters studded with floating ice that had calved with thunderous roar from the glittering white wall. With such recent memories of an avalanche, the party could not settle until they found the cause of the rumbling sound that echoed around the rock-bound inlet.

Bligh Island was reached on the morning of the 11th, and with it came the completion of the survey of the perimeter coasts of Prince William Sound. Whidbey, unsure whether or not Johnstone would have examined the inlet named Port Fidalgo completed its survey before returning to the *Discovery* on the 15thTo his initial disappointment, Vancouver had been unable to careen his ship. The neap tides he experienced had not provided the range he required to beach the vessel in order to get at the lower hull. Now, with no evidence of serious damage, he considered the question *'more as a matter of curiosity than as an object of real necessity.'* Consequently, the *Discovery* sailed on the early morning of the 17th – and promptly ran on to a submerged rock. To make matters worse, the tide was falling, leaving the bows of the ship rising as the stern began to lower. This time, however, the low tidal range came to Vancouver's assistance. Within a few hours, the tide turned and began to lift the ship clear. The time in between had been used to replace the copper sheets around the stem that had been wrenched off by the ice in Cook's inlet.

Weak winds delayed the ship's departure from the sound and it was not until the 20th (two days before his 37th birthday) that she reached Cape Suckling and the open sea. Vancouver had spent part of the time in continuing his newly-awakened – albeit reluctant – criticism of Cook. The single position fix taken by Cook, and his failure to survey, or even describe, the islands within the sound was, according to Vancouver, a *'great deficiency of nautical information'*. He felt that the failure to record the area in detail could only be put down to the editor of Cook's journal (an incorrect assumption). Once again, he overlooked that fact that Cook's only interest was in searching for an entrance to a north-west passage. Clearly, no such passage existed in the sound, and Cook was eager to press on to the 65th parallel, leaving behind a jumble of islands of no interest to vessels on passage to Bering's Strait.

Chapter Fifteen

PORT CONCLUSION

*'as dreary and inhospitable an aspect as the imagination
can possibly suggest.'*

The *Discovery*'s voyage south was made tedious by contrary winds. With the exception of Mount St.Elias (*'majestically conspicuous in regions of perpetual frost'*) and the ice-fringed coast, there was little to add interest to the cold, choppy, waters. At last Admiralty Bay (Yakutat Bay) was reached and the boom of a cannon announced that the *Chatham* was safe inside. A native kayak arrived alongside bearing Manby, sent by Puget to pilot the *Discovery* in. The winds, however, prevented both her entry and Manby's return to his ship, so Vancouver continued on towards the next appointed rendezvous, Cross Sound.

On the 3rd July, the monotony forced by the baffling winds, was broken by the sight of a strange sail. She proved to be the *Jackal*, commanded by William Brown, last seen in command of the *Butterworth*. Brown brought disturbing news he had picked up on a trading trip to China. France had declared war on Great Britain, the French king had been murdered on the guillotine, and the country was in a turmoil of terror and anarchy. Even worse, Brown brought news of *'the attempts which the discontented were making in Great Britain, by the promulgation of French doctrines, to subvert our inestimable constitution.'* The murder of a rightful sovereign, and the spread of treason in England, was news of the gravest kind, but the outbreak of war was of especial import. Not only was the country at risk from French regicides and British traitors, but the war would bring the chance of both glory and prize money. The effect of the news on Vancouver and his ship's company *'will be infinitely easier for the reader to conceive than for me to describe, and I shall therefore only say, that they became the subjects of our most serious and painful reflection'*. The options available to Vancouver were limited. He could have broken off his survey immediately and returned home via Cape Horn. A more practical proposition might have been to have crossed the Pacific in the hopes of offering his services to whoever was commanding the East Indies fleet. His instructions, however, had not been framed with the outbreak of war in mind and ordered him *'not to do anything which may give occasion to any interruption of that peace which now happily subsists between His Majesty and all other powers.'* Unhappily, *'that peace'* no longer existed, and it would have been Vancouver's duty to engage any French vessel he might come across. But, in the absence of any further instructions, the completion of the survey, followed by a prompt return home, was the best course of action.

They reached the ice-strewn waters of Cross Sound on the 7th July and, after naming the northern point of its entrance 'Cape Spencer', the *Discovery* was anchored at 'Port Althorp' off the southern shore. She was joined shortly afterwards by the *Chatham,* and Puget presented Vancouver with the charts he had drawn up of the coast south of Prince William Sound. With no time to waste, Whidbey and Menzies were sent off with three boats and a fortnight's provisions to examine the coast from Cape Spencer.

Vancouver, whose health had been *'too indifferent'* to take part in the boat surveys for some time, set off on the 14th to examine a number of islands that were likely to be missed by Whidbey. By noon that day, he was forced to return having been *'seized with a most violent indisposition, which terminated in a bilious cholic, that confined me for several days to my apartments.'* He was, therefore, in no mood to have three Indians – one man and two women – steal part of the rudder chains. The thieves were chased by one of the ships boats as they tried to escape towards the shore, only for the canoe to turn over with the loss of the stolen chain. Angered by the theft, Vancouver ordered all three natives to be put into irons. Soon afterwards he listened to a plea from the women that they would never steal again if he set them free. This he agreed to, but continued to keep the man secured. His anger was aroused again when he learned that thefts had occurred in the *Chatham.* Now with a prisoner already in his hands he ordered that the man be given four dozen lashes before allowing him and the two women ashore bearing bloody evidence of what would happen if thefts were to continue. All the Indians in the anchorage promptly took flight in their canoes and disappeared for four days before a nervous approach to the ships demonstrated that, unless they stole, they were not to be given a flogging. Among those returning was one of the two women who had helped in the theft of the rudder chains. During the struggle to get her on board after the theft, a traditional cosmetic slit in her lower lip was damaged. Vancouver ensured that the surgeon's mates tended to her injury until it was healed.

Whidbey returned on the 26th. Plagued by fog and drifting ice, he had managed to make his way across the sound to Cape Spencer. A bay to the north (Taylor Bay) was found to be blocked by a glacier fed by mountains to the rear. From there, Whidbey was faced with a sea of broken ice and he was forced to send the strongest boat – the pinnace – on ahead to clear a path for the other vessels. Fog and ice continued to cause them difficulties. One night, having gone ashore to camp, they found the boats under attack from a huge field of drifting ice. By the time they reached the shore, the cutter had been wrenched from its grapnel and was drifting, at great risk of being crushed. The boat was recovered after a struggle with the current but the grapnel was lost. With no spare being available, Midshipman William Le Mesurier earned wide praise for constructing a replacement out of wood and stone.

Another opening ('Glacier Bay') could be entered only as far as two enormous walls of ice that blocked further progress and Whidbey was concerned that he would continue to meet such obstructions as he made his way around the coast. However, a passage leading to the south-east ('Icy Strait') provided open water. It also afforded the temporary companionship of a small group of Indians who used their canoes to ferry Whidbey's party to and fro from their anchored boats and lent a hand when the cutter ran aground.

The strait ended at a wide waterway that stretched both to the north and to the south. Whidbey rounded a point of land that led him northwards – a point that Vancouver chose to name 'Point Couverden' *'after the seat of my ancestors.'* Pulling hard against a fresh northerly wind, and with the current against them, the three boats found themselves passing shores lined with pines and backed by snow covered mountains (the passage was named 'Lynn Canal' by Vancouver, *'after the place of my nativity'*). Its spectacular beauty, however, was lost on the straining men. The prospect of exhausting work in examining a waterway that appeared to have no end put *'almost everyone in bad humour at the extent & direction it was likely to carry us.'* It took two days of hard work before the end was reached. The main passage divided into two arms (Chilkoot and Chilkat inlets), both supplied by meltwater streams.

If the voyage up the waterway was a test of endurance, the return was one fraught with menace. A large number of Indians were encountered. All seemed to be friendly and peaceable, and a large canoe containing twenty of the natives stayed in company with the boats. The two groups met ashore and Whidbey was impressed by one of the Indians – clearly a chief – who demonstrated a cordial manner towards the visitors. On leaving, the canoe remained in company and the chief put on a colourful outfit and danced and sang from the top of a box placed in the centre of his flimsy craft – *'We stopt on our oars to gaze at this ludicrous enterainment with astonishment, which made him repeat it.'* Despite this gesture of friendliness, Whidbey felt that there was more to the chief's actions than merely providing entertainment for his crews. That night he ordered the watch to be particularly attentive. As the light dawned the next day they were alarmed to see that four more canoes had arrived – all unobserved by the watch.

Taking to the water once again, Whidbey could see that the Indians were being reinforced by yet more canoes. Soon almost two hundred Indians began to paddle their way towards his party of about twenty-five men in three boats. The first contact came when the chief, who only the day before had kept them amused with his dancing, came alongside and jumped into the pinnace *'with no other intent than that of plundering the boat.'* His audacity was met by a push which sent him back into the canoe. The canoe itself was fended off with boat-hooks, but kept station as the Indians shouted abuse. A second large canoe, steered by an old woman yelling encouragement, approached and began to threaten the pinnace with a variety of spears, muskets, and brass blunderbusses. A bizarre refinement was added when a chief stood up in the canoe and began to harangue the pinnace through a speaking trumpet. To this he added the occasional squint through a telescope, or picked up a blunderbuss which he pointed at Whidbey. There was no denying the clear intentions of the natives, and Whidbey was forced to take action, either in the form of an assault, or of a defensive posture. He chose the latter and ordered the three boats to close up. This completed, the oars were brought inboard, and fire-arms primed and loaded. Then, in silence, and surrounded by scores of yelling and taunting Indians, the boat's crews waited for the attack. It never came. The determined show of resistance seemed to have un-nerved the natives and, gradually, the canoes were backed away. As soon as it was safe to do so, the oars were put out and the boats got under way. The Indians followed them at a distance for about three miles before giving up and turning away. Whidbey had shown leadership and courage. He could have easily opened fire and created devastation in the midst of the natives; by not doing so, he had also shown great humanity. The boats followed the eastern shore of Lynn Canal and, instead of continuing on to the southern passageway ('Chatham Strait'), found themselves being led along an eastern inlet that appeared to terminate at the foot of mountains looming ahead of them. They were not, however, to be given the opportunity to examine the inlet in detail. A canoe containing twelve Indians came up but kept their distance. Shortly afterwards, another, larger canoe joined the first and, once again, Whidbey felt himself under threat. The weather began to close down, the wind increased and heavy rain started to fall. He was given the choice of spending a miserable night in the boats, or trying to shake off the potential threat and set up camp ashore. To this end he ordered some of his men to fire their muskets over the heads of the Indians, despite previous experience demonstrating that the discharge of weapons without effect merely encouraged the natives. Again, the empty show of force had the wrong effect and the Indians began to close with the boats. Whidbey then tried a different tack. He gave orders that the boats should pull hard towards the shore in the hope of setting up a defensive base which would allow his men to rest. As soon as the movement was seen, the natives, in the much lighter canoes, raced ahead and reached the beach first. Whidbey then found himself faced with a large number of Indians who had leapt from their canoes and were now lined up on the shore with spears held ready for an attack. Once again, a fusillade from the boats would have swept the beach clear but, rather than cause an horrific number of casualties, Whidbey sheered off and returned to the middle of the inlet. Having spurned the opportunity to attack the Indians, Whidbey's alternatives were limited. He could wait in the boats until the dawn before directing them to the head of the inlet, or he could retire to its entrance and explore the much more promising Chatham Strait. So, with the inlet apparently *'unworthy of any further examination, at the risk of a serious dispute with these troublesome people'*, Whidbey chose to leave. Vancouver, generally impressed by Whidbey's actions, was not too pleased with the withdrawal and named the western entrance to the inlet 'Point Retreat'.

The eastern shores of Chatham Strait were, for the most part, surveyed in pouring rain which reduced visibility to a mile or less. Yet again, Indians approached in canoes and seemed to offer yet another threat. With his fire-arms having been loaded in preparation for some days, Whidbey ordered their discharge and re-loading in case the powder had become damp. The resultant harmless bangs was greeted by a round of fire from the canoes – fortunately, without incident. The Indians then paddled off to a village which could be seen being built on the shore.

Close by the native village, much to the botanist Menzies' excited curiosity, they observed an area of land that had been cultivated – the first time such a native endeavour had been encountered. His excitement, however, was somewhat blunted when it appeared that the Indians were growing tobacco. *'Here then we see'* he noted, *'the first dawns of Agriculture excited amongst these savages, not in rearing any article of real utility either to their comfort or support, as might naturally be expected, but in cultivating a mere drug to satisfy the cravings of a fanciful appetite that can be no ways necessary to their existence.'*

The dawn of agriculture, nor the use of tobacco, appeared to have little effect upon the war-like attitude of the Indians who followed up their precipitate retreat with a show of force as a large number of canoes were launched from the shore and steered towards the boats. This time, however, as the leading canoe approached, a chief stood up with his musket and made a deliberate act of putting it down again. He repeated the action several times until Whidbey ordered his crews to lower their fire-arms. At this, the chief sent a single canoe over with a request that Whidbey and his men join him ashore. Using sign-language, Whidbey refused but explained that a supply of fish would be welcome. The chief sent over a few small fish and was rewarded by the gift a few trinkets in return. With astonishing speed, the news of this transaction raced ashore, and many more canoes were launched as men, women, and children all came out to meet the visitors. Eventually, over five hundred natives jostled amiably around the boats trading food for needles, mirrors, beads, and articles of clothing. Whidbey, alarmed at the threat of his boats being swamped with the eager throng, was forced to shout at them to keep back. Unsure of his meaning and intentions, the canoes returned to the shore. Shortly afterwards the chief returned with a large supply of fish, for which he was well rewarded before the boats continued along the coast.

The 22nd July saw the boats arrive at a position ('Point Gardner') where the coast turned sharply to the north-east, opening up a into wide inlet (Frederick Sound). At that point, despite the rain-restricted view, Whidbey knew two important things. Firstly, the swell under the boat's keel told him that he was being affected by the motion of an open ocean – the strait down which he had passed clearly led to the sea. And secondly, that ahead of him, obscured by curtains of grey rain, lay Cape Decision; the point where the survey had reached the previous year, and the final link in the entire survey.

Now over a hundred and twenty miles from the ships and short of food, Whidbey was forced to conclude his examination. A survey of the strait's western shore was carried out as he made his way back to the *Discovery* at Cross Sound. He arrived sixteen days after his departure, having surveyed over five hundred miles of coast, and having survived the repeated attentions of hostile natives.

Before the survey was completely finished, there still remained the unanswered question posed by the opening seen by Whidbey heading north-east from Point Gardner. To deal with this, Vancouver took the ships along the western shore of the land revealed to be an island by Whidbey's survey (in fact, two islands – Chichagof and Baranof islands). The southern tip (Cape Ommaney) of the island was rounded and the ships put into a secure harbour just up the eastern shore.

The final part of the survey was to be carried out by Whidbey picking up from where he had left off at Point Gardner. Johnstone was sent to Cape Decision and told to work his way to the north following the continental shore until he met up with Whidbey who was expected to return along that coast. Each party was to take two boats and a fortnight's provisions. They set off in the early morning of the 2nd August.

With the boats' departure from 'Port Conclusion', Vancouver set about ensuring that the ships were ready for the voyage home. Sails and rigging were repaired, the hulls caulked, and spars and planks cut from the pine forests along the shore. Menzies spent his time collecting plants to put in the glass frame erected on the quarterdeck for that purpose. With care and attention, many of the plants might survive to be *'added to his Majesties valuable collection of Exotics at Kew.'*

By the 16th, a fortnight after their departure, no sign had been seen of returning boats, and Vancouver began to grow concerned. The stories brought back by Whidbey of hostile Indians caused him *'irksome anxiety'* as he thought of the *threatening danger to which I was conscious they must necessarily be exposed.'* All he could do was move the ships closer to the harbour entrance in readiness to leave immediately on their – hoped for – safe arrival.

On reaching Point Gardner, Whidbey had followed the northern shore of the inlet until it turned northwards into another waterway ('Stephens Passage'). A 35-mile narrow branch ('Seymour Canal') off the main channel proved to be a dead-end, but the waterway itself surprised Whidbey by trending sharply to the west and bringing him to the site of his first conflict with the Indians. What had seemed to him – when approaching from the Lynn Canal – to be an inlet, had proved to be a wide passage that curved southwards as far as its junction with Frederick Sound. Consequently, the land which he had kept on his larboard side was an island ('Admiralty Island'). Although an interesting point in geography, his voyage had brought him back to the hostile Indian territory – and the natives lost no time in taking to their canoes to resume their confrontation. Now with the probability of a passage home just a few short days away, Whidbey was in no mood to place his life and the lives of his men in jeopardy. When a musket shot fired over the heads of the rapidly closing Indians failed to have an effect, Whidbey ordered the next shot to be aimed directly at the leading canoe. The effect of the ball hitting the vessel was dramatic. All the occupants fell back and, once the canoe had drifted so that its high stern was facing the boats, the hands of the occupants was seen to emerge over the gunwales clutching paddles which were then dipped in the water. Thus protected by the stern and the canoe sides, they afforded the strange sight of a canoe in flight being paddled by men lying down. That night, having reached Point Retreat and returned along the passage, the boats were close enough to the native village to hear the combined yelling and wailing of a ceremony that suggested the musket fired at the canoe had found a victim.

Returning along the continental shore, Whidbey came across an inlet (Taku Inlet) from which poured a continuous flow of broken ice. The sheer sides of its lofty, snow-covered, mountains were joined by a towering wall of ice (the Taku Glacier). Such majestic scenery meant little to Whidbey who merely felt that it *'exhibited as dreary and inhospitable an aspect as the imagination can possibly suggest'.*

The eastern coast of Stephens Passage was followed until it merged with Frederick Sound. There, on the sound's southern shore, Whidbey yet again fell in with a canoe bearing sixteen men and a few women and children. His party had gone ashore to cook a meal and dry their clothes when the canoe landed close by them. A brief sign-language conversation took place before the natives retreated into the woods behind the beach. Whidbey felt that something was not quite right about the Indian's demeanour and became very concerned when he saw the men strapping knives to their arms – a practice usually carried out just before combat. Unwilling to risk being caught out, he ordered his men to return to the boats. They had only just pushed off, and were still within a few yards of the beach, when a number of Indians burst from the woods yelling and screaming. At the same time a canoe with more Indians appeared around a corner and rapidly closed with the shore. A trap had been sprung, but too late. Realising that they had missed their quarry, the Indians ran to board the canoe and give chase as the boats crews prepared to repel the inevitable attack. Then suddenly, and unaccountably, the natives stopped what they were doing and began to melt away in the woods. It was not until someone looked out into the sound that the reason for this abrupt retreat became clear – pulling towards them with their best endeavours were the two boats of Johnstone's party.

With three cheers from each of the parties echoing around the cove, the boats came together in a flurry of shaken hands and congratulation. The final link had been made in a voyage stretching from the 30th to the 60th parallel. The *'joy that was manifested in every countenance, on thus meeting their comrades and fellow-adventurers'* was marked that evening by an extra ration of rum and *'no small portion of facetious mirth'* over an expedition sent out on April Fools Day to look for a north-west passage up mythical passages.

The following day, the 17th August, 1794, to the breaking out of the Union Flag and the salute of muskets, Whidbey took possession of all the lands from New Georgia (itself extending south to 45 degrees north) northwards to Cape Spencer, just north of 58 degrees. The ceremony taking a huge area of land in the name of *'His Britannic Majesty, his heirs, and successors'* was completed by the issue of a double allowance of rum to all concerned. The date of the possession being the same as that of the birthday of one of the king's sons, the waterway was given the name 'Prince Frederick's Sound' (Frederick Sound). As they returned to the ships the boats passed down the coast surveyed by Johnstone and his team. They had covered a much shorter distance than Whidbey, but it had been achieved over an extremely difficult coastline. At one stage, Point Protection had been seen across Sumner Strait and, with its sighting, the insularity of Kuiu Island had been established. Some Indians had been encountered but, when they had become a threat, they had been driven off by the discharge of muskets.

To Vancouver's relief, the boats reached the ships on the 19th August. Now it was the turn of the ships to salute the boats with three cheers. Not only did their arrival mean the safe return of shipmates, but it also meant the time had come when the ships could leave for home, and a chance to get into the war (assuming it was still being fought).

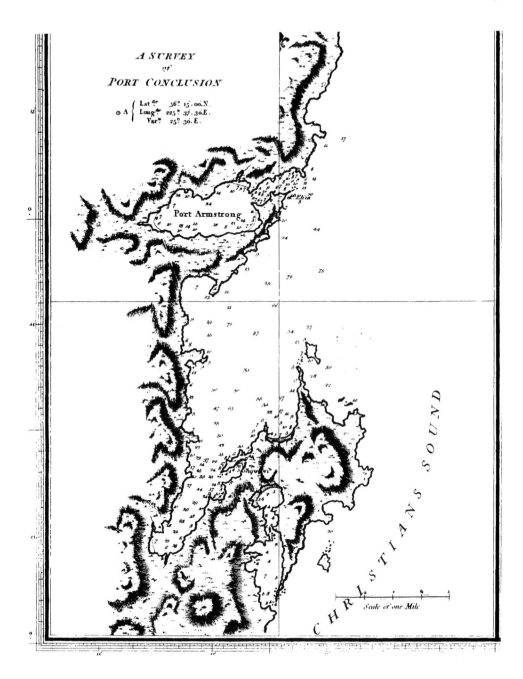

A SURVEY
of
PORT CONCLUSION

Lat⁴ᵉ 56° 15.00.N.
⊙ A { Long⁺ 225° 37.30.E.
Var? 25° 36.E.

Port Armstrong

CHRISTIANS SOUND

Scale of one Mile

To Vancouver, their arrival also meant the end of one of his greatest tasks. The diplomatic mission over Nootka had not gone as well as he had hoped, but the survey had gone far better than expected: *'I trust the precision with which the survey of the coast of North West America has been carried into effect, will remove every doubt, and set aside every opinion of a north-west passage, or any water communication navigable for shipping, existing between the North Pacific, and the interior of the American continent, within the limits of our researches. The discovery that no such communication does exist has been zealously pursued, and with a degree of minuteness far exceeding the letter of my commission or instructions; in this respect I might possibly have incurred the censure of disobedience, had I not been intrusted with the most liberal, discretionary orders, as being the fittest and most likely means of attaining the important end in question.'* All that now remained was to sail his ships home.

Chapter Sixteen

DELAYED DEPARTURE

*'once more entrapped in this infernal Ocean, and I am totally
at a loss to say when I shall be able to quit it.'*

If, as was highly likely, anyone on board the *Discovery* or the *Chatham* was hoping for a fast voyage home to England, they were destined for disappointment. Vancouver knew that the question of taking back the property at Nootka remained to be resolved. Lieutenants Broughton and Mudge had been sent back to London to ask for more instructions. Neither had been heard from since, nor had instructions arrived by other means. There was always the chance, however, that dispatches awaited him at Nootka, and to have sailed by the port without inquiry would have been seen as a dereliction of duty.

The ships left Port Conclusion on 24th August, 1794, and sailed into the paths of storms and massive fog banks that placed both ships in peril on a lee shore. At one stage, the boats had to be used to tow the ships out to sea and, as they were being hoisted inboard, a seaman – Isaac Wooden – fell overboard and was drowned. This melancholy incident was marked by Vancouver's naming of a rock off Cape Ommaney, 'Wooden's Rock' (Wooden island).

Friendly Cove in Nootka Sound was reached just over a week later. There, to his deep regret, Vancouver learned that Quadra had died the previous March. The amicable Spaniard's place in the negotiations had been taken by a man of equal disposition – Brigadier General Don Jose Manuel Alava. Once again, Vancouver found himself dealing with a man who was sympathetic to his predicament, and who went out of his way to assist both himself and his ships whilst they were in his area of responsibility.

Alava was waiting for a new set of instructions to be sent up from St. Blas and there was always the possibility that similar despatches might arrive for Vancouver on the same vessel. In the meantime, the rigging of both his ships badly needed attention. To that end, several coils of rope were obtained from the *Phoenix*, a British trading vessel at anchor in the sound. Trees were felled to provide planks and spars, an observatory was set up ashore, and contact with the local Indians re-established. Despite the activity, however, the possibility of a long delay was beginning to put a strain on the ships' companies. Menzies wrote to Banks that they were all *'in perfect health, & in high Spirits, with the idea of returning home but we are now detained, God knows how long.'* Seamen, allowed ashore for a walk, got into a fight with some Spaniards and only narrowly escaped injury when the Spaniards drew their knives. Vancouver, not immune from the tensions, wrote to his agent saying that he was *'once more entrapped in this infernal Ocean, and I am totally at a loss to say when I shall be able to quit it.'* He already was beginning to make plans for the *Chatham* to visit China to obtain supplies for an extended stay.

To provide a diversion for the officers, Vancouver and Alava accepted an invitation from the Indian chief, Maquinna, to visit his house. Greeted by drumming on hollowed logs, three boat loads of British and Spanish officers (with an extra boat to carry their luggage), arrived at the Indian village. There they were entertained (and somewhat alarmed) by dancers brandishing a variety of weapons. This display was followed by the chief wearing a costume to which were attached shells and pieces of copper. As he danced, his costume, the drums, and the singing; *'produced a savage discordant noise, as offensive to the ear as the former exhibition had been to the eye.'* Nevertheless, a diplomatically loud applause was *'bountifully bestowed'* to the gratification of the chief.

After six weeks of wearying delay, Alava and Vancouver came to the conclusion that they were unlikely to receive any instructions from St. Blas and decided to set sail for Monterey in the hope that any despatches might have reached there. The weather continued to be difficult and the *Chatham* and the *Discovery* were soon separated. Alava's ship – the *Princessa* – was seen briefly, but then soon lost in the heavy rain. High seas continually broke over the *Discovery*, flooding the gun-room, opening seams, and restarting an old leak at the bows. It took four weeks, much of which was spent at the pumps, to reach Monterey. There – to his mixed pleasure and annoyance – Vancouver found the sluggish *Chatham* waiting for him. However, to his *'great disappointment, anxiety, and concern'* nothing else awaited his arrival. There was just the chance that instructions had reached as far as San Diego, so the Governor agreed to send a courier there to see if anything was waiting at the settlement. Another two weeks delay seemed inevitable.

One good item of news that the Governor was able to impart confirmed that Lieutenant Broughton had reached Madrid. This was followed a few days later by another great disappointment. Despatches arrived for Alava containing his instructions for the continuation of the negotiations. The two governments had come close to agreeing with Vancouver's objections regarding the amount of land and property to be handed over. That might have been a cause for some slight self-congratulation, but for the fact that Alava was also informed that Vancouver had been relieved of his duties regarding the diplomatic mission, and that someone else was to be appointed to receive the Nootka territory from the Spanish.

Such news must have come as a severe blow to Vancouver's morale. Under difficult circumstances he had tried his best to represent his Country and her interests. From the alterations and amendments evident in Alava's latest instructions, it was clear that he had been right to demand that his interpretation of the treaty be observed as correct. Now – his actions having been justified – he found himself humiliated by his removal from the negotiations. He tried desperately to rationalise his position; *'Having maturely considered the several parts of this intelligence, I concluded that from the length of our voyage, and the various accidents to which the service in which we were employed would necessarily render us liable, Government did not expect we should remain longer in these seas, than the survey of the American coast might require; and in truth we were not now in a fit condition to protract out stay in these regions.'* Such a contrived view would have done little to ease the hurt he felt at being discarded by a government he had tried so hard to serve. With his reason for delay now removed, he *'did not long hesitate, but determined on making the best of my way towards England.'*

Monterey could not be left immediately as Vancouver had to wait for the return of the courier from San Diego. The delay gave him the opportunity to re-organise his ships' officers now that it was clear that Broughton would not be returning. Puget was confirmed as captain of the *Chatham,* with Johnstone as his first lieutenant; Manby was promoted to acting lieutenant and appointed as the *Discovery*'s third lieutenant. In Manby's place as Master, Vancouver appointed the American-born Master's Mate Henry Humphrys. Joseph Baker was confirmed as the *Discovery*'s first lieutenant with Spelman Swaine appointed as second.

The San Diego courier returned with nothing to add to what was already known and Vancouver made plans to put to sea immediately. With a plentiful supply of *'Indian corn Beans Pease cabbage &c'* and with live cattle to provide fresh meat, the ships sailed from Monterey on the 2nd of December, 1794.

The voyage south proved to be a troubled journey. Amongst other problems, Vancouver was accused of using his additional role as ship's purser to line his pockets at the expense of the ship's company. This, in itself, would not have been remarkable – pursers were expected to turn their appointment to good account by obtaining the cheapest food available and making it last for as long as possible, any resulting profits being retained as a perquisite. Food that came free of charge was especially welcomed by a purser. Coconuts were collected at Cocos Island (with Surgeon's Mate Hewett complaining that the trees were cut down to collect the fruit rather than the seamen being allowed to climb them), and turtles were picked up whenever the chance offered itself. Turtles collected at sea were dragged into the boats using a 'turtle peg', taken on board and kept on the upper deck for a few days until their bowels had emptied. They were then stowed below where they would remain alive for months without food or water, providing the ship with a source of fresh meat. Like other pursers, Vancouver would refuse to supply fresh provision until the old stock had been used up. Hewitt complained bitterly that beef purchased and salted down in Monterey had rapidly gone bad, but Vancouver would insist on its use before the cattle were slaughtered to provided fresh meat. According to the surgeon's mate, whenever a joint of rotting meat was taken back to Vancouver, he would exchange it for another piece from the same cask. The original decaying meat was then returned to the cask and handed out to the next complainant despite being *'so highly Putrid as to swim in Water'*. Hewett also claimed that when water was in short supply, Vancouver would have a cask of good water delivered to his cabin for his sole use whilst the rest *'could not get sufficient of the bad to quench their Thirst'*.

If any of Hewett's accusations were true, Vancouver's mean-spirited displays did not alter his kindly approach to the world in general. Whilst the coconuts were being collected at Cocos Island, the ship's boats were surrounded by fearsome, threatening, sharks. After a few boat loads of coconuts had been collected it was noticed that the sharks would instantly turn on and devour any of their own kind that was injured. A sport then arose among the seamen and midshipmen where they would lean over the gunwales and, by hooking or stabbing one of the sharks as it closed with the boat, cause it to become a meal for the other sharks. However, after a seaman and one of the young gentlemen were nearly lost overboard after they had hooked a shark, Vancouver put a stop to the activity – *'I thought it proper to prohibit further indulgence in this species of entertainment; which independently of its being likely to be attended with serious consequences, was in itself of too cruel a nature to be witnessed without pain.'*

The issue of food rose again when Vancouver, to his *'utter astonishment and surprize'* learned from Menzies that scurvy had broken out in the *Discovery*. The outbreak was considered *'inexplicable'* after the *'rigid observance'* that had been made in supplying what was considered to be vital anti-scorbutics. Fresh green vegetables, of a wide variety, had been obtained whenever possible and spruce beer had been brewed at every opportunity. The mystery was brought to an end when the culprit made his way to the quarterdeck to confess that he had been responsible for the outbreak. The *Discovery*'s cook, John Brown, a Scotsman from Dundee, had first entered the ship as a quartermaster, but had been discharged at the Cape of Good Hope. The following day Vancouver re-entered him, this time as acting cook in place of Nathaniel Ridley who had been sent home as 'unserviceable'. To be appointed as a ship's cook was a considerable advance in a man's social standing. Although a petty officer, he could be appointed only by a warrant from the Navy Board, thus making him a warrant officer of equal standing to the Chaplain, Armourer, Schoolmaster, Master at Arms, and Sailmaker, but without the quarterdeck privileges of the other warrant officers, the master, surgeon, boatswain, and purser. As Brown had been appointed by his captain – who was not entitled to issue a warrant – he could only be made an acting cook. Vancouver had always found the *Discovery*'s cook to be a *'steady, grave, and valuable man'*, and was surprised by his admission that he had been the cause of the scurvy. For many generations, cooks had been allowed the privilege of keeping the 'skimmings' which rose to the surface when salt meat was being boiled. This fat had a number of valuable uses for which the cook could sell it at two shillings and six pence per pound to his shipmates, keeping the extra income as a perquisite of the job.. It could be employed to grease moving mechanical parts in pumps, capstans and blocks, etc. It was also frequently used on bread as a substitute for butter, used to fry fish, or mixed with beans as an anti-scorbutic. Vancouver had no time for the latter use, believing that it had the opposite effect, actually causing scurvy. He had, therefore, ordered the cook not to supply the ship's company with the fat. The cook, however, had not only been urged by all and sundry to ignore the order, but was also *'acquainted with the opinions of the president of the Royal Society ... who stated, that he conceived that pulse with any kind of grease was not only a wholesome food, but also very antiscorbutic.'* As the President of the Royal Society was Sir Joseph Banks, a man of enormous influence, but no friend to the captain of the *Discovery*, Vancouver took great delight in applying the logic that – as his orders had been disobeyed, and scurvy had broken out – he must be right, and Banks must be wrong. So pleased was Vancouver at his *'satisfaction in recording, from* (the cook) *having been the means of establishing a fact of so much importance to maritime persons'* that he let the man off without punishment.

With the supply of skimmings cut off, and with the health of the invalids restored by a supply of fresh fruit at the first opportunity, Vancouver's logic remained unimpeachable.

A brief landing on the Galapagos Islands provided Menzies with the high point of his voyage. He had been frustrated at Cocos Island by the loss of the seeds and seedlings he had collected on the island when the surf washed them out of his boat. Now, despite the equatorial islands being the *'most dreary barren & desolate country I ever beheld'* he was astonished to find penguins and seals living alongside turtles, snakes, and lizards. The reason behind such a mixture of animals normally associated with extremes of temperature proved beyond his powers of deduction, but he came away with the satisfaction that he had discovered a new dove to which he gave the name *'Columba leucoptera'*.

With the Galapagos Islands well astern, Vancouver gave more thought to his immediate future. His instructions told him that he was to survey the western coast of South America from 44 degrees South to its tip at Cape Horn, but his removal (and the means by which he learned of his removal) had made him lose both heart and interest in the work. Instead, with the outbreak of war in Europe, he decided that he would add *'our little strength to the means adopted for the restoration of good order and tranquillity at home.'* A coastal survey might get his name on a few charts, but a war could give him the chance of prize money – and a share in the glory falling to his contemporaries. There was, however, a problem. The *Chatham*, with her poor sailing qualities, was holding him back. He decided, therefore, that his consort should be left to make her own way home. A rendezvous would be made at Juan Fernandez Island (the source of Daniel Defoe's 'Robinson Crusoe') but, if the *Discovery* had left by the time she arrived, Puget should set a course for England via St. Helena. Regrettably, in his instructions to Puget, Vancouver seemed to suggest that Puget's ship-handling skills were the reason for the *Chatham*'s poor performance. The instructions – according to Puget – contained a *'Sort of Complaint of animadversion* (ie. unfavourable observation) *on our conduct in not strictly following the Motions of the Discovery since quitting Monterey'* Although unable to reply to this criticism, Puget was deeply offended by the accusation that he was failing somehow as a ship-handler – especially as the *Chatham* had, after separation, frequently arrived at a destination ahead of the *Discovery*. He noted in his private journal that he had: *'no guide but the Discovery & no signal was made for a change of Course - her distance in many Instances … has been so great during the Course of the Night, that She had not been discernable & I have as often wondered that a separation did not take Place. Where the blame lies is obvious & and any impartial person would see That Superiority of Sailing gives the choice of Distance. Since our meeting with the NE trade it will be found that the Foretop Mast & the Top Gallant Steering Sails have mostly been set & that we have followed the Motions of the Discovery whenever She could be seen … whatever Detention the Chatham has caused arose solely from her sailing & not any Inattention to the Orders I received to prevent a separation.'*

Puget's wounded pride was soon healed. Two weeks after the *Discovery* had sunk beneath the southern horizon another sail was sighted. The stranger was showing no colours and Puget steered for her to investigate who she was. After a six hour chase, with still no colours showing, the cannons and swivel guns were prepared for use and the ensign and jack were hoisted. Closing with her, Puget could see that she was cramming on sail in an effort to escape. He gave orders to clear the ship for action. The guns were run out, the surgeon prepared his instruments, the marines climbed into the tops with their muskets, and the galley fire was doused. Within a few short hours, *HMS Chatham* had changed from a survey vessel on its way home to a warship bearing down on a possible enemy. Apart from the sounds of the sea and the rigging the only other thing to be heard was Puget's voice as he gave orders to the master, Humphrys, and his first lieutenant, Johnstone. Two hours later, with the stranger in range of his guns, Puget order a cannon shot across her bow. Even before the smoke had cleared, a Spanish merchantman's ensign was broken out on the other ship. Puget sent Johnstone across in a cutter to board the Spaniard. He discovered that Antonio Joseph Valaro – the captain of the *Rosario* – had tried to escape rather than risk being run down by a Frenchman wearing false colours. He was carrying cocoa and 'Jesuit's bark' (the bark of the cinchona – the source of quinine) from the Equadorian port of Guayaquil around Cape Horn to the Rio de la Plata. When Johnstone told Valaro that the *Chatham* was on her way to Juan Fernandez, the Spanish captain urged that they should go instead to one of the Spanish ports on the coast of South America. English ships were welcomed at any of the ports, whereas Juan Fernandez provided a very poor anchorage and had little in the way of supplies.

Two weeks later, to the north of Juan Fernandez, another sail was seen. This time it was the *Discovery*, limping along with a sprung main-mast. Vancouver was faced with a serious problem. To attempt to go around Cape Horn with the damaged mast would have been unthinkable, and yet he knew of nowhere he could call in to have it repaired. It was unlikely that Juan Fernandez would have the facilities or the timber for such a task, and his instructions forbade him from visiting the ports to the north of 44 degrees South along the western coast of South America *'unless, from any accident, you shall find it absolutely necessary, for your immediate safety, to take shelter there.'* Puget's news, however, put matters in a different light. If, as the captain of the *Rosario* had suggested, the Spanish ports would offer a welcome, there was hope of getting the repair done. Puget, Baker, Swaine, and Whidbey were called to the *Discovery*'s great cabin for a conference. They heard Vancouver go over the options open to them – they could sail across the Pacific and hope to fall in with a British fleet; take a chance that the work could be carried out on Juan Fernandez; take the risk of going around Cape Horn with a defective main-mast; cut the mast away, thereby massively reducing the sail that could be carried; abandon the *Discovery* and all go home in the *Chatham*; or – bearing in mind the situation in Europe – risk a visit to the nearest Spanish port – Valparaiso. The decision was unanimous, the ships would call at Valparaiso.

Chapter Seventeen

HOMEWARD

*'I do not recollect that my feelings ever suffered so much
on any occasion of a similar nature, as at this moment.'*

The coast of Chile, with the Andes mountains providing a far-off, broken, horizon, was reached on the 24th March, 1795. With no chart to guide him, Vancouver had only a note by Richard Hawkins written in 1593 – over two hundred years earlier. He had to look for: *'a great rock or small island a league or better to the south of, and a good mark and sure sign of, the port.'* With just those few words, the rock was found the following day and Valaparaiso Bay safely entered. As they sailed around the point, Vancouver's men saw *'a scene to which we had long been intire strangers.'* A large town with houses, Churches, several forts, and with seven sailing ships riding at anchor. Finding a secure anchorage, Vancouver sent Manby ashore to inform the local senior officer of the reason behind his unannounced visit. Whilst Manby was away, a Spanish officer came alongside and boarded the *Discovery*. He was carrying a message of greeting from the governor of the port, Don Lewis Alava – none other than the brother of Don Jose Manuel Alava, the kindly officer who had taken over the Nootka negotiations on the death of Quadra.

Manby returned shortly afterwards having had an audience with the Governor. Alava, like his brother, had proved to be a genial host who was keen to provide what he could for the visitors. Some matters, however, particularly regarding the stores required to repair the *Discovery*'s main-mast would require the personal permission of the representative of the Spanish Crown, the President and Captain-General of Chile, Don Ambrosio O'Higgins. Born in Ireland, O'Higgins had served with the British army before entering the service of Spain. His rapid rise through the ranks of the Spanish army saw him appointed as President of Chile in 1789. When a reply was received from the Captain-General, it turned out that, not only was he delighted to be able to help Vancouver, but he also invited him and his officers to his palace in the capital city St.Jago (Santiago) whilst the repairs to the ship was being undertaken. It was not the sort of invitation that could be lightly turned down. Quite apart from any assumed diplomatic snub, a refusal might affect the goodwill shown to Vancouver's immediate difficulty, that of getting his ships into a condition to face the rigours of Cape Horn and the South Atlantic. The journey to St.Jago was, in itself, no small undertaking for naval officers unused to lengthy journeys on horseback. The city was about ninety miles from Valparaiso and most of the distance had to be covered over rough tracks through broken country. Only two months earlier Vancouver had been in *'a very feeble and debilitated state'*. Since then he had been at sea with little time for recuperation or exercise and the thought of such an arduous journey must have seemed onerous.

There was a further complication. Having spent months in an area where pine and fir trees were beyond number, he now found that, nowhere in Valparaiso, or in the surrounding country, was there a single length of timber long, or stout, enough to provided the *Discovery* with a replacement main-mast. The only answer, it seemed, was to lift the existing mast out and reverse it so that the part that had sprung could be secured below the decks and 'fished' with strengthening battens.

The mast was removed and taken ashore where, at the Governor's request, it was placed under the guard of the *Discovery*'s marines '*a very unprecedented and extraordinary circumstance, that a guard should be requested by the governor from an English man of war, to do duty in the dominions of his Catholic Majesty.*'

Having ensured that all the ship's companies had access to an ample supply of fresh beef, green vegetables, bread, grapes, apples and onions, Vancouver set of for St.Jago in the company of Puget, Johnstone, Baker, Swaine, and Menzies. They were to be escorted by two Irish dragoons in the Spanish service and a gang of muleteers driving mules carrying tents and baggage. Vancouver, with the support of the muleteers, thought the tent poles were too large for the animals, but the Irish dragoons thought otherwise. When it looked as if a fight was about to break out between the dragoons and the muleteers, Vancouver withdrew from the scene. The Irish won the dispute and the tent poles were carried.

During the journey, stops were made at wayside houses where a meal could be taken. The tumbledown condition of the outside of these building prepared the visitor for the utter dilapidation that was to be found on the inside. Usually the furniture consisted of '*a dirty table, a stool, a wretched bed in one corner, and five or six crosses.*' Regarding the latter items, Puget, allowing his Huguenot background to emerge, felt they were '*emblematical of their Religion & to which they seem infinitely more superstitiously attentive, than to Domestic Comfort; it appears to erase Happiness from their Mind every Consideration of Social or Civil Society, bent or devoted to that one Object, they lose all Idea of attaining those numberless Comforts, which are only to be purchased by Industry.*' Vancouver was more disappointed in the lack of self-sustenance: '*The land about these miserable hovels was, like the surrounding waste, in a perfect state of nature, without the vestige of any labour having been ever bestowed upon it, not even in the cultivation of a garden*'. The occupants of the dwellings, however, used domestic utensils made from pure silver.

After two days of travelling through country that Vancouver thought '*possessed little to entertain, and less to interest*' they spent a night beneath blankets on the earthen floor of a mud-built hut. Their sleep was cut short by the dragoons who insisted that they start the final journey at three in the morning in order to avoid the midday heat (the naval officers, however, believed that the Irishmen merely wanted to '*insure a resting place the next evening among their particular friends.*'). Shivering in the early morning cold, the party wound its way up the foothills of the Andes until, from the top, they could see the city laid out before them, its rising spires no match for the towering snow-capped mountains amongst which it nestled. A two hour trot brought the party to within a mile of the city and Vancouver dispatched one of the dragoons to inform the Captain-General of their arrival. In his absence, the

W. Alexander del. from a Sketch taken on the Spot by J. Sykes.

J. Heath Sculp.

The TOWN of VALPARAISO on the COAST of CHILI.

party dressed themselves in their threadbare best uniforms in preparation for the meeting with His Excellency Don O'Higgins.

The dragoon returned accompanied by two Spanish officers and five extremely well-bred horses, each bearing an elegant saddle over a saddle-cloth fringed with gold and silver lace. To Vancouver's disappointment, their entry into the city was to be a public spectacle and his pleas for a more private visit were ignored. A note of friction was introduced when the visitors were requested to wear spurs which had been brought from the city by the officers. The naval party refused on the grounds that none of them were horsemen. They were not prepared to take the risk that *'some embarrassment or mischance should take place from their being unintentionally applied'*. The officer first pleaded, then demanded that the spurs be worn. When this failed to move the naval officers, he tried to persuade them that spurs were considered an essential part of dress, and to be seen without them would be considered an *'impropriety'*. The refusal remained adamant, and *'to his great mortification we mounted without them, and proceeded towards the capital, with a true military step, attended by the two officers, and our former guides the dragoons.'*

The cavalcade made its way through curious crowds until it reached the palace where they were greeted by a guard of honour before being taken to the audience chamber. There they met Lieutenant General Don Ambrosio O'Higgins who greeted them without a hint of formality, and with a delight at being able to speak in English once again. Two officers were appointed to act as their hosts for the visit and supper was enlivened by the arrival of a number of ladies who offered nosegays and invitations. The night was spent in beds beneath *'thin gauze, as a protection against the musquitos'*. The bedrooms themselves, however, were so littered with rubbish that *'it would rather have required a shovel than a brush for its removal.'* On requesting brooms to help tidy the rooms, they were told that such things were not readily available in St.Jago, and all that could be offered was water for sprinkling on the floor to keep the dust down.

The following day, feeling very dowdy amongst a glittering throng of Spaniards in military uniforms and court dress, they attended levees given by the Captain-General and the Bishop before enjoying a strange custom known as a *'siesta (or afternoon's nap)'*. The evening was spent at a concert and ball during which the visitors were invited by the ladies *'to join their party on the cushions: with this we instantly complied.'* By the end of the event, Vancouver was able to describe the womens' *'under linen garment, the bottom of which, as well as the tassels of their garters, was fringed with lace.'* Any attraction to the ladies was, however, muted by their *'scandalously neglected'* education and their *'total neglect of their teeth, which are suffered to become intolerably dirty.'*.

For the next six days, their hosts took them to the mint, the cathedral, and to the houses of the city's leading citizens. Under the leadership of the amiable and generous Captain-General, the natives had been subdued, the country's silver mines had fed the Spanish treasury, and its people had been brought to peace and prosperity (his illegitimate son, Bernardo O'Higgins, would lead the revolt that brought about the creation of the Chilean republic).

Vancouver and his officers took their leave on the 13th April and arrived at
Valparaiso three days later. The main-mast of the *Discovery* had been successfully
inverted and strengthened but, much to Vancouver's distress, the main-yard had
been found to be rotten throughout its length. All that could be done was to make
a temporary, fragile, yard out of a spare main-topmast and the yard-arms of the
defective main-yard. Whereas previously he had intended to avoid a survey of the
western coast of South America out of pique at his dismissal from the Nootka affair,
he could now use the legitimate excuse of the *Discovery*'s defects: '... *under all the
circumstances of both the vessels' condition, I did not consider myself warranted to indulge
my inclinations at the hazard of His Majesty's ships under my command, and at the risk
of the lives of so many valuable men, who had cheerfully endured the fatigues of our former
survey, and who, after so long an absence from their native country were intitled, in a peculiar
manner, to every care and protection that were in my power, for the purpose of insuring them
a safe return to their families and friends.*' Nevertheless, whilst the final repairs were
being carried out, Vancouver undertook a closely detailed survey of the port and
town ('*A door, in that side of the wall which faces the market-place, is the only entrance,
and leads by a winding staircase to different parts of the fortification.*' The governor earned
'*four thousand dollars per annum.*').

To a thirteen gun salute exchanged with the fort, Vancouver's ships left Valparaiso
on the 7th May with enough provisions to take him straight to St.Helena, thus
avoiding a call at the Cape of Good Hope. Three weeks later they were subjected
to heavy snow as they reached well to the south of Cape Horn. The *Discovery* had
many sails split during the voyage south of Valparaiso, decayed ropes parted, and the
gib-boom snapped in half. Nevertheless, tacking to the north-east in squally weather
on the 29th May, Vancouver set out to find Isla Grande, an island supposed to have
been discovered in 1674 but not seen since. He intended to reach South Georgia and,
from there, shape a northern course in search of the island but, once out in the
southern Atlantic, a north-easterly wind delayed his passage, threatened his masts and
rigging, and saw the *Chatham* become separated. Giving up the search, he felt
confident enough to report (correctly) that '*no such island exists*' and set off for
St.Helena. Two weeks later, a Welsh seaman, Richard Jones fell into the sea from
the main chains. A grating was thrown overboard to help him keep afloat but, by the
time the cutter was lowered, no trace of the man could be found.

The hills of St.Helena rose above the horizon on the 3rd June at the same time
as the *Chatham* appeared to the south-east. As the ships closed, Vancouver sent a
message across to Puget ordering him to read out an Admiralty instruction
demanding that all log books and journals kept during the voyage, along with all
charts, drawings and sketches, should be handed in before landing at St.Helena.
Furthermore, the entire ship's company of both vessels were to be ordered not to
disclose to anyone ashore where they had been for the past four years. Only the
surgeon-biologist, Menzies, objected to the order, asking – and getting Vancouver's
agreement – for more time to get his notes into order.

To Vancouver's disappointment, as they grew nearer to the island, a large fleet
could be seen standing to the north. He had hoped to be able to join such a fleet

and gain its protection for the last leg home, but it seemed as if he had missed his opportunity and would be forced to make an unprotected dash through seas alive with French men of war.

On anchoring in St.Helens Bay, Vancouver paid his compliments to the Governor of the island, Colonel Robert Brooke. From the Governor he learned that the fleet he had seen leaving was, indeed, heading for England under the command of Captain William Essington in the 64-gun *Sceptre*. Brooke also told him that war had broken out between Holland and Great Britain as a result of Holland's subjugation by France. What made this news of particular interest was that, as Vancouver and the Governor were discussing this turn of events, a Dutch ship, the 34-gun *Macassar*, sailed into the bay and dropped anchor – her captain unaware that war had been declared. '...as the Commanding Naval Officer of the Island of St.Helena' (there being no other naval ships in the bay), Vancouver agreed on a course of action with the Governor. Returning poste haste to the *Discovery* he ordered two boats, one commanded by Baker, the other by Swaine, to board the Dutchman and take possession of her. At the same time, in case the Dutchman should resist, he sent men across to the *Arniston*, a well-armed, but weakly manned, East Indiaman. In the event, the *Macassar* surrendered without a fight, and Vancouver found himself with a handsome, and valuable, prize.

Three days later *HMS Sphinx* sailed into the harbour under the command of Captain George Brisac. From Brisac, Vancouver learned that the British Government had decided that the Dutch-owned Cape of Good Hope was at risk of falling into the hands of the French, an event that would place British trade and other maritime movement around the Cape under grave threat. To counter this, a fleet was sent out to the Cape under the command of Vice Admiral Sir George Keith Elphinstone as a fleet of transports carrying three thousand men was sent to Brazil, there to await instructions from the admiral. Those instructions were now being carried by the *Sphinx* and Brisac sailed after just an overnight stay at the port. Vancouver had also learned from Brisac that a fleet was due to leave Salvador for England some time after the *Sphinx*'s intended arrival at Brazil. This information gave Vancouver the idea that, once her repairs had been completed, the *Chatham* should be sent in the wake of the *Sphinx* and make her way home under that fleet's protection. The plan was re-enforced when, four days after the *Sphinx* had sailed, a merchantman – the *Orpheus* – arrived at St.Helena carrying a copy of Elphinstone's despatches and letters. The despatches had to be sent on to the army waiting at Salvador in case the 20-gun *Sphinx* came up against the enemy whilst on passage. In consultation with the Governor, Vancouver confirmed that the *Chatham* would sail for Brazil, taking the despatches with her. He would take the letters on to London in the *Discovery*. The *Chatham* sailed on the 12th leaving behind Lieutenant Johnstone, who with seventeen seamen, was placed in command of the prize, *Macassar*.

Vancouver's decision to take the letters for London came as a result of an interesting news item brought by Captain Bowen of the *Orpheus*. According to Bowen, the French National Assembly had given orders to its naval forces that, if

Vancouver should be met at sea, he was to be allowed to continue unmolested. If such an order actually existed, it had been given as a result of the survey work Vancouver had been doing (a similar dispensation had been given by the French to Cook on his final voyage). Whether Vancouver believed the information or not, it clearly did not mean that he could sail with impunity. Some of the enemy ships might be unaware of the order, or the order itself might have been revoked as the result of some subsequent action (for example, Vancouver had sent spare supplies – including weapons and ammunition – to Elphinstone). Order or not, Vancouver knew that he had a good chance of catching up with the fleet that had left just prior to his arrival at St.Helena, before it entered an area where he would be at a greater risk of *'any thing unpleasant from the enemy's ships of force.'* With a new main-yard rigged, and with his ship's company exercising with the cannons and other firearms, *Discovery* sailed from the island on the 16th July in pursuit of the homeward bound fleet.

Less than two weeks out of St.Helena, Vancouver found himself faced with a difficulty which, being close the end of his voyage, must have rankled far beyond mere irritation. Against his judgment and instinct, Vancouver had been directed by the Admiralty – after pressure from Sir Joseph Banks, the President of the Royal Society – to take on board as 'Supernumary for Victuals Only', Dr Archibald Menzies. Menzies was clearly Bank's man and, as Banks and Vancouver had a marked disagreement before the ships left England, could be guaranteed to take any opportunity to represent the *Discovery*'s captain in a less than favourable light. At best, Menzies' botanical achievements during the voyage could be described as 'modest' – an achievement he took care to blame on what he saw as Vancouver's lack of co-operation; *'I believe I have not had, a boat from the Ship, on the particular duty of my department, above four or five times during the Voyage, & that only for a few hours each time.'* He had, however, accompanied Vancouver, and other officers, on many surveying boat journeys, all of which were required to spend some time ashore. Any plants collected during the voyage were to be protected in a glass frame built on the quarterdeck of the *Discovery*. Vancouver's orders from the Admiralty told him that, in addition to providing water for the botanical specimens, he was to allow Menzies to; *'have the sole charge & custody of the Plants which he may collect, and to direct that care may be taken that neither Dogs, or any other Animals, or property belonging to other Persons be suffered to be put into the Frame within which the plants are intended to be deposited; and that particular care be taken, in case the Glass of such Frame should, from any Accident be broken, and that the same may be immediately repaired, and that, during the time it may be necessary to keep the frame open, for the Convenience of admitting air or Rain to the Plants, no animals likely to do mischief to them, be suffered to be loose in the Sloop.'*

Over two years later, after complaining with a sneer to Banks that Vancouver had named the great island off the north-west coast as 'Quadra and Vancouver Island', Menzies continued: *'I have not yet been able to get plants to succeed, to my mind in the frame on the Quarter Deck - for if it is uncovered in rainy weather to admit air, the dripping from the rigging impregnated with Tar & Turpentine hurts the foliage & soil - and if the Side lights are opened Goats - Dogs - Cats - Pigeons - Poultry &c. &c. are ever creeping in & destroying the Plants. I am now however contriving to pass a strong Net round it in hopes with due attention it will answer better.'* The constant complaining by Menzies about the frame clearly did little to improve Vancouver's temper at a time when the Spanish were showing hostility to his presence off the Californian coast in November, 1793. In a letter to Vancouver (copied to Banks), the surgeon-botanist wrote:

> *'It is really become so unpleasant to me to represent to you verbally any thing relative to the Plant-frame on the Quarter-deck that I have now adopted this method to mention to you all the alterations or rather additions which I wish to be made to its original plan, for the security of the plants within it, together with the occasional aid that may be required to look after it, in my absence; that my solicitations for its success may not subject me hereafter to such treatment.*
>
> *I beg leave then to acquaint you that the Fowls have been in it again last night, and have done irreparable damages. It is therefore absolutely necessary to have the upper part of the frame as well as the sides covered over with netting of sufficient strength and sized-meshes, and to be constantly kept in due repair, to prevent Poultry, Pigeons and other Animals from destroying the Plants, while they are receiving the necessary advantages of light and air.*
>
> *It will likewise in future be necessary that you appoint a Man, who will be suffered from his other duty to look after it, and execute my orders concerning it, while I am out of the Ship or pursuing my duty on shore.'*

Instead of throwing the whole contraption overboard (as many other captains would have done), Vancouver agreed to supply a man from his ship's company to help with the frame – despite that fact that Menzies had his own servant, an Irishman, James Coote, whom Menzies preferred to take with him on boat voyages. The note to Bank's continued: *'You will see by the Above* (letter) *that Captain Vancouver's disinclination for the Success of the garden, has been pretty evident for sometime back, and that it was no unusual thing with him to be passionate & illiberal in his abuse whenever any thing was represented to him relative to its safety, which made me always cautious in giving him as little trouble as possible.'*

The early arrival at Cook's Inlet had killed off most of the Californian and Hawaiian plants in the frame. They were replaced by seedlings from Nootka Sound. A boat-load of plants was lost in the surf at Coco Island, and Menzies lost the chance to collect more than just a few plant specimens when he spent most of the time in Chile being entertained by the Captain-General. Blaming the *'dry scorched state of the country'* for the few specimens collected he, nevertheless, assured Banks that the plants would have his *'utmost attention & endeavour to save them.'*

The *'attention & endeavour'* were sadly missing on the 28th July. With a shortage of seamen as a result of manning the *Macassar*, Vancouver had reclaimed the man he had given to Menzies to help look after the frame, and had put him into one of the ship's watches. He was still available to work for Menzies when off watch, or when not required to work elsewhere when actually on watch but, on that particular day, he was ordered to join the other seamen in whatever evolution was then being carried out. Unfortunately, the covering of the frame was off at the time and the plants were subjected to a downpour of heavy rain. Now that the *'heavy and sudden deluge of rain crushed down the tender shoots of many of the plants'* thanks to the seaman being *'guilty of a very notorious neglect in disobedience of my particular Orders'*, Menzies demanded the infliction of *'punishment or disgrace'*. The surgeon-botanist insisted that Vancouver punish the seaman despite his being placed *'in a situation where he was so liable every moment to disobey my orders by being as it were obliged to obey others.'* The captain looked into the matter, and after consideration sent the man back on watch without any punishment – he had, after all, only been obeying the orders of his superior. When Menzies learned of this he (in his own words) *'coolly & without Insolence or contempt'* went again to complain to Vancouver. This time the captain – no doubt impatiently searching the horizon for a sail, and on finding one, hoping it would not be the enemy; *'immediately* (again according to Menzies) *flew in a rage, and his passionate behaviour and abusive language on the occasion, prevented any further explanation'*. The outcome, Menzies continued to inform Banks, was that he: *'was put under Arrest.'* The surgeon-botanist had – by accident or design – manoeuvred Vancouver into a position where, as captain of a man of war, he had no choice but to defend his rank and authority against a warrant officer who was intent on telling him when he could and could not order the employment of his own men. Menzies, on the other hand, now had an excuse for his poor botanical work. He also flatly refused to hand over his journal as requested by Vancouver.

Three weeks after Menzies' arrest, a lookout saw a sail followed rapidly by two more. The next day found the *Discovery* in the midst of the fleet of twenty-four East-Indiamen and a number of Dutch prizes, all under the protection of the *Sceptre*. Upon closing with the solitary escort, Vancouver took a boat across and reported to Captain Essington. Although it had taken six weeks to catch up with the fleet, it would have taken considerably longer had the prizes not been attached. Most were in a very poor state and some were on the point of foundering. Although to stay under the protection of the convoy would mean a protracted voyage to England, Vancouver was not over concerned as his own ship had masts and rigging in a *'shattered condition'*. He had already reconciled himself to the idea that if he had fallen in with a Frenchman he would not have been able to outrun him and *'of necessity we must have yielded.'* Essington also expressed the opinion that Captain Bowen's suggestion of Vancouver's ships being allowed to pass unmolested by any French man of war was, at best, *'premature'*. Vancouver, he believed, would have been more likely to have found himself facing *'the horrors of a French prison.'*

Ten days after joining the convoy, a Dutch prize near to the *Discovery* hoisted a distress signal. The cutter was sent across and found that the ship was in such a bad state that Essington ordered its abandonment prior to its being burnt. When the cutter returned, she was hoisted out of the water and brought inboard to be lowered on to her stowage. Just as this was being done, the tackle gave way and the boat crashed to the deck, wrecking it entirely. Vancouver was badly affected by the loss of the small but sturdy vessel that had served him so loyally for four years; *'I do not recollect that my feelings ever suffered so much on any occasion of a similar nature, as at this moment. The cutter was the boat I had constantly used; in her I had travelled many miles; in her I had repeatedly escaped from danger; she had always brought me safely home;*

Nepean, all had places named for them during Vancouver's voyage. Middleton –
now the head of the professional service – had received no such honour.

What Vancouver's actual reception at the Admiralty was like is not recorded.
It is likely that he met Nepean, but the distinct lack of celebration (no introduction
to the king, no dinner with the First Lord, no vote of thanks in Parliament etc)
suggests that the conduct of the war had taken firm priority over remote coastal
surveying. The country needed heroes, not another navigator. It certainly was not
interested in the acquisition of yet another island in the Pacific – even if it was the
strategically important Hawaii. If he had met Nepean, the interview seems to have
been short as the logs and journals he had brought were not handed over at the
time, but were delivered by messenger some five weeks later. An appeal to
Stephens was also likely to have been unproductive. The former secretary had been
the probable author of a memorandum in which he noted his belief that Vancouver
had failed in the Nootka negotiations. Instead of arguing about the size of the land
to be handed over; *'I regret ... it was not closed on those terms for We would have been
in Possession and under those Circumstances would have been on a better footing for
negotiating at home ... All that We really are anxious about in this particular part of the
business is the Safety of our National honour which renders a Restitution necessary. The
Extent of that Restitution is not of much moment.'*

Vancouver almost certainly learned two things of note. On his return home,
Broughton had been promoted to Master and Commander and given command
of *HMS Providence*, William Bligh's former ship on his second breadfruit expedition.
Lieutenant Zachary Mudge – who had arrived home a month after Broughton –
was appointed as first lieutenant, with Lieutenant James Vashon (son of Vancouver's
captain in the *Europa*) as second. The *Providence* sailed in February, 1795, with
instructions for her captain to take over the surveying task from Vancouver.
Broughton was probably rounding the Cape of Good Hope as Vancouver was
making his way north from Cape Horn.

Secondly, no doubt to his great pleasure, Vancouver found that he had been
promoted to captain, the actual advancement being back-dated to the 28th August,
1794. Such a promotion was of singular importance to a naval officer. It meant that,
even if he never went to sea again, and spent the rest of his life on half-pay,
providing he survived long enough he would be promoted to flag-rank. The
promotion from captain to rear admiral was achieved simply by advancing up a
list – on reaching the top, the promotion was made to fill a vacancy caused by
death. Every promotion from then on up to Admiral followed the same path. The
only variation from this method came about when the list of captains was so long
that those at the bottom would be in their dotage by the time they were due to
be advanced. On these occasions 'dead wood' clearances were made by offering
the senior captains a chance to be promoted to rear admiral and transfer to the
'Retired List' with a rear admiral's pension (considerably better than their
captain's half-pay). Just as the 'Active List' flag officers would become admirals of
the red, white, or blue; the dead wood admirals were known as 'Admirals of the
Yellow'.

Secure in his new rank and with his – recently introduced – single gold epaulette on his right shoulder and slashed cuffs with their double row of gold lace, Vancouver met the *Discovery* at Longreach to oversee her de-commissioning. Much of the time was spent in attending to the needs of his ship's company. Thomas Manby and Spelman Swaine had passed their lieutenant's examinations before sailing with Vancouver. He had promoted them to fill vacancies and the Admiralty confirmed them in the rank with seniority dated from 27th October, 1795. Four master's mates and three midshipmen were recommended to take the lieutenant's examination. The examining board passed them all without questions on the grounds that their experience under Vancouver was enough to merit their advancement. Another obligation was settled when Vancouver wrote to the Navy Board and the Admiralty asking for Joseph Whidbey to be promoted to Master Attendant – an appointment at one of the great dockyards with responsibility as harbour-master, pilot, and for dockyard vessels. The request was eventually granted. It was not just the officers that Vancouver attempted to help. One seaman had entered the *Discovery* whilst she was at Nootka. It turned out that he was a deserter from *HMS Alfred* who had taken work with the fur-traders. Desertion could be a hanging offence, but the man had proved to be a good seaman and had caused no trouble throughout his time on the voyage. Vancouver pleaded his case with the Admiralty and succeeded in having him listed as a member of the *Discovery*'s ship's company. As was usual in time of war with its shortage of manpower, the ships ratings were turned over to another ship (*HMS Caroline*), but Vancouver managed to have two deserving seamen exempted from the transfer.

Puget brought the *Chatham* safely home on the 17th October. His deviation to Brazil was not entirely without incident. An out-break of scurvy cost him £4 for the purchase of 3000 oranges, and practice with the muskets saw a burning paper cartridge fall on to a stack of four-pound gunpowder charges. One caught fire immediately and disaster was only averted when Able Seaman James Robinson snatched up the burning charge and threw it overboard. His bravery earned him an instant promotion to Quartermaster. The *Macassar*, under Johnstone's command reached port on the 22nd October thus ensuring the prize-money to which many (Vancouver not being the least) were looking forward to with great anticipation.

On the 3rd November, with the *Discovery*'s stores landed, and her ship's company turned over or dispersed, Vancouver was placed on half-pay. A fit, active, Royal Naval captain would have gone immediately to the Admiralty waiting room to see if another ship was available. There was a war on, captains were being killed, new ships were being commissioned, and appointments were becoming available. Vancouver, however, was not fit. The increasing effects of the illness he had borne for many months had worn him down. The crushing disappointment of his lukewarm reception at the Admiralty would not have helped, and there were some loose ends to be tidied up.

Two disciplinary matters required his urgent attention. Menzies, still under arrest, was due to face a court martial. However, upon his making an '*ample apology*', Vancouver wrote to Nepean requesting that the application for court-martial be withdrawn. It was, but Menzies continued to take every opportunity to denigrate his former captain. His journal – having never been handed over to Vancouver – was sent to Sir Joseph Banks, but if he had hoped that the President of the Royal Society would put his name forward for a Fellowship, he was to be disappointed.

On the 17th November, Vancouver was present at the court-martial of Henry Phillips, the ship's carpenter who, in March 1792, had rounded on his captain after Vancouver had criticised his workmanship on a new foretopgallant yard. Phillips was charged with 'General inattention to the duties of his employment', 'Neglect of Stores committed to his charge', 'Disobedience of his captain's order', and 'Contemptuous and disrespectful behaviour'. In his defence, the carpenter claimed *'a want of experience this being the first time of my having had the Honor of serving in the Navy the discipline of which I had not been acquainted with or accustomed to, neither did I conceive that I should have been treated with such language.'* No doubt much to his anger, Vancouver sat and listened as the Court-Martial Board found Phillips guilty only on the charge of 'Contempt and disrespectful behaviour.' The warrant officer had his Navy Board Warrant taken from him and was order to serve out the war as a seaman on whatever ships the local Commander in Chief decided.

At this stage Vancouver turned his attention to his failing health and repaired to Bristol Hot Springs to take the cure. Even there, however, he could not break free of controversy. Two seamen who had deserted from the *Chatham* during the first visit to Monterey had been captured by the Spaniards and held until the ships returned. They were then handed over along with one man who had deserted from the *Daedalus*, and a convict who had stowed away on the same storeship. Neither Vancouver nor the Spanish could decide how the costs (325 dollars) incurred by the deserters could be paid (especially as he did not have that amount of money in the ship) so, with agreement on both sides, it was decided that it would be left to the different governments to arrange payment. On his return, Vancouver had, on three occasions, brought the matter to the attention of the Admiralty, but nothing had been done. Now the Spanish Ambassador had lodged a complaint against him with the Foreign Secretary and was demanding payment. The matter was dealt with quickly by Nepean when Vancouver pointed out the facts of the matter, but the small furore had not reflected well upon his name and character.

In February, 1796, Vancouver moved to the village of Richmond, Surrey, where he took rooms in the Star and Garter Hotel, high on Richmond Hill. From there, access to London was easily made by coach or by hired boats along the River Thames. Apart from his poor health, one of Vancouver's most pressing problems was his finances. As yet unpaid for his time in the *Discovery*, he was living on his half-pay and on loans from his navy agent, James Sykes. In an attempt to raise money he sent his journal to the Board of Longitude pointing out that, as the *Discovery* did not carry an astronomer (the official astronomer, William Gooch, was murdered at Hawaii), he had carried out the duties of astronomer himself. The Board was welcome to the information he had amassed, and any recompense they felt was owed in return would be gratefully received. The journal was returned, without thanks, and without money. A year later, Whidbey approached the Board with the claim that he had been carrying out the duties of astronomer in the *Discovery*. He was paid £180 for his trouble – there was, of course, no record of Whidbey ever having a disagreement with Sir Joseph Banks.

The next hoped-for source of income was the *Macassar* and the prize-money she had brought. To his surprise, the Admiralty Prize Court brought to Vancouver's attention the unwelcome news that Colonel Robert Brooke – the Governor of St.Helena – and the captain of the *Arniston* East Indiaman, were also claiming a share in the prize money. An outraged Vancouver pointed out that the Governor's sole contribution was a number of soldiers who were put on board the prize to act as 'Centinels', and the *Arniston* had merely loaned one of her ship's boats. After months of deliberation it was decided that half of the prize-money would be divided between the three claimants, the remaining half to go to the Crown. But, just as the money was about to be distributed, Vice Admiral Sir George Keith Elphinston returned from his expedition to seize the Cape, and laid a claim against the prize-money on the grounds that the *Discovery* had been in his area of operations and, therefore, he was entitled to a share. The case was to drag on for many more months.

There remained one further method of raising money. Earlier explorers had done well out of writing their account of their expeditions – or of getting someone else to write it for them. In Vancouver's case, the suggestion seems to have come from the Admiralty itself as he began a letter to Nepean; '*It having been communicated to me that it is the wish of the Lords Commissioners of the Admiralty, that I should prepare for Publick information the results of the labours of the Voyage I had lately the honor of executing in His Majesty's Sloop Discovery accompanied by the Chatham Armed Tender*'. After asking Nepean for the return of his journals, and the return of his charts from the Hydrographer of the Navy's office, he brought the Admiralty Secretary's attention to the fact that '*in the instances of Captains Cook & King, the Government defrayed certain expenses of the Publications.*' Nepean replied that the Admiralty meant '*to give you every reasonable advantage to you which they can*' but added that any payment would be consistent '*with a due attention to the Claims of other Persons employed during the Voyage.*' Enquiries revealed that the '*other Persons*' was Menzies who, supported by Banks, was about to write his own account of the expedition. To his sponsor, Menzies had written that '*the finishing of my Journal before Captain Vancouver's is published is what I most ardently wish.*' Even worse – again with Banks' prompting – Menzies was claiming a share in any profits from Vancouver's book on the grounds that it would be referring to the botanical work done by him. Infuriated by this attempt to profit by his work, Vancouver wrote a stiff letter to Lord Chatham reminding him that Menzies' pay during the voyage '*was much more than double mine which together with his expenses, has been paid him since his return; and hence it is natural to conclude; since he has been so amply paid by Government that the results of his employment are the entire property of Government and totally at their disposal.*'

With the help of his brother, John, and with contributions from Lieutenants Puget and Baker, Vancouver set about writing his account of the voyage. Money became an increasing problem and three months after starting, he had to write to Nepean *'hoping through their Lordships generous aid, to be enabled to lay out a sufficient sum of money on the publication in question to render it a more finished work than my own private finances will allow.'* In the end, apart from covering the costs of eighteen plates, no money ever came to Vancouver from the Admiralty.

In August, with his health deteriorating, suffering from the stress of writing, and with his debts piling up, there could have been no worse time for Vancouver to receive a letter from Italy. Inside was a challenge to a duel, issued by Acting Lieutenant Thomas Pitt, Lord Camelford.

The 19 year old Camelford had learned of his father's death when the *Deadalus* reached Port Jackson. He had inherited a huge fortune, estates, large houses, and a seat in the House of Lords. His cousin was the Prime Minister, and his sister had married another cousin, the Foreign Secretary, Lord Grenville. Another cousin (the Prime Minister's brother) was Lord Chatham – at that time the First Lord of the Admiralty. Rather than wait for the next transport home, Camelford took the chance of making his own way back using whatever transport he could find. Stopping only for a series of dalliances in the Spice Islands, he arrived at Malacca eight months later to find the 44-gun *HMS Resistance* at anchor beneath the fortress walls. Reporting on board, he found that her captain was Edward Pakenham, a son of Lord Longford, and brother of Captain the Honourable Sir Thomas Pakenham after whom Vancouver had named Point Pakenham in Prince William Sound. The captain of the *Resistance* took his fellow nobleman on to his ship's book immediately and, within three weeks, had appointed him acting lieutenant. Unlike Vancouver, as an aristocrat, Pakenham knew the rules of the game. Head-strong young men like Camelford had to be given their head, and allowed to run wild. They could easily afford to pay for any damage caused on the way, and could buy themselves out of trouble without a second thought. If, in the meantime, his companionship should lead to promotion for his friends and for those who had helped him in his career, then so be it. Soon Pakenham was writing to the Admiralty praising Camelford as *'a most promising Officer, every way qualified for Promotion, and bids fair to prove a credit to the service.'* A subsequent letter to the Foreign Secretary urged an early confirmation of Camelford's rank as he would be *'an ornament to his profession, and too honourable an Acquisition for the service to lose.'* The provincial, boorish, Vancouver, whose background would have barely allowed him entry into the middle classes of the nation's capital had clearly been vindictive against such a promising young man.

After eight months in the *Resistance*, the station's Commander in Chief, Rear Admiral Peter Rainier (in whose honour Vancouver had named a volcano), confirmed Camelford's commission as lieutenant.

A year after he entered the *Resistance*, Camelford left to continue his journey home. Buying a ship at Prince of Wales Island (Penang) and providing it with a crew of twenty seamen gathered up from the port, he reached the coast of Ceylon (Sri Lanka) as the ship, riddled with leaks, sank beneath his feet. Making it safely ashore in the ship's boat, Camelford reached Colombo from where he took an East

India Company ship to Suez. He crossed the desert by camel until he reached Alexandria and found there a ship bound for Venice. The Egyptian port had been visited by the plague and, consequently, Camelford and his fellow travellers were placed in quarantine for forty days. Whilst kicking his heels waiting for permission to continue his journey, Camelford wrote to his mother begging her to use her influence to gain him promotion; *'For God's sake make haste to get me the rank of Post Captain that I may not throw away any more time.'* His next letter was to Vancouver demanding that he meet him in a duel at Hamburg. To ensure that his former captain could not plead poverty as an excuse to avoid the challenge, Camelford enclosed a draft for £200 (equivalent to more than a month's pay for Vancouver).

The first problem that Vancouver encountered on receiving the letter was that the date chosen for the duel – the 5th August – was already a fortnight behind. Secondly, he had no intention of catering to the outraged whims of a petulant thug. In his reply, Vancouver pointed out that he was not *'called upon in a private capacity to answer for his Public conduct in the exercise of his official duty'*. Furthermore, he would be happy to have his conduct examined by any flag officer in the Royal Navy.

Two weeks later, the rattle of a post-chaise was heard outside the Star and Garter Hotel. Minutes later, the sound of hammering on Vancouver's door echoed through the building. On the door being opened, Camelford stormed in and began to bellow insults at Vancouver. Trying to calm the towering figure down, Vancouver explained once again that he could not be held personally responsible for his official actions and that the young man should seek advice about his behaviour. Frothing with rage, Camelford roared back that it had only been the idea of spilling Vancouver's blood that *'had kept him alive'* on his journey home and that, one way or another, he was to have the satisfaction of a duel.

After Camelford had stamped his way out of the building, a shaken Vancouver wrote to a number of people asking their advice. All agreed with his action, and one of the correspondents – Lord Grenville, Foreign Secretary and cousin and brother-in-law of Camelford – supported his view that *'a commanding officer ought not to allow himself to be called upon to answer personally for his conduct in command.'*

Vancouver then wrote to Camelford reiterating his willingness to have his actions examined by a flag-officer. The letter was delivered by his brother Charles, who like John Vancouver, had come in support of their ailing brother. Charles's reception by Camelford was one of abuse and insult rounded off by the threat of a public insult to his former captain in a coffee house, thus forcing a duel. If that failed to call Vancouver out, Camelford would *'drive him from the Service, would compel him to resign his commission, and would finally, wherever he should meet him, box it out and try which was the better man.'* His temper was little improved with the knowledge that his promotion to lieutenant had not been confirmed and, instead of being advanced to the glittering rank of captain, he had to return to the rating of midshipman. The next day, Vancouver received a note from Camelford: *'When a man of honor has the misfortune to be embroiled with a Poltroon the line of conduct he ought to pursue is too obvious to occasion him the smallest embarrassment.'*

With such a threat hanging over him, Vancouver met Grenville to ask for advice on dealing with his rogue kinsman. The Foreign Secretary then wrote to Camelford, advising him that Vancouver had, if necessary, legitimate recourse to the law. His cousin replied immediately that, as for as he was concerned, *"the whole affair to be now concluded, at least for the present."* This clearly unsatisfactory answer gave Vancouver no other option but to apply to the courts for protection. Unfortunately, as Camelford was a peer of the realm, any such action would require the involvement of Lord Loughborough, the Lord Chancellor.

On the morning of the 21st September, Vancouver and his brother Charles were making their way to the Lord Chancellor's house in Bedford Square. They were walking up Conduit Street when, much to their shock and consternation, they saw Midshipman Thomas Pitt, Lord Camelford, on the opposite side. Just at that moment, Camelford caught sight of the brothers and, leaving his two companions, raced across the road wielding his walking cane over his head. Any attempt at reason was out of the question as Camelford began to rain blows down on Vancouver. Charles managed to grab Camelford and pushed him away before wading in with punches at the young man. Breaking away from this counter-attack, Camelford once again turned on Vancouver who was now more prepared for the assault and fended the midshipman off with his own walking stick. At this, Camelford backed away whilst threatening to do the same to Vancouver the next time they met, and whilst challenging Charles to a duel (Camelford later confronted Charles with the claim that his enemy's brother had given him *'a damned good hideing in Conduit Street,* (and) *that my arm and shoulder are still black and blue.'*).

An account of the incident soon appeared in the press and Charles was moved to write a letter to the *Morning Chronicle* giving his and Vancouver's side of the affair: *'whatever respect his Lordship might consider himself an injured man, it was solely and alone to be ascribed to his own misconduct, and that the personal inconveniences he had incurred were (though with the greatest reluctance, imposed by his commanding officer) indispensably necessary to the maintenance of discipline and good order on board the Discovery.'* The letter earned Charles the sneering nick-name 'Charles Rearcover' and brought out Camelford's friends in his defence. By far the worst result, was the publication of a cartoon by the famous caricaturist, James Gillray, entitled *'The Caneing in Conduit Street'*.

Amongst those eager to see a wide distribution of the caricature was Archibald Menzies. Knowing that Lady Camelford was keen to know what her son had undergone during *'the unexampled species of tyranny and cruel oppression, exercised during several years by my son's wretched commander'*, Menzies wrote to Whidbey enclosing a copy of Gillray's work. In his reply, Whidbey demonstrated the sad lack of moral character needed to ensure that his 'interest' – and thus his future advancement – was both protected and enhanced. The cartoon had caused him *'much laughter'* and he could not *'hesitate a moment in informing you everything that occurs to my memory respecting the treatment Lord Camelford received'*. After commenting on the punishments that Vancouver had awarded the midshipman, Whidbey answered the query concerning 'what crimes Lord Camelford was guilty of, during his stay with us; to that request I can easily answer - I know of none - excepting what are incidental to Boys in general. I ever conceived Lord Camelford to be a well-disposed young man; and I make not the least doubt but he will prove an Ornament to his profession - that was always my opinion, which you must have heard me say, both before Lord Camelford left the Ship and likewise after.' He then went on to say that Captain Pakenham and Lieutenant Manby were of the same opinion as himself. Menzies forwarded a copy of the letter to Sir Joseph Banks along with a print of the cartoon.

Just in case Vancouver's character was not blackened enough by these comments, the President of the Royal Society, not wishing to left out of an opportunity to attack Vancouver, added his comments in a note circulated to anyone who wished to read it. Vancouver had 'ordered the midshipmen birth to be pulled down by which they were exposed to the men & had no between decks to separate them.' Camelford was '4 times Punished by V's orders the 3 Whippings were done in the Cabbin by the Boatswain's mate in the Presence of all the midshipmen who were summoned on the occasion.' Midshipman Stuart 'experienced much inconvenience from the Captain's Revenge … he was often sent to the mast head as a punishment for trifling or supposed offences & kept there an unreasonable time but his Spirit never gave way he did his duty to the utmost of his Ability & bore the injustice he received patiently.' Menzies (no doubt to his great satisfaction) deserved mention for saving 'Vancouvers Life by putting him upon a nutritive diet when he thought himself within a few days of his dissolution by having adhered to a shore one.' And, of course, the glass frame on the quarterdeck could not go without mention: 'The Fowls & Pigeons &c were frequently in the garden & little attention was paid to it on the Part of the Commander.'

Beset on all sides by his adversaries, his health declining rapidly, and with his debts piling up, Vancouver left his rooms at the Star and Garter Hotel and moved down Richmond Hill into a cottage at River Lane, Petersham. With a sweep of the River Thames less than two hundred yards down the tree-lined lane, his new quarters were an ideal retreat where he could, with the help of his brother John, press on with the mammoth task of completing his account of his voyage to the north-west of America. It was a task made, no doubt, considerably easier with the knowledge that Camelford (who owned Petersham Lodge, just a two minute walk from River Lane) had been appointed to *HMS London* and was at that time patrolling in the Channel.

But just as one irritant was removed another took its place. Word had been spreading for some time that there had been a mutiny in the *Discovery*. When he heard of this, Vancouver demanded that a board of enquiry should be formed to look into the accusation. His agent, worried about Vancouver's health, pleaded with him not to pursue the matter. The reply he received gives some indication of the poor condition to which Vancouver had been reduced: 'If the investigation is to stand over until I can attend personally to it, most likely the whole business will be settled long ere that period arrive, as although I am undoubtedly in a recovering state it will be some months before I shall be able to venture a visit to London.' When his agent again asked that he consider his health rather than pursue an unlikely enquiry, Vancouver was

adamant: *'the ascertaining & refuting the falsehood in Question is an indispensable duty, which I owe to all those, whom at the time I had the honor to command.'* It was an important point as all the officers with whom he had served could have their future careers affected by the taint of mutiny. It was, he felt, his *'duty'* to them that he should clear them of the charge. In the end, despite his request for an enquiry, the matter was never tested.

In October, 1797, just over two years after his return to England, Vancouver learned that he was to receive his pay for the time he had been away in the *Discovery*. To his disappointment, he found that the Admiralty proposed to pay him at the basic Commander's rate of six shilling and six pence per day. Vancouver appealed to their Lordships for an increase on the grounds that (like all other Masters and Commanders in command of their own ships) he was also acting as his own purser. The lowest rate of pay for a purser – that of a purser serving in a sixth-rate – was two pounds a day. Using the precedents set for William Bligh after his *Bounty* voyage, the Admiralty agreed to raise Vancouver's pay to eight shillings and sixpence – minus sixpence a day in contribution to the Chatham Chest, a fund for naval charities. A month later, Vancouver was informed that the Privy Council had agreed the distribution of prize-money from the capture of the *Macassar*. He informed his agent that the long-awaited money would *'place me most completely on velvet'*.

On the 28th April, 1798, after almost half a million words, the long toil over the account of his voyage had reached the time when Vancouver's ships had entered Valparaiso harbour. At that point he broke off the writing and, sending for his lawyers, told them that he wished to make out his will. After leaving twenty-five pounds to his agent, Vancouver left all his money to his brother John who was to pay his other brother, Charles, fifty pounds a year and twenty-five pounds to each of his sisters, Sarah and Mary.

Exactly two weeks to the day after completing his will, Captain George Vancouver drew his last breath. He was forty years old.

The navigator of the north-west coast of America was buried in the grounds of St.Peter's church, Petersham, his grave marked by a simple, unadorned, headstone bearing just the words 'Captain George Vancouver Died in the year 1798 Aged 40'. The parish register recorded 'Captain George Vancouver of the Royal Navy aged 40, of this parish. Bd. May 18th, 1798.' It was a plain, unvarnished end to a life that was, at times, plain, and at other times, unvarnished. But a life, nevertheless, that shone a light into some of the earth's dark corners for the benefit of mankind in general, and of his country in particular. He was mourned by few, and forgotten by many. His achievements, however, stood the test of time, and his name, and the names of his companions, provide beacons of enterprise and endeavour along an often bleak and forbidding coast – a memorial truly earned through courage and the call of duty.

Chapter Nineteen

AFTERMATH

*'A degree of minuteness far exceeding the letter of
my commission or instructions.'*

For the majority of Vancouver's officers and young gentlemen, the voyage
had not only left their names on the charts of the American north-west coast,
but had provided a successful launch for their further careers in the Royal
Navy. **Commander William Broughton** – with Zachary Mudge as his first
lieutenant – took the *Providence* to the Pacific via the Cape and Australia with orders
to survey the west coast of South America if not already charted by Vancouver.
Nootka Sound was reached in early 1796 and letters left for Broughton by
Vancouver were presented by the Indian chief Maquinna. From the letters,
Broughton assumed that the South American survey would have been carried out
by the *Discovery* and *Chatham* on their way south. Accordingly, he then turned to
his instructions which allowed him to select a course of action *'to be carried out in
such a manner as might be deemed most eligible for the improvement of geography and
navigation.'* After consulting his officers, it was decided that the *Providence* should
be used to survey the little-known Asian coast from Sakhalin (north of Japan) to
the Yangtze River. With the season well advanced, Broughton decided to run
down the eastern coast of Japan and Formosa (Taiwan) before wintering at Macao.
There he decided that a second vessel should be purchased to act as tender to the
survey. He found a schooner that tradition suggested had been built by the *Bounty*
mutineers but was, in fact, a former fur-trader, the *Prince William Henry*. On the
17th May, 1797, off the southern coast of Japan, the *Providence* was wrecked on a
reef and the ship's company were transferred safely into the tender. Broughton
made for the Yangtze where he was fortunate in finding *HMS Swift* under the
command of Captain Thomas Hayward. Hayward, as a midshipman, had been
with Bligh on his extraordinary boat journey following the mutiny and had
suffered another long open boat journey when the ship sent to search for the
mutineers – the *Pandora* – was wrecked. Forty of Broughton's men were
transferred to the *Swift* whilst others (including Mudge) moved into an East
Indiaman for the voyage home. Those who left in the *Swift* lost their lives when
Hayward's ship sank with all hands on her way home to England.

Broughton continued his survey with thirty-five men and the tender. The
coastline of east Asia from the Gulf of Tartary to the southern point of Korea was
successfully charted before he set off for home in late 1797. On arrival he found
that he had been promoted to captain a year earlier. In 1807, Broughton was
appointed as commodore of a squadron operating in the East Indies. Given orders
to attack Java in support of the army, he carried out the assault out with a lack of
conviction and was replaced by a rear admiral whom Broughton accused of

'behaving in a cruel, oppressive and fraudulent manner unbecoming the character of an officer, in depriving me of the command of the squadron.' Nevertheless, Broughton was made a Companion of the Bath in 1815 and appointed as Colonel of the Royal Marines three years later. He died in Florence in 1821.

Lieutenant Zachary Mudge, having picked the right ship to sail home in 1797 found, on his arrival, that he was promoted to commander. Three years later he was advanced to captain and gained a reputation as an aggressive challenger of anything floating that was French. In July, 1805, whilst in command of *HMS Blanche* he fell in with a French squadron and was quickly battered into submission, however, the subsequent court-martial for the loss of his ship praised him for his *'very able and gallant conduct'*. After two more commands, the war against the French was over and he was offered no further service at sea. Mudge was promoted to rear admiral in 1831, vice admiral in 1841, and to admiral eight years later. He died in 1852.

On his return with the *Chatham,* Lieutenant Peter Puget found he had been promoted to commander. He was soon appointed to the *Adelphi* with instructions to escort a convoy to Gibraltar and, after discovering that there was no spare stowage for gunpowder on the rock, packed his ship with 4500 barrels of gunpowder rather than have it sent back to England. Six extremely risky weeks were spent at a buoy in Rosea Bay fending off Spanish attacks with fire ships before space for stowage was found ashore. Puget then begged the Governor to be allowed to take another convoy home rather than waste time in inactivity. He was given the tiny 6-gun *Esther* and told to take charge of four merchantmen. He had not long been out with his small convoy when he ran into a 44-gun French frigate. As the convoy escaped he turned toward the far heavier ship and was forced to lower his colours. Then, extraordinarily, Puget offered the French captain money rather than have his ship taken as a prize. The Frenchman agreed, and Puget handed over £94. Having avoided capture by the enemy, Puget sailed after his convoy only to fall in with a Spanish merchantman, *El Conde de Galbez,* which he promptly captured. Unfortunately, the Admiralty decided that the prize-money from the capture should go to the Crown. Puget was promoted to captain in April, 1797, and commanded a number of first-rates over the next seven years. This was followed by a period of bad luck during which time he was appointed to the command of three successive ships, only to have the command taken from him at the last moment. He finally managed to succeed in his appointment to the *Goliath* and earned high praise for his conduct at the second Battle of Copenhagen. Between 1810 and 1818 he served as Naval Commissioner at Madras and Trincomalee and was made a Companion of the Bath on his return. Puget was advanced to rear admiral in 1821 and – as recorded on a plaque attached to his tombstone – *'terminated his earthly career in the arms of his family on the 31st day of October 1822.'*

Lieutenant Joseph Baker, who had earned Vancouver's praise for his *'zeal for the service and abilities as an officer',* was promoted to commander in 1799 and to captain three years later. In 1809 he was appointed to the frigate *HMS Tartar* and played an active part in the Baltic operations of that year before his ship was wrecked on Anholt Island. He died in 1817.

In 1796, it was decided that the 44-gun *Charon* should be removed from her harbour service role and refitted for sea. **Lieutenant Thomas Manby** was appointed to oversee the refit. In February, 1797, he was promoted to commander and given command of the ship for convoy escort duties. Over the next two years, Manby successfully escorted 4,758 ships between the Downs and Ireland without a single loss. Appointed to the 38-gun *HMS Africaine* on the West Indies station, he was ferrying home invalided soldiers when an outbreak of yellow fever struck. A third of all those on board died and Manby only narrowly escaped death. He was later sent in the 36-gun *Thalia* to protect the Greenland whaling fleet from French men of war, but the combination of the cold and the effects of yellow fever led to his leaving the sea. He was promoted to rear admiral in 1825 and died in 1834.

In 1802, Lieutenant Spelman Swaine was promoted to commander and appointed to the 14-gun sloop *Raven* and earned the praise of Vice-Admiral Lord Nelson by leading the admiral's fleet through the uncharted Straits of Bonificio (between Corsica and Sardinia). Two years later, the *Raven* was lost in the North Sea off Cuxhaven. Having survived the shipwreck, Swaine was made an acting captain and appointed as one of the three captains of the Sea Fencibles based at King's Lynn. There he was responsible for the coast-line from Cromer to the Wash along which, in case of invasion, he was to repel the enemy using any vessel and any men that he could find at the time. Confirmed in the rank of captain in 1810, he was appointed to the 38-gun *Statira* only to be shipwrecked again, this time off the coast of Cuba. The length of the captain's list at that time may be judged by the fact that Swaine was finally advanced to rear admiral in 1846 – thirty-six years after he was confirmed as a captain. He died in 1848.

The first master of the *Chatham*, **James Johnstone**, was confirmed as a lieutenant on his return and later appointed to the 80-gun *Sans Pareil* for service in the West Indies. He was promoted to commander in 1802 and to captain four years later. In 1810 he was given command of the 74-gun *Scipion* and took Rear Admiral Robert Stopford out to replace Broughton off Java. Johnstone was made Commissioner of the Navy at Bombay and had been intended to replace Puget at Madras, but ill-health forced his return home. He died in 1823.

Joseph Whidbey, promoted to master attendant on Vancouver's recommendation, was appointed to Woolwich Dockyard. In 1805, the President of the Royal Society (Sir Joseph Banks) made him a Fellow of the society – the honour he had withheld from Menzies. The following year, a survey was needed of Plymouth Harbour where a breakwater was to be built for the protection of the sound. Whidbey was appointed for the task and, with the civil engineer, John Rennie, developed a proposal for the construction. The plan was accepted and, in 1806, the work started with Whidbey as resident superintendent. He was to remain with the project until illness forced his retirement in 1830. He died in 1833, eight years before the breakwater was finished.

After the threat of court-martial had been lifted following his apology to Vancouver, **Archibald Menzies** was appointed to the Royal Yacht *Augusta* – an appointment arranged by Banks so that the surgeon could finish his journal ready for publication before Vancouver's account was published. The dictates of the war, however, soon saw Menzies being sent to join Johnstone in the *Sans Pareil*. It was to be his last naval appointment. After qualifying as a Doctor of Medicine, he moved to London where he established a medical practice. Menzies survived to the age of eighty-seven and died in 1842, the year before naval surgeons ceased being warrant officers and were finally granted their sovereign's commission. His journal was never published.

Of all those who served in the *Discovery*, none achieved – or even approached – infamy in the manner of Thomas Pitt, Lord Camelford. Prevented from tormenting Vancouver by his appointment to sea, and whilst serving in the West Indies, Camelford was promoted to lieutenant in April, 1797. Just five months and one week later he was given command of the sloop *Favourite* over the head of the ship's first lieutenant, Charles Peterson. With his own date of promotion giving him nineteen months seniority over Camelford, Peterson's discontent led to him leaving the ship. On 13th January, the following year, the *Favourite* sailed into English Harbour, Antigua, to join the only other British ship, the *Perdrix*, now commanded by Lieutenant Peterson. Camelford, claiming to be the senior officer, sent Peterson a written order which his former first lieutenant ignored on the grounds that he was the senior officer. Eventually, both officers met on the quayside backed up by seamen and marines from their respective ships. Peterson gave his men the order to load their muskets. Camelford responded by snatching a pistol from one of his officers and placing the gun against Peterson's chest. Three times he demanded that Peterson obey his orders. When, after the third demand, Peterson still refused, Camelford pulled the trigger and Peterson fell dead.

The first response of the Admiralty was to promote Camelford to commander – and to back-date it to a month before the murder. The subsequent court-martial – despite Peterson being clearly the senior officer – gave Camelford an honourable acquittal.

On his return home Camelford tried to get himself another ship but was met by Admiralty indifference. Two months later, his brother-in-law, the Foreign Secretary, Lord Grenville, under pressure from his wife and Lady Camelford, managed to persuade the Admiralty to give Camelford a ship. It was to be the *Charon* and he would be taking over command from Commander Thomas Manby. Then, much to everyone's surprise, in January, 1798, Camelford was arrested as he tried to reach France in a hired boat. He was carrying no luggage, and in his pocket was found a letter of introduction to Citizen Paul Francois, comte de Barras – the leading member of the French Directory and chief sponsor of a young artillery officer named Napoleon Buonapart. When examined, Camelford claimed that all he was doing was going to visit Paris to see what changes had taken place since his last visit. The Privy Council (which had three of his close relatives on it) were faced with a dilemma. It was a capital offence for any British citizen to visit France, an offence which had only recently led to a hanging. The only course of action they could find was to mount an appeal to the king for a free pardon. The appeal worked and Camelford was set free. But there was a sting in the tail, the pardon came with an instruction that Camelford was not to be given the command of any of the king's ships. Outraged by this slight upon his honour, Camelford wrote to the Admiralty offering that his name should be removed from the commander's list. The Admiralty accepted his offer.

Camelford then embarked upon a dissolute, loutish lifestyle. Within weeks he had been fined £500 for violently attacking a defenceless man, and soon achieved a reputation for drunken excesses in which he delighted in pushing over night-watchmen's boxes, trapping the unfortunate workmen inside. In October, 1801, when a peace treaty was signed with the French, all the houses in London were illuminated by candles at their windows. All, that is, except for Camelford's house in Bond Street. A cheering mob soon spotted the discrepancy and began shouting abuse at the front of the building. Suddenly the door burst open and out ran Camelford swinging a large cudgel to drive the crowd back. His reward was to have all his ground floor windows smashed.

In March, 1804, Camelford got into an argument with an army officer, Captain Thomas Best, over 'a strumpet'. He angrily issued a challenge which was accepted, and the antagonists met at Kensington at dawn on the 7th. Both men levelled their pistols as they waited for the command to fire. Camelford, knowing his opponent to be a good shot, pulled his trigger before the command was given – and missed. Best took aim and fired, hitting Camelford in the chest. Thomas Pitt, Lord Camelford died two days later. At his bedside was Captain Robert Barrie, like Camelford, one of Vancouver's midshipmen.

So ended the misspent life of a man born to every advantage except moral strength. He was an intelligent, wealthy, bully who used his social standing to browbeat anyone of lesser status who did not fawn in his presence – hence the description as 'an ornament to his profession' from such as Pakenham. It took two of Cook's former midshipmen to display the courage needed to stand up to him. Both Edward Riou and George Vancouver refused to countenance his advancement in the service – and both were proved correct.

Battered almost into a state of unserviceablity, *HMS Discovery* lay unused at Deptford until it was decided to convert her into a bomb-vessel. Her hull was strengthened throughout and a huge high-angle mortar placed amidships. In this role her moment of glory came on the 2nd April, 1801, when, with other 'bombs' she took her place eastwards of the centre of the line of battle at Copenhagen. The great mortar was used to hurl mortar-bombs over the mast-heads of the British ships to fall amongst the Danish line. Abreast of the *Discovery*, lay the *Elephant*, Vice Admiral Lord Nelson's flagship. Rejoicing in the heat of the battle, Nelson was less than pleased when his signal-lieutenant brought his attention to a signal from the commander-in-chief, Admiral Sir Hyde Parker. On hearing that the signal read 'Discontinue Action', Nelson snapped back '*Mr Langford, I told you to look out on the Danish commodore and let me know when he surrendered. Keep your eyes fixed on him.*' Lieutenant Colonel Stewart of the Royal Marines asked Nelson what the signal from the commander-in-chief meant: '*Why to leave off action*' replied an outraged Nelson, '*Now damn me if I do.*' Turning to address his captain, Thomas Foley,

The *Discovery* hulk in the Thames. Wrongly described by the artist as "Captain Cook's ship", this vessel was actually "Captain Vancouver's ship"

Nelson remarked 'You know, Foley, I have only one eye, I have the right to be blind sometimes.' Then, putting a telescope to his sightless eye, he added with heavy humour, 'I really do not see the signal.' One man who had seen the signal was Captain Edward Riou of the Amazon, Vancouver's midshipman companion in the Resolution. Although under very hot fire from the Trekroner Battery, he and the frigates he commanded were determined to stick it out and trade shot for shot. Now, to his dismay, he was being ordered to retire. Reluctantly, he gave the order and followed it with the words 'What will Nelson think of us?'. Seconds later he was cut in half by a cannonball.

The Discovery was converted into a prison hulk in 1818 and used to hold convicts before their transportation to Australia. She was finally broken up sixteen years later. HMS Chatham survived in service with the Royal Navy until she was sold off in Jamaica in 1830.

It was mainly upon the shoulders of John Vancouver that fell the 'arduous task' of completing his brother's account of the voyage to north-west America. Puget assisted with the writing and Baker completed the charts which were to accompany the volumes. The illustrations were selected from a large number of sketches done by the midshipmen, the only exception being Lieutenant Mudge's drawing of the Discovery heeled over on the rocks of Queen Charlotte Sound. Vancouver's 'A Voyage of Discovery to the North Pacific Ocean and Round the World in which the Coast of North-West America has been carefully Examined and Accurately Surveyed. Undertaken by His Majesty's Command, principally with a view to Ascertain the Existence of any Navigable Communication between the North Pacific and North Atlantic Oceans; and Performed in the Years 1790, 1791, 1792, 1794, and 1795, in the Discovery Sloop of War, and the Armed Tender Chatham, under the Command of Captain George Vancouver.' was published in late 1798. Foreign language editions and abridged versions soon appeared and the work remained in print until 1984.

Although generally comprehensive, the Voyage left some aspects of the expedition without mention. Punishments awarded to wrongdoers are glossed over. There may appear to be good reason for this when it is realised that over fifty per cent of the Discovery's ship's company were flogged, and just under fifty per cent of the Chatham. To later generations, such figures seem excessive and to reflect badly upon the ships' captains. In fact, they do not reach far above the average for the period, and there are few other examples of such a long voyage with which to compare them. The quality of the seamen Vancouver started out with was not of the finest- the possibility of a war had seen the best men seek berths in ships likely to see action. Hewett, the malcontent surgeon's mate, regarded the ships companies as 'a ragged Complement of Fishermen's Boys and other Fresh water Sailors'. The recent mutiny in the Bounty had graphically illustrated what could happen if seamen were not kept fully aware of their obligations to the service and to each other. All the recorded floggings in the Discovery were awarded for crimes deemed to be beyond naval law – disobedience, theft, fighting, neglect of duty, drunkenness. Vancouver was aware that his ship's company was made up of young, competitive, men, held together in a close environment, far from home, and at risk from the elements and the native peoples they encountered. Only by strict discipline could they, and the ships in which they sailed, be kept safe. There is another, frequently forgotten aspect of naval punishment. The men who served on the lower deck had broadly the same aspirations as the officers. They wanted a happy voyage, free from threat, and the prospect of a safe return home. They did not want to suffer theft, violence, or unnecessary discomfort. They wanted the thieves and bullies to be punished as an example to others of a like mind. Where that did not happen, they would take their own revenge, often with catastrophic results, both to them and to their ship. In the great mutinies of 1797, the complaints were about conditions, food, and pay. Not only was there no complaint about punishment, the mutineers carried out their own floggings against men who broke the basic rules of their community. Vancouver was an humane man who had to keep his ships companies together for their own welfare, and for the task he had been given – in that he was eminently successful.

The many pages of the *Voyage* give little clue to Vancouver's illness, and Menzies – the surgeon – none. Clearly, his inability to take part in the inshore surveys came about through illness. Menzies (via Banks) claimed to have *'saved Vancouver's Life'* early in the voyage, and Vancouver himself notes that, by the time of the voyage home, he was *'in a very feeble and debilitated state.'* Suggested causes of this ill-health – from both experts and laymen – range from tuberculosis to a thyroid gland disease (with either an over- or an under-active thyroid), and to chronic glomerulonephritis (or 'Bright's Disease'). In fact, any chronic renal failure – especially if aggravated by an intake of salt – or even diabetes, would produce the same symptoms of increasing weakness. Whatever the cause was, it has often been linked to the numerous outbursts of temper to which Vancouver was said to be prone. Such incidents, however, on examination, were all severe trials upon the patience of a man weighed down with heavy responsibilities. His angry ejection of a native Hawaiian chief from his cabin was as a result of theft- the chief's action flying in the face of his strenuous efforts to treat the natives fairly. When Manby became separated from Vancouver in Jervis Inlet and *'suffered every hardship fatigue and hunger could inflict'*, Vancouver's reaction on finding his errant midshipman safe was no more than that of any captain relieved at the survival of any of the young men for whom he was responsible. Equally, there can be no doubt that Menzies frequently tested Vancouver's patience to the limit. When, at great risk of encountering an overwhelming enemy, the petulant surgeon's continual complaining about his plant-frame would have tested the patience of the mildest of men. Even the symptoms of panic exhibited by Vancouver at Hawaii could have been the result of mental scarring brought about by – as a young man – being present at the death of Cook on the island. None of these and similar incidents need have any bearing on the illness which eventually caused Vancouver's death.

That death brought about no statues, no memorial from a grateful nation. Consequently, no confirmed image of Vancouver is known to exist. The National Portrait Gallery, London, is in possession of a portrait – claimed to be of Vancouver and painted by Lemuel Abbott – which was purchased in 1878. The name

'Vancouver', however, was already on the map. 'Quadra and Vancouver Island', with the loss of Spanish influence in the region, and thanks to the penetration of the west coast by the Hudson's Bay Company, saw the loss of the 'Quadra' element by the early 19th century. Victoria, the chief city of British Columbia, is situated on the southern tip of Vancouver Island – the dome of its Parliament building graced by a gilded statue of Captain George Vancouver.

In 1825, the Governor of the Hudson's Bay Company, Sir George Simpson, in the belief that the eventual border between the United States of American and British North America would be drawn along the Columbia River, built a fort on its northern bank. To three cheers, and the breaking of a bottle of rum against the flag pole, Simpson announced *'In behalf of the Honourable Hudson's Bay company I hereby name this establishment Fort Vancouver, God save King George the 4th'.* He then went on to explain why he had chosen the name: *'The object of naming this fort after that distinguished navigator George Vancouver is to identify our claim to the soil and trade with his discovery of the Columbia River and the coast on behalf of Great Britain.'* It was a bold but presumptuous act. Seven years earlier, the United States and British governments had agreed to the drawing of a boundary between their territories along the 49th parallel of latitude from Lake Superior to the Rockies, and for the next twenty-seven years Oregon was jointly administered between the United States and Great Britain. Finally, in 1846, using the charts prepared by Vancouver, it was agreed to extend the border along the 49th parallel until it reached the Strait of Georgia, passing just to the north of Point Roberts. From there it passed down the centre of the strait until it turned westwards along the centre of the Straits of Juan de Fuca. Only the ownership of the San Juan Islands (in the centre of the Strait of Georgia) were left in doubt – an omission later leading to some comic opera sabre rattling between the two countries. The place of the Hudson's Bay Company – now forced to withdrew to the north – was taken by the United States' army who took over Fort Vancouver and re-designated it as 'Vancouver Barracks'. Among its commanders during the succeeding years can be found the names of Ulysses S. Grant (later a civil war leader and President of the USA), Phillip H. Sheridan and George B. McClellan (both civil war leaders), and George Armstrong Custer of civil war and Little Big Horn fame. Around the army post grew an ever increasing civil population which took for itself the name 'Columbia City'. However, sometime in the early 1850s, the whole settlement was named 'Vancouver'. Over the years, what had begun as a trading post, developed into a thriving city which, in the year 2000, erected an eight-foot bronze statue of Captain George Vancouver. Far to the north, near the head of Yakutat Bay, Alaska, 'Mount Vancouver', rises in appropriately close company with 'Mount Cook'.

The low ground between Burrard's Inlet and the Fraser River saw a number of settlements develop during the early 19th century. The Hudson's Bay Company built Fort Langley and the community of Queensborough was founded. In 1858, the region was named 'British Columbia' and Queen Victoria requested that Queensborough become the colonial capital under a different name – 'New Westminster'. 'Port Moody' – at the head of Burrard's Inlet – was named after a

Colonel R.C. Moody of the Royal Engineers who, in turn, named the island at the mouth of the Fraser River 'Lulu Island' after an American actress, Lulu Sweet. Another settlement 'Granville' was known locally as 'Gastown' after its most prominent citizen, saloon owner John 'Gassy Jack' Deighton. In 1866, the colonies of Vancouver Island and British Columbia were united under the name of the latter and, five years later, British Columbia was accepted as a province of the Canadian Confederation. At that time the Canadian Pacific Railway Company were looking for a western terminal for its transcontinental railway and decided on Port Moody. However, on visiting the area in 1884, the railway's general manager – William Van Horne (a name, like Vancouver suggestive of Dutch extraction) – decided that Granville would make a better terminal. Not liking the 'Gastown' nickname, he suggested that the new railhead should be renamed 'Vancouver'. The 400 residents of Granville, keen to see the profits associated with the railway coming their way, happily agreed. A new town sprang up immediately, only to be completely burnt down in less than an hour the following year. Showing the enterprise that was to become its hallmark, Vancouver was immediately rebuilt and soon began to flourish. By 1891, the population had leapt to 13,000, a figure to be doubled ten years later. In time, Vancouver became a city of world renown, a centre for commerce, industry, art and leisure set against the great splendour of snow-capped mountains.

Australia had not forgotten its debt to Vancouver, and a promontory between King George Sound and Princess Royal Harbour was named 'Vancouver Peninsular'. An islet in the sound was named 'Vancouver Rock', and another islet, off Mount Gardner, was distinguished with a 'Cape Vancouver'. In New Zealand's South Island, Dusky Bay is extended by 'Vancouver Arm'.

An unusual, and frequently unrecognised memorial to Vancouver, came about as the result of the United States of America's acquisition of Hawaii. Following the lack of interest shown by the Foreign Office in Vancouver's efforts in obtaining the island for the British Crown, nothing was done about Hawaii until 1843. That year the French occupied Tahiti, an act which probably led to Captain Lord George Paulet RN of the 50-gun *Carysfort* countering with a vigorous response to *'certain indignities'* allegedly inflicted against British subjects on Hawaii by King Kamehameha III. For the second time in its history – although this time by force – Hawaii was ceded to the British Crown. Paulet held the island for six months until he was ordered by Rear Admiral Richard Thomas – the commander-in-chief in the Pacific – to hand the island back to the king. The forced cessation, although entirely illegal and unauthorised, prevented further French Pacific expansion when France became a signatory, along with Great Britain, guaranteeing the island's independence. The action of Thomas in overturning the work of his subordinate earned him the British Government's highest approbation for *'the whole of proceedings at the Sandwich Islands, as marked with great propriety and admirable judgment throughout, and calculated to raise the character of British authorities for justice, moderation, and courtesy of demeanour in the estimation of the natives of those remote countries, and of the world.'* King Kamehameha requested a portrait of Thomas in order that he *'might have and preserve in his palace the likeness of a British officer, who, in restoring to him his kingdom, dared to act on his own sense of right, counting upon the approval of his magnanimous Queen, in which he was not disappointed.'* Fifty years later a revolution replaced the monarchy with a republic. After just four years the republic collapsed and the island was annexed in 1898 by the United States of America without opposition from either Great Britain or France. In 1959, Hawaii became the fiftieth state of the United States and adopted for its state flag the same flag designed for King Kamehameha I in 1816 – the British Union flag against stripes of red, white, and blue. The flag that Vancouver had hoisted on Hawaii in 1794 thus became part of the heraldry of one of the world's great democracies.

Kings Lynn, however, despite being proud to be the assumed birthplace of George Vancouver, paid him the strangest of compliments. Next to hearing the news from a Spanish officer that he had been removed from the Nootka Sound negotiations and that he had been replaced by a Marine Lieutenant, Vancouver's greatest humiliation was, almost certainly, the attack upon him in Conduit Street by Midshipman Lord Camelford. Nevertheless, the authorities at Kings Lynn saw fit to change the name of the street on which he had lived – Fincham Street – to 'New Conduit Street'. During his lifetime, Captain George Vancouver RN did not strive for recognition beyond the approval of his contemporaries. The only time he gave his own name to a feature was in compliance to a request from Quadra, the leading Spanish Nootka Sound negotiator – even then, Vancouver put his own name second to the Spaniard in suggesting 'Quadra and Vancouver Island'. He was much more interested in carrying out his duty with compassion and humanity, in producing charts of great accuracy and precision, and in proving – or disproving – that a north-west passage existed on the north-west coast of America between 30 and 60 degrees north. His only guilt was in working to *'a degree of minuteness far exceeding the letter of my commission or instructions'*.

Grateful for having been selected *'in pursuance of his Majesty's pleasure'* for a task of immense proportion and importance, Vancouver applied himself with dedication and rigour to its completion. Therein lay his greatest monument, therein lay his memorial – *'ne plus ultra!'*

BIBLIOGRAPHY

A Voyage of Discovery to the North Pacific Ocean by Captain Vancouver
London 1798

Ibid., edited by W. Kaye Lamb, Hakluyt Society   London 1984

Dictionary of National Biography

The Half Mad Lord, Nikolai Tolstoy, Jonathan Cape   London 1978

People of the Totem, Bancroft-Hunt & Forman, Orbis   London 1979

The Influence of Sea Power upon History 1660–1805, A. T. Mahan, Bison
London 1980

The Influence of Sea Power upon the French Revolution and Empire, A. T. Mahan
London 1983

The Life of Captain James Cook, J. C. Beaglehole   London 1974

James Cook Maritime Scientist, T. & C. Stamp   Whitby 1978

Naval Records for Genealogists, N. A. M. Roger, PRO   London 1988

Exploring Alaska & British Columbia, S. E. Hilson   Seattle 1997

The Royal Navy Day by Day, A. B. Sainsbury   London 1994

The Commissioned Sea Officers of the R.N., Scolar Press   Aldershot 1994

Nelson, A Personal History, C. Hibbert   London 1994

Vancouver's Voyage, Marshall   Vancouver B.C. 1967

Cooks
Inlet

1795

Nootka Sound

Teneri

Sandwich Islands
(Hawaii)

Cocos Island

Galapagos Islands

St.

Salvador

Tahiti

Oparo Island
(Rapa Island)

Dusky
Bay

Valparaiso

Chatham Island

Cape Horn